Can Creative Writing Really Be Taught?

ALSO AVAILABLE FROM BLOOMSBURY

Composition, Creative Writing Studies, and the Digital Humanities,
Adam Koehler

Creative Writing in the Community: A Guide, Terry Ann Thaxton

Creative Writing in the Digital Age: Theory, Practice, and Pedagogy,
edited by Michael Dean Clark, Trent Hergenrader and Joseph Rein

Creative Writing Innovations: Breaking Boundaries in the Classroom,
edited by Michael Dean Clark, Trent Hergenrader and Joseph Rein

Can Creative Writing Really Be Taught?

Resisting Lore in Creative Writing Pedagogy

10th Anniversary edition

Edited by
Stephanie Vanderslice and
Rebecca Manery

Bloomsbury Academic
An imprint of Bloomsbury Publishing Plc

B L O O M S B U R Y
LONDON · OXFORD · NEW YORK · NEW DELHI · SYDNEY

Bloomsbury Academic

An imprint of Bloomsbury Publishing Plc

50 Bedford Square
London
WC1B 3DP
UK

1385 Broadway
New York
NY 10018
USA

www.bloomsbury.com

BLOOMSBURY and the Diana logo are trademarks of Bloomsbury Publishing Plc

First published 2017

© Stephanie Vanderslice, Rebecca Manery, and Contributors, 2017

British Library Cataloguing-in-Publication Data

A catalogue record for this book is available from the British Library.

ISBN:	HB:	978-1-4742-8505-6
	PB:	978-1-4742-8504-9
	ePDF:	978-1-4742-8507-0
	ePub:	978-1-4742-8506-3

Library of Congress Cataloging-in-Publication Data

Names: Vanderslice, Stephanie, editor. | Manery, Rebecca, editor.
Title: Can creative writing really be taught? : resisting lore in creative writing pedagogy / edited by Stephanie Vanderslice and Rebecca Manery.
Description: 2nd edition, 10th Anniversary Edition. | London ; New York : Bloomsbury Academic, [2017] | "New chapters on identity and activism Can Creative Writing Really Be Taught? is supported by a companion website at www.bloomsbury.com, including extensive links to online resources, teaching case studies and lesson plans" | Includes bibliographical references and index.
Identifiers: LCCN 2016052120| ISBN 9781474285049 (pb) | ISBN 9781474285056 (hb)
Subjects: LCSH: Creative writing (Higher education) | English language--Rhetoric--Study and teaching (Higher)
Classification: LCC PE1404 .C327 2017 | DDC 808/.0420711--dc23 LC record available at https://lccn.loc.gov/2016052120

Cover design: Alice Marwick

Typeset by RefineCatch Limited, Bungay, Suffolk
Printed and bound in India

To find out more about our authors and books visit www.bloomsbury.com. Here you will find extracts, author interviews, details of forthcoming events and the option to sign up for our newsletters.

CONTENTS

ACKNOWLEDGMENTS

Stephanie Vanderslice would like to acknowledge once again, the early support of her mentor, Dr. David Harvey, whose leadership and encouragement of her pursuit of this field at the beginning of her career has made all the difference, and to thank Graeme Harper for responding so kindly to her first email years ago. While bringing this manuscript to fruition, she was also fortunate to work with insightful editors and brilliant contributors and to enjoy the love and support of her family, often accompanied by achingly beautiful cello refrains and the affections of two loyal dogs. For all of this, she is grateful.

LIST OF CONTRIBUTORS

Janelle Adsit is an assistant professor of creative writing at Humboldt State University. Her poetry, reviews, and essays have appeared in literary journals such as *Cultural Society*, *Mid-American Review*, *Colorado Review*, and *Requited*. She is the author of *Unremitting Entrance* (Spuyten Duyvil, 2015) and a chapbook *Press Yourself Against a Mirror* (Porkbelly, 2015). Her research on writing pedagogy is available in *Creative Writing in the Digital Age* (Bloomsbury, 2014), *Feminist Formations*, and elsewhere.

Stephen B. Armstrong is an associate professor of English at Dixie State University in St. George, Utah. He is the author of *Pictures about Extremes: The Films of John Frankenheimer* (2007) and *Andrew V. McLaglen: The Life and Hollywood Career* (2011). He also edited *John Frankenheimer: Interviews, Essays and Profiles* (2013). His biographical study of film director Paul Bartel has been accepted for publication by McFarland & Co. and will be forthcoming.

Wendy Bishop was the former Kellogg Hunt Professor of English at Florida State University and the author or editor of a number of essays, and articles on composition and creative writing pedagogy and writing research, as well as twenty-two books including *Acts of Revision*; *The Subject Is Writing, Third Edition*; *The Subject Is Story*; *The Subject Is Research*; and *The Subject Is Reading*, as well as *Ethnographic Writing Research*, *Elements of Alternate Style*, *In Praise of Pedagogy*, *Teaching Lives: Essays and Stories*. She was also a prolific poet whose posthumus book of poetry, *My Last Door* was published by Annhinga Press in 2007. A generous colleague and mentor, she pioneered the field of creative writing studies until her untimely death in 2003 and her influence continues today.

Patrick Bizzaro has published eleven books and chapbooks of poetry, most recently *Poems of the Manassas Battlefield* from Mount Olive College Press and *Interruptions* from Finishing Line Press. To Bizzaro's credit are two critical studies of Fred Chappell's poetry and fiction with LSU Press, a book on the pedagogy of academic creative writing with NCTE, four textbooks, and a couple hundred poems, reviews and review essays in literary magazines. He has won the Madeline Sadin Award from *NYQ* and *Four Quarter's* Poetry Prize as well as a Fulbright to visit South Africa during 2012. Bizzaro, first Director of the University Writing Program at East Carolina University in Greenville, NC, is a UNC Board of Governor's Distinguished Professor for Teaching and ECU Scholar-Teacher Award winner. He lives with Resa Crane and their son, Antonio, in Indiana, PA, where he recently retired as a full professor from Indiana University of Pennsylvania's doctoral program in Composition and TESOL, after retiring in 2008 from ECU as Professor Emeritus of English. During his last year on the ECU faculty, he received the "Outstanding Professor" award from the ECU Department of Disability Support Services, the ninth award for teaching he has received during his career. His articles on Creative Writing Studies and composition have appeared regularly in *College English* and *College Composition and Communication*. His co-edited book on poet and pedagogue Wendy Bishop, *Composing Ourselves as Writer-Teacher-Writers*, was published spring 2011 by Hampton Press. He is at work on a new book of poetry and a literary study, *The Rhetoric of the New Southern Writing*.

Mary Ann Cain's fiction, nonfiction essays, and poems have appeared in literary journals ranging from venerable standards such as *The Denver Quarterly*, *The Sun: A Magazine of Ideas*, *The Bitter Oleander* and *The North American Review* to experimental venues such as *First Intensity* and *LIT*. Her novel, *Down from Moonshine*, was published by Thirteenth Moon Press in 2009. She has received two Indiana Arts Commission Individual Artist grants. Her recent critical work on writing theory and praxis includes a collaborative book (with Michelle Comstock and Lil Brannon), *Composing Public Space: Teaching Writing in the Face of Private Interests* (Heinemann, 2010). She has also published a monograph on writing workshops, *Revisioning Writers' Talk* (SUNY Press, 1995), as well as numerous articles and book chapters about writing and writing instruction. She is currently Professor of English at Indiana University Purdue University Fort Wayne where she teaches fiction, creative nonfiction, rhetoric and women's studies. Her latest project is a nonfiction book about the legacy of Chicago artist-teacher-activist Dr. Margaret Burroughs.

Katharine Haake is the author of five works of fiction, including a dystopian eco-fiction, *The Time of Quarantine*, a hybrid prose lyric, *That Water, Those Rocks*, and three collections of stories. Her writing has long appeared in such magazines as *One Story*, *Crazyhorse*, *The Iowa Review*, *New Letters*, and *Witness*, and has been recognized as distinguished by *Best American Short Stories* and *Best American Essays*, among others. A long time contributor to the scholarship and theory of creative writing, Haake is also the author of *What Our Speech Disrupts: Feminism and Creative Writing Studies*, and, with Wendy Bishop and Hans Ostrom, *Metro: Journeys in Writing Creatively*. She teaches at California State University, Northridge.

Graeme Harper is a Professor of Creative Writing and Dean of The Honors College at Oakland University, Michigan. He is editor of *New Writing: The International Journal for the Practice and Theory of Creative Writing*, of *New Writing Viewpoints* and of the *Approaches to Writing* series. Graeme was the inaugural chair of the Higher Education Committee at the UK's National Association of Writers in Education (NAWE). He founded and directs the Great Writing International Creative Writing Conference, now in its twentieth year. Formerly a Commonwealth Scholar in Creative Writing, he is an award-winning fiction writer. His latest novel is *The Japanese Cook* (Parlor, 2017).

Tonya Cherie Hegemin grew up in West Chester, Pennsylvania and Rochester, New York. She majored in poetry at the University of Pittsburg and received her MFA in Writing for Children at The New School University. Her book, *Most Loved in All the World*, won New York Public Library's Ezra Jack Keats Award in 2009 and a Christopher Award for Positive Media that same year. Her young adult novel, *M+O 4evr*, was short listed for the ALA Best Books for Reluctant Readers prize and was featured on CosmoGirl.com's Best Summer Reads '08. Her novel *Willow* was a finalist for the Phyllis Wheatley award. She has also published criticism and poetry. She is currently Assistant Professor and Creative Writing Coordinator at Medgar Evers-College, City University of New York.

Trent Hergenrader is an Assistant Professor of English at the Rochester Institute of Technology. His research resides at the intersection of creative writing studies, digital pedagogy, and games and game-based learning. In addition to his short fiction publications, he has published numerous articles and chapters on role-playing games and fiction writing. He is co-founder and Secretary of the Creative Writing Studies Organization, a senior editor for the *Journal of Creative Writing Studies* and co-edited the collections *Creative Writing in the Digital Age* and *Creative Writing Innovations*. His current project is a book entitled *Collaborative World Building for Writers and Gamers*, published by Bloomsbury, due out in 2018.

Petra Kuppers is a disability culture activist, a community performance artist, and a Professor at the University of Michigan. Her *Disability Culture and Community Performance: Find a Strange and Twisted Shape* (2011) explores arts-based research methods. She is editor of *Somatic Engagement* (2011) and author of *Studying Disability Arts and Culture: An Introduction* (2014), a book full of practical exercises for classrooms and studios. Her most recent poetry collection, *PearlStitch*, appeared with Spuyten Duyvil Press (2016), and her previous books include *Disability and Contemporary Performance: Bodies on Edge* (2003), *The Scar of Visibility: Medical Performance and Contemporary Art* (2007) and *Community Performance: An Introduction* (2007).

Anna Leahy is the author of the poetry collections *Aperture* (Shearsman, 2017) and *Constituents of Matter* (Kent State University Press) and the nonfiction book *Tumor* (Bloomsbury, 2017) and the co-author of *Generation Space* (Stillhouse, 2017), *What We Talk about When We Talk about Creative Writing* (Multilingual Matters, 2016), and *Conversing with Cancer* (Peter Lang, 2017). She teaches in the MFA and BFA programs at Chapman University, where she directs both undergraduate research and Tabula Poetica. See more at www.amleahy.com.

Gregory Light is a senior fellow and the former director of the Searle Center for Advancing Learning and Teaching and a professor in the School of Education and Social Policy at Northwestern University. He completed his PhD (on Learning Creative Writing in higher Education) at the University of London in the UK where he was a faculty member of the Lifelong Learning Group at the Institute of Education (UCL). His teaching and research focuses on the theory and practice of learning, teaching and assessment in higher and professional education. He has published over fifty papers and chapters in national and international peer-reviewed publications and given over 100 invited talks, workshops and conference presentations in North and South America, Europe, Africa and Asia. He is the author, with Susanna Calkins, of *Learning and Teaching in Higher Education: The Reflective Professional* (Sage, 2001, 2009); and, with Marina Micari, of *Making Scientists: Six Principles for Effective College Teaching* (Harvard University Press, 2013).

Rebecca Manery is Assistant Professor of English at Ball State University. She completed a PhD in English and Education at the University of Michigan in 2016 and an MFA in Creative Writing at Bennington College in 2009. Her dissertation, "The Education of the Creative Writing Teacher: A Study of Conceptions of Creative Writing Pedagogy in Higher Education" is an investigation of variation in conceptions and practices of creative writing pedagogy teachers in U.S. graduate creative writing programs. Her article, "Revisiting the Pedagogy and Theory Corral: Creative Writing Pedagogy Teachers' Conceptions of Pedagogic Identity" appeared in the June 2015 issue of *New Writing: The International Journal for the Practice and Theory of Creative Writing*. She has presented at numerous national and international conferences including the Association of Writers and Writing Programs, the Conference on College Composition and Communication, and Great Writing. Her poetry, dramaturgy, and arts journalism have appeared in numerous print and online publications. Her debut poetry collection, *View from the Hotel de l'Etoile*, was published in 2016 by Finishing Line Press.

Tim Mayers is associate professor of English at Millersville University of Pennsylvania, where he teaches courses in creative writing, composition, writing studies, and the disciplinary histories of English studies. He is the author of *(Re)Writing Craft: Composition, Creative Writing, and the Future of English Studies*. He is also a published poet and an award-winning novelist.

Joseph Rein is co-editor of *Creative Writing in the Digital Age, Dispatches from the Classroom*, and the forthcoming *Creative Writing Innovations*. His creative work has appeared in over twenty journals and anthologies, most recently *Ruminate, Iron Horse Literary Review* and *Pinch Literary Magazine*, and has been nominated for a Pushcart Prize. Two of his screenplays have also been produced into award-winning festival films. He is currently an Assistant Professor of Creative Writing at the University of Wisconsin-River Falls.

Ben Ristow writes and teaches at Hobart and William Smith Colleges (Geneva, New York). His scholarship, short fiction and poetry has appeared or is forthcoming in *New Writing: The International Journal for the Practice and Theory of Creative Writing, Praxis: A Writing Center Journal, Writing on the Edge, Gray's Sporting Journal, Indiana Review, BOMB Magazine.*

Phil Sandick is a PhD candidate in Rhetoric and Composition at The University of North Carolina-Chapel Hill, where he teaches writing, literature, and film. Formerly a fiction editor at *The Carolina Quarterly*, Phil received an MFA in fiction from the University of Wisconsin-Madison.

Stephanie Vanderslice edited the first edition of *Can It Really Be Taught: Resisting Lore In Creative Writing Pedagogy* with Kelly Ritter in 2007. Her most recent books are *Studying Creative Writing Successfully* and *Rethinking Creative Writing* (Frontinus, 2016, 2012). She has published fiction, nonfiction and creative writing criticism in numerous venues. Professor of Creative Writing and Director of the Arkansas Writer's MFA Workshop at the University of Central Arkansas, her column, *The Geek's Guide to the Writing Life* appears regularly in the *Huffington Post* and will be forthcoming soon in expanded book form from Bloomsbury. She is founding chair of the Creative Writing Studies Organization. Updates about her projects and pursuits can be found at www.stephanievanderslice.com.

Jen Webb is Distinguished Professor of Creative Practice at the University of Canberra, and Director of the Centre for Creative and Cultural Research. Her most recent scholarly books are *Researching Creative Writing* (Frontinus, 2015) and *Art and Human Rights: Contemporary Asian Contexts* (with C Turner; Manchester University Press, 2016), and her recent creative books are the poetry collection *Stolen Stories, Borrowed Lines* (Mark Time

Publishers, 2015), and the poetry and photography collection *Watching the World: Impressions of Canberra* (with P. Hetherington; Blemish Books, 2015). Jen is co-editor of the scholarly journal *Axon: Creative Explorations* and the literary journal *Meniscus*. Her current research focuses on creative labor studies, and material poetics.

Can it Really be Taught? Influential Essays Revisited by Their Authors

Introduction—Lore Past, Present, and Future:

The Tenth Anniversary of *Can Creative Writing Really Be Taught?*

Stephanie Vanderslice

Story and history are important to our field, and to the world, and you will find much written in this new edition of *Can Creative Writing Really Be Taught?* about disciplinary histories and where to find them—hidden and in plain sight. Indeed, any historian interested in the rise of Creative Writing could learn much from two stories in my own history, the story told by the comparison of our efforts to get the first edition of this book published versus the second, and the story told simply by the book orders for the creative writing pedagogy course I founded and began teaching in 2002, one year after my first co-author, Kelly Ritter, made her famous plea for more of such courses in creative writing programs in College English.

As you might imagine, these stories are connected.

When I first began teaching my creative writing pedagogy course—which has always filled and sometimes been oversubscribed—of only three books available, I chose: Wendy Bishop, Kate Haake and Hans Ostrum's edited collection, *Colors of a Different Horse: Rethinking Creative Writing*, and Bishop's book *Released into Language: Some Thoughts on Teaching Creative Writing* (which I made special arrangements to purchase directly through Bishop herself, since it was out of print). (The third, Joseph Moxley's *Creative Writing in America*, while a trailblazing book, was already thirteen years old at that point). These books dominated for three years, until 2006, when I could finally add Anna Leahy's *Power and Identity in the Creative Writing*

Classroom: The Authority Project and suggest Tim Mayers's and Kate Haake's single authored books about the field as supplemental texts. *Power and Identity* served as my core text for the next several years—at least five—and is even now still a favorite supplemental text with my students—although starting in 2007 I could also augment the list with the first edition of *Can It Really Be Taught*. By 2012, however, the number of texts available to support the course had grown significantly, with notable collections such as *Does the Workshop Still Work?* by Dianne Donnelly and *Dispatches from the Classroom: Graduate Students on Creative Writing Pedagogy*, by Chris Drew, Joseph Rein and David Yost becoming new favorites in my own course. And even now, anyone ordering texts for one of the dozens of courses taught today (thanks again, Kelly Ritter) has a veritable feast of books to select from.

A great deal had to happen behind the scenes to bring this feast to the table. I'm not privy to what went down between Wendy Bishop, Kate Haake, Hans Ostrum, Mary Ann Cain, Pat Bizzaro and others in the 1990s and early 2000s. But I do remember how hard Anna Leahy, Kelly Ritter and I worked to convince traditional academic publishers at the time that there *was* an audience for a book about creative writing pedagogy. Anna Leahy ended up going with the very wise Graeme Harper over at Multilingual Matters, a press that has turned out to be a leader in our field, while Kelly Ritter and I, after years of persistence, finally managed to persuade Heinemann that people really *would* read this book. We turned out to be right too—it was a consistent seller for them that never went out of print, until we pressed for a second edition. Heinemann had gone in an entirely different direction by then. They released the book to Bloomsbury, who had already agreed enthusiastically to the new vision Rebecca Manery and I had about a second edition.

Fast forward ten years and all that work, writing and proposing at times, it seemed, into the abyss, has indeed paid off. Anna has just marked the tenth anniversary of the New Writing Viewpoints series with the publication of *What We Talk About When We Talk About Creative Writing*, a stellar new volume; Professional and Higher has ventured forth with the Creative Writing Studies imprint (launched with my own book, *Rethinking Creative Writing*) and Bloomsbury Academic has shown the kind of vision and foresight that has led to a number of critical works in the field, not the least of which is the volume you hold in your hands.

The second edition of *Can Writing Really Be Taught: Resisting Lore in Creative Writing Pedagogy*, newly revised and expanded, stands at this moment at a critical juncture between the past and the future, looking productively back at where we've been and turning, sanguine and sage, toward all the possibilities yet to come. And they are rich indeed. What is perhaps most notable about these essays, in addition to their depth and breadth and the ways in which many of them are able to surface entirely new ways about thinking about creative writing, is how much they speak to one another, truly capturing the current synergy of our field. Tim Mayers' revision of "(Re)Figuring the Future," for example, in its renewed focus on lore, creative writing and institutional and disciplinary history, offers one vision for creative writing in the academy going forward, while Pat Bizzaro's "Finding Truth in the Gaps," offers another and Phil Sandick's "Lore 2.0" speaks to both of these visions by considering the critical nature of lore in understanding disciplinary history itself.

Conversely, in "Against Reading 2" Katherine Haake worries about the "untheorized" nature of the claim that writers are readers first, and proposes the creative writing classroom as a natural site for "questions about language, authorship, power, writing itself," a proposal that very much presages Janelle Adsit's essay, "Polemics against Polemics: Reconsidering Didacticism in Creative Writing," which urges that the writing classroom, "put a diverse range of texts into conversation and ask what is possible." Moreover, in revising "Charming Tyrants, Faceless Facilitators," Mary Ann Cain looks at problems that arise when the two personas (charming tyrant, faceless facilitator) influence the way students receive and learn course materials, while Anna Leahy picks up that very same thread when she interrogates the different ways she has approached student resistance to course readings over the years in, "It's such a good feeling: Self-esteem, the Growth Mindset and Creative Writing'." And again, Stephen Armstrong winds up the first section, as he did the first book, by invoking his late co-author, Wendy Bishop, and calling upon us all to watch movies about writers with the same interrogative eye that Haake or Adsit would ask us to cast upon iconic texts.

The second section enjoys some of the voices I've already mentioned, such as Janelle Adsit and Phil Sandick, as well as several more new voices in the field and some national and international leaders in areas the first volume did not include. Australian scholar Jen Webb complicates the subject of lore from a new perspective, one that is perhaps less skeptical and more aligned with Phil Sandick as well, noting that academics tend to look askance at lore because "academics are committed to knowledge that is won," while, "lore is given," or perceived as given. She also suggests, echoing some of what I have said in my own work on Anglophile writing pedagogy, that lore is less of a problem in Australia and the UK because for some time now, "institutional demands have propelled writing teachers into the logic of the academy." "It is a long time," Webb adds, "since anyone [in Australia] seriously wondered, for example, whether it is possible to teach creative writing." Tonya Cherie Hegamin, moreover, challenges the lore that the creative writing classroom is a neutral space and in an essay that is both memoir and academic study, explores what it really means to make space for creative writing, in a culture where it may still be considered a "white endeavor," in "'We don't need no creative writing': Black Cultural Capital, Social (In)Justice and the Devaluing of Creativity in Higher Education'." And disability studies expert Petra Kuppers further challenges this idea of neutrality when she offers classroom exercises that "shift myth and disability stereotypes" in "Disability Culture and Creative Writing Pedagogies: When having Fun Together is Radical Practice."

Trent Hergenrader shatters another myth—that genre fiction does not belong in the creative writing classroom—in "Genre Fiction, and Games and Fanfiction! Oh my! Collaborative Creative Writing in Pre-existing Fictional Worlds," an essay that not only looks at how and why genre fiction can fit in the creative writing classroom space but also considers benefits to student writing development from making room for fanfiction and collaborative world building as well. And Joseph Rein considers the effect of the lore of "authorship" on the creative writing classroom, including the representation of authorship in movies and popular culture described by Armstrong and Bishop, especially the ways this lore may hinder the revision process of student writers and his own methods for resisting it in, "'It's my story and I'll revise if I want to': Rethinking Authorship Through Collaborative Workshop Practices." Ben Ristow, meanwhile, takes a close look at the stories writing programs tell in their own promotional videos and the ways in which these videos can re-inscribe lore and provide disciplinary history (also recalling Sandick's suggestion that lore can be a source of history) in "Toward a Digital Historiography of Creative Writing Programs in our Millennium."

Taking a playful turn, in, "Creative Writing with Godzilla: Welcoming the Monster to your Creative Writing Classroom," leading British creative scholar Graeme Harper notes that in our educational institutions (Western English language classrooms) "the equality of creative knowledge and critical knowledge is constantly challenged, quite frequently with work encouraged, responded to and graded according to a struggle or sense of hostility" and offers "Godzilla, the monstrous, the abject, . . . untainted by the baggage of much current and dubious creative writing lore . . . existing before we imposed symbolic, representational, constructed and frequently reactionary notions on our creative writing teaching and learning," as a symbol for bringing together oppositional theories in the creative writing classroom in order to breathe.

In his essay "Investigating Creative Writing: Challenging Obstacles to Empirical Research," Greg Light adds another dimension to the title of the book itself when he examines lore and authentic research into what students actually learn in their actual study of creative writing, significantly illuminating our understanding of our students' development and calling for more of this kind of research. Finally, Rebecca Manery's work returns us to the creative writing pedagogy course, now established enough to be a subject of resource itself. "Myths, Mirrors, and Metaphors: The Education of the Creative Writing Teacher," undertakes a thorough analysis of the creative writing pedagogy course, where teachers are presumably taught and our discipline is preserved and extended. Her results offer a thoughtful critique of the course as it is taught now that both circle us back to where we started and serve to mark again, how far we have come. What is most promising, however, is that, in spite of our gains, and they are many, as this book and the talented authors within it demonstrate, we stand at the threshold of a truly exciting future.

1

(Re)Figuring the Future:

Lore, Creative Writing Studies, and Institutional Histories

Tim Mayers

> *In history, things always hide other things.*
> JOHN MCCUMBER, *ON PHILOSOPHY: NOTES FROM A CRISIS*

Roughly a decade ago, I began my chapter in the first version of *Can It Really Be Taught?* by noting that creative writers in academe often existed in a kind of "privileged marginality" (privileged because their activity was regarded as rare and mysterious, marginalized because by producing poetry and fiction rather than analysing it interpretively—or at least by prioritizing production over analysis—they stood outside the mainstream of the English departments in which they were almost always housed). Today, I don't find that characterization (which even back then I admitted might be a bit overgeneralized and stereotypical, albeit accurate enough to elicit nods of agreement from many of those familiar with creative writing's position in the academic world) quite so apt any more. Yes, some pockets of privileged marginality remain. Yes, there are still quite a few creative writers (mostly well-published poets and fiction writers who have also won numerous and prestigious awards) teaching in MFA programs, dealing solely or mainly with graduate students, and living comfortably enough to devote large amounts of time and energy to their own writing without worrying about, or perhaps even paying attention to, the daily administrivia and toils of the departments and universities where they work. But I suspect that for the vast majority of newer academics and aspiring academics with a background and/

or interest in creative writing, the attainment of such a position is a virtual impossibility: a nostalgic hope that may have been possible in the past but not now, something not much more attainable than making a comfortable living by writing alone, or by winning a multi-state lottery jackpot.

Indeed, for many today the reality is much different. People with MFAs (or PhDs) in creative writing and numerous publications can sometimes find academic work (if they can find it at all) only as low-paid adjuncts with no benefits, no job security, and very little academic freedom. Sometimes this adjunct work does not even involve teaching creative writing, but rather teaching first-year composition: a task for which the MFA holder may or may not be well prepared or temperamentally suited. While creative writing courses and programs thrive at both the graduate and undergraduate levels, drawing record numbers of students, the number of well-paying, tenure-track jobs in creative writing is miniscule in comparison to the number of people seeking them, and thus competition for those jobs is fierce. The irony is striking. On one hand, creative writing's move into the academy, begun (depending which historian's account you find most persuasive) in the late nineteenth or early twentieth century, accelerated after the Second World War, and consolidated from roughly the 1960s onward, has been a smashing success. On the other hand, while colleges and universities produce more and more credentialed creative writers every year, they provide fewer and fewer viable employment opportunities for those very writers—at least if those writers conceptualize viable employment according to models established by the creative writers who found academic employment between the early and middle decades of the twentieth century.

I do not mean to suggest that the current situation of creative writing in the academy developed only over the course of the past ten years. There were warnings about the number of good academic jobs available for holders of MFAs or PhDs in creative writing long before that. There were also questions raised (at least in some corners) about the wisdom and viability of the workshop as the sole or primary model for creative writing pedagogy. What is significant about the past ten years is the sudden coming together of forces that have exacerbated or made more visible the issues that swirled around creative writing in prior decades: the lingering effect of the economic downturn of 2008 on an already-poor academic job market, aggravating the decades-long erosion of tenured or tenure-track employment for many academics; the role of blogs and online social media in circulating old and frequently disingenuous critiques of creative writing programs to wider audiences than ever before; the reshaping of the publishing landscape through the continuing emergence and viability of electronic alternatives to traditional print publication of literary works; the renewed popularity of so-called "genre fiction," especially among younger readers who eventually find themselves in college or university creative writing classrooms; and the rapid proliferation in the United States of scholarly publications in an emerging subfield many are calling "creative writing studies." The publication of a revised and expanded version of *Can It Really Be Taught?* might be read, on one level, as a response to all of these developments.

Thrown into history

For nearly twenty years now, I have been writing, talking, and thinking about creative writing's actual and possible places in the academy. Looking back today on "Figuring the Future: Lore and/in Creative Writing," it becomes both easy and difficult to see that chapter in the earlier version of this book as part of a dynamic and unfinished project—as part of an argument that has been developing over time, and continues to develop. Perhaps the most stable, fixed point in that argument is the crucial importance of disciplinary and institutional history. Virtually all of my published work in the field now called creative writing studies has hinged in some way on the insistence that in order to assess creative writing's current place in the academy, and to chart viable paths for its future, we must study and come to terms with its institutional history. And in doing so, we inevitably must broaden our focus not simply to include creative writing, but also the other subfields of the English departments which have most often housed it; the educational institutions that have housed those English departments; the ideological and material dimensions of the subfields that make up English studies at the local, national, and global levels; and the larger sweep of political, philosophical, economic, and cultural ideas in which the contemporary academy is embedded.

My own journey toward understanding the importance of institutional histories was spurred in part by two jarring realizations I made during my time as a student in an MA program in creative writing. The first was that outside the small liberal arts college environment where I had spent my undergraduate years, creative writing was often separated by a wide intellectual chasm from other subfields of English studies and other fields and disciplines in the university. The second realization was that the likelihood of obtaining a tenure-track job in an English department, if I chose to align myself solely with creative writing, was slim at best. And this was a quarter century ago! It pains me today still to see people shocked, angered, and feeling betrayed that their MFA degrees—and now, often, their publication of books as well—do not land them tenure-track jobs in English departments. Whatever we want to say in the ongoing debate over whether the MFA is a terminal degree or not, the fact remains that for a long time now, the MFA has not been a guarantee (or anything close to it) of a decent academic job. Of course there are still individual success stories even today. But in the bigger picture, they are becoming exceedingly rare.

The triple desire to find stable academic employment, to maintain an active connection to creative writing as a practitioner and a teacher, and to understand how things had gotten the way they were, led me (after a few years teaching composition, creative writing, world literature, and business writing as a low-paid adjunct) to the study of English studies' institutional history, which led me to a PhD program in rhetoric and composition, which was then, in the early 1990s (and probably still is today) the best place for an aspiring academic to engage in such work. I became energized, at the time, by some of the theoretical scholarship being done in rhetoric and composition—scholarship that dug beneath the surface question of how we teach students to write better toward the deeper question of what it means to want students to write better. I was struck by the way composition scholarship asked crucial questions about where our conceptions of what writing is and how writing works originated, and how those conceptions affect the way we practice writing and evaluate it. (My interest in philosophy, which dated back to my undergraduate years as a double major in English literature and philosophy, also came into play here.) Quite often, such investigations were steeped in institutional histories both of English studies and of higher education in the U.S.—histories that revealed there is usually nothing natural or inevitable about how writing is treated, assigned, and evaluated in our institutions of higher learning. Many of the problems we face in our classrooms and our institutions are not new, even though they may appear to be. And if we falsely continue to believe that these issues are new, we are likely to repeat the mistakes of the past. Understanding our histories may not help us solve all of our problems immediately, but it does offer us a more productive vantage point from which to keep trying.

As a PhD student, I became convinced that the kind of historically-infused theory about writing that I found in composition studies might profitably be brought to creative writing. My 1998 doctoral dissertation, after much revision and reorganization, became *(Re)Writing Craft: Composition, Creative Writing, and the Future of English Studies*, published in 2005. In that book, I argued that creative writers in the academy ought to pursue one of two paths, depending on the exigencies of their local situations: 1. Join with their colleagues in composition and rhetoric to secede from literature-dominated English departments and form departments of their own, departments that might operate under the banner of "writing studies." This course of action would, for all intents and purposes, split English studies apart; or 2. Join with their colleagues in composition and rhetoric to remain within English departments and challenge the dominance of interpretive literary study within pedagogy, curricula, and hiring practices—also under the banner of "writing studies," in this case as a means to reconfigure the larger enterprise of English studies from the inside. This course of action would not split English studies apart but keep it together, albeit in a radically changed form, by challenging many of the assumptions that have historically defined it. In "Figuring the Future,"—the chapter I am revisiting here, published two years after *(Re)Writing Craft*—I focused more on the second path, concluding with three related pleas for more integration of creative writing into other strands of English studies, and more attention among historical disciplinary scholars to the roles that creative writing has played (or could have played, or could yet play) within the broader realm of English studies. Although I critiqued creative writing then for many of its practices, and still do so today, I was convinced then and remain so now that the rest of the subfields of English studies ignore creative writing—or, in some cases, critique it in reductive and dishonest ways—to their own detriment. Creative writers in academe have much to offer to English studies, and to the university itself. But we must position ourselves carefully in order to do so. Our colleagues elsewhere in the English department and elsewhere in the university have proven reticent to accept our claims of specialness and distinctiveness at face value.

The past becomes present

And so where are we now, nearly a decade after the first version of this book was published? On one hand, signs of change abound. At least two disciplinary historians have sought to place creative writing within the broader universe of English studies—not ignoring it entirely, not mentioning it only in passing, and not simply treating it as a niche area deserving its own isolated treatment. Thomas P. Miller, in *The Evolution of College English: Literacy Studies from the Puritans to the Postmoderns*, locates creative writing together with composition and rhetoric in the broader field of "writing studies" and considers writing studies to be one of the "four corners" of English studies, along with linguistics, literary studies, and English education. And Bruce McComiskey, in *English Studies: An Introduction to the Discipline(s)*, identifies creative writing as one of six distinct but occasionally overlapping subfields of English, along with linguistics, rhetoric and composition, literature, critical theory and cultural studies, and English education. Both Miller and McComiskey, from different angles, argue that creative writing needs to be acknowledged in disciplinary histories, and that it needs to be integrated more visibly into English studies in the twenty-first century. So, at least in some arenas of scholarly discussion, the longstanding belief (often unspoken and, by implication, unquestionable) that English studies is essentially nothing more than interpretive literary studies, and the somewhat related beliefs that literary studies forms the natural and unquestioned center of English studies even if there may be other (subservient) subfields, or that the history of English studies can be read only as the story of the relationships and struggles between literature and composition, are being challenged and eroded. How much reach and influence these developments have at the moment, though, is still an open question.

Another sign of change is that venues for scholarship in creative writing studies, and the sheer amount of such scholarship being written and published, appear to be on the rise. When *Can It Really Be Taught?* first appeared, creative writing studies was barely recognized as a describable entity, at least in the United States. My College English article naming and describing the emerging field would not appear until 2009 (though it should never be forgotten that Katharine Haake used the phrase "creative writing studies" quite some time before this, in the subtitle of *What Our Speech Disrupts,* published in 2000). Two years after my article appeared, Dianne Donnelly's *Establishing Creative Writing Studies as an Academic Discipline* offered a book-length argument about what the field might be and where it might go. The New Writing Viewpoints series from Multilingual Matters, inaugurated in 2005 by Anna Leahy's *Power and Identity in the Creative Writing Classroom: The Authority Project,* now features more than a dozen titles, and Bloomsbury Academic has also begun to establish itself as a viable and welcoming home for scholarship in creative writing studies. A new generation of teacher-writer-scholars, many of them having gone on to earn PhDs in composition and rhetoric after earning MFAs in creative writing, has arrived on the scene. And their energy and passion, along with a sense that English studies' established major professional organizations (MLA, CCCC, and AWP) do not provide welcoming enough spaces for the kinds of work they wish to do, have led directly to the formation of the new Creative Writing Studies Organization (CWSO), which promises to make the work of creative writing studies more visible in the coming years.

On the other hand, signs of resistance to change (or of outright ignorance of change) abound also. There are vocal groups both inside and outside the academy that appear insistent on characterizing creative writing only as an enterprise dedicated to the training of writers for success in the traditional literary print marketplaces via the singular pedagogical method of the workshop. While these groups share a shallow and unreflective notion of what creative writing is, they differ dramatically in their assessment of what should be done. Those reactionaries inside the academy tend to assert that creative writing is fine just the way it is, not in need of any kind of reflection or examination or revision. Business as usual, they say, must continue. Those reactionaries outside the academy (or inside the academy while paradoxically occupying an anti-academic stance) tend to assert that creative writing programs, by training too many allegedly mediocre writers and providing too many of them with stable employment, clog the literary marketplace with an excessive number of publications and cut off writing from the "real world" outside the academy. Based on these assumptions, they argue that MFA programs, and creative writing instruction generally, ought to be abolished or dramatically scaled back. Because the reactionaries both inside and outside the academy are so vocal, and so steadfastly locked into their positions, many discussions of creative writing often still seem bogged down in the old unproductive commonplaces: Can creative writing really be taught?; and Are MFA programs destroying contemporary literature? And even worse—participants in those discussions often seem not to know, or not to care, that there exists a significant history of scholarship and discussion around those issues that might help us get beyond repeating worn out slogans.

Lore, with and without history

Lore is still a key lens through which many view creative writing pedagogy. Indeed, for some practitioners it seems that pedagogy is implicitly defined as lore, and not much more. Consider, for instance, the Facebook group "Creative Writing Pedagogy," which, at the time I am writing this chapter, has more than 4,000 members. A significant number of the discussion thread-starters there take one of two forms. The first is what might be called a "seeking models" question, something like, I'm looking for examples of short fiction, set in suburban locations, using more than one first-person narrator and preferably published online. In this kind of question/discussion, the originator presumably believes that a key way to teach creative writing is through "model texts," and is asking others in the online community to offer examples of texts that fit the model, probably so that they can be assigned for students to read, either individually or as a whole class. Sometimes the kinds of text asked for are more broadly defined than the one above (which is not quoted directly from the Facebook group but "invented" here by me as an amalgam: a typical sort of request that might be seen there, based on my having seen scores of them over the past couple of years) and sometimes they are defined even more narrowly. Crucial to my point here is that this kind of request appears often enough in the Facebook group to be considered a recognizable subgenre there. A second such subgenre might be called the "problem student/problem situation" question, which (again, this is not a direct quote but an invented one, generated by the type) usually goes something like this: There's a student in my workshop who won't follow directions and insists on submitting "genre fiction" for every assignment even though I've insisted that s/he supply realist fiction instead. This kind of question appears to assume that problematic teaching situations can be addressed by applying the proper kind of pedagogical "fix," which can be provided, if the teacher does not yet know what it is, by other teachers who have experienced and solved similar problems before. Rarely is this kind of question posed in such a way that assumes perhaps the problem situation is a manifestation of the ways in which the teacher has (perhaps unwittingly) framed the enterprise of creative writing narrowly or contradictorily. Questions within these two subgenres are nor "bad" sorts of questions, but they certainly are limiting sorts of questions— questions that implicitly define creative writing pedagogy within a quite narrow framework, as a bag of tricks or collection of techniques that can be deployed on an ad hoc basis, often without considering any context larger than fixing a day-to-day problem.

I should be abundantly clear here: the Creative Writing Pedagogy group on Facebook is a wonderful and productive online space that brings together a wide variety of voices for discussions that could not happen otherwise, or at least could not happen with the same immediacy as they do there. My own thinking about creative writing pedagogy has been immeasurably enhanced by many of the conversations that happen there. The trends I note in the previous paragraph do not, by any means, characterize all of the discussions that take place within the group. They do, however, illustrate that lore-oriented conceptions about the nature of pedagogy exhibit an extraordinary staying power, as they continue to proliferate alongside other sorts of notions that extend and complicate the idea of what pedagogy is.

Probably the most significant problem with lore is—and long has been—that the conditions of its emergence tend to make it appear natural and neutral, as though it is purely pragmatic and outside the realms of history, ideology, and culture. Yet lore is never outside such realms, and its perceived naturalness can serve to limit—sometimes severely—our field of vision. Excellent examples can be found in the recently published *Workshops of Empire: Stegner, Engle, and American Creative Writing during the Cold War*, where Eric Bennett demonstrates meticulously how so many of the aesthetic preferences and practices encouraged in the creative writing workshop (especially a preference for concreteness over abstraction) have deep roots within the turbulent swirl of competing Cold War ideologies and cannot fully be understood if divorced from this crucial originating context. There is nothing natural or neutral about an aesthetic preference for concreteness over abstraction (just as there would be nothing neutral or natural about an aesthetic preference for abstraction over concreteness). Such preferences frequently serve political ends, or originate in political ends that later become forgotten; sometimes writers are intentionally aware of these ends, sometimes not. Teachers of creative writing at the college level need to know, I would argue, something about the historical backgrounds of the aesthetic features of texts that they advocate or oppose (or even remain neutral about) in their classrooms.

None of this should overshadow the value we might often find in lore, nor should it suggest that lore should be completely abandoned. Sometimes, that little piece of advice we pick up from a colleague, or that exercise or assignment we design to deal with a particular classroom frustration we've been experiencing, works. Yet if we don't understand why or how it works (and with lore, we sometimes don't), or if we do not make some attempt to understand, we are back to square one if at some point in the future, with different students or in a different situation, it stops working. Another argument against the complete abandonment of lore, as I noted in the first version of this chapter, can be found in Patricia Harkin's "The Postdisciplinary Politics of Lore." Harkin argues that because lore often operates outside the "disciplining" constraints of a traditional academic discipline, it harbors the potential for generating "postdisciplinary" knowledge. But then again, this requires not only using lore or purveying it for the short-term benefit of ourselves and others, but also understanding—or at least attempting to understand—where that lore came from and what purposes it may have served in the past.

(Re)placing lore

How might we avoid lore's dangers while taking advantage of its promises? At least one obvious place is in graduate education for creative writers. Every MFA program serving students who wish to pursue academic careers, every PhD program in creative writing, and certainly (if these emerge in the near future) every PhD program in creative writing studies, should include at least one course on the disciplinary histories of English studies. (An alternative approach would be to weave disciplinary history into all, or nearly all, of the courses in a program. Such an approach would be more difficult to design and implement, though potentially more effective at achieving the overall aim. In the context of this current chapter, I will focus on the single-course approach.) A foundational graduate course in disciplinary history, as I envision it, would provide students with both broad views and narrowly focused views of history, and enable students to toggle back and forth between these views as necessary. For broader views of English studies, two texts I mentioned above—Bruce McComiskey's *English Studies* (which includes an excellent chapter by Katharine Haake on creative writing) and Thomas P. Miller's *The Evolution of College English*—would be essential. An even wider historical net, which would ensnare English studies in the broader fields of the humanities, could be provided by James Turner's *Philology: The Forgotten Origins of the Modern Humanities*. Interpretive literary study, so long the dominant center of English studies, would need to be approached not from the "inside," as it is in the vast majority of graduate courses in literature, but from the "outside," as in Gerald Graff's *Professing Literature*, which provides the groundbreaking argument that the yearning for a "direct experience" of the literary text, unmediated by "theory," has been a fantasy at the heart of literary study ever since its acceptance as a viable academic field, but that such an unmediated experience is actually impossible.

Composition, so long the economic engine of English departments via the required first-year composition course, and so much an influence on creative writing studies via its scholarship from the 1960s onward, would be due a large chunk of attention also, through archival histories (tinged with argument) like James Berlin's *Rhetoric and Reality* and Robert Connors's *Composition-Rhetoric*. But also important would be works that more explicitly combine history and polemic, like Sharon Crowley's *Composition in the University* and Susan Miller's *Textual Carnivals*.

And obviously, creative writing's academic history would have to play a prominent role in any disciplinary history course geared toward MFA and PhD students. D.G. Myers's *The Elephants Teach* would be essential as background, even though it stops just at the point when MFA programs began to multiply after the middle of the twentieth century. Stephen Wilbers's history of the Iowa Writers' Workshop before 1980 would be interesting, if only to demonstrate how the field's most historically prestigious program represented itself shortly after mid-century. More recent and focused histories would be useful too: books like Mark McGurl's *The Program Era* and Eric Bennett's *Workshops of Empire*, which both examine the ways in which creative writing programs have both shaped and been shaped by the literary and political cultures with which they dwell. Dianne Donnelly's *Establishing Creative Writing Studies as an Academic Discipline* is essential for understanding how creative writing's signature pedagogies have drawn from and been influenced by modes of scholarship and theory from other subfields of English studies, especially literary and composition studies. Paul Dawson's *Creative Writing and the New Humanities* usefully compares and contrasts the historical trajectories creative writing has taken in the U.S. and in Australia, and also unearths some of the complicated ways in which creative writing has been influenced by theories of literary criticism.

Our history shapes our present—and our future

The epigraph to this chapter comes from John McCumber's *On Philosophy: Notes From a Crisis*. One strand of argument in that book is that philosophers who simply wish to "do philosophy," and who consider the history of philosophy unimportant or peripheral to their own interests, are at the mercy of what is hidden from them within philosophy's history. In fact, McCumber argues, the history of philosophy is philosophy, or at the very least is an essential element of philosophy that cannot be bracketed aside in pursuit of some allegedly purer aim. I would like to suggest here that creative writers in the academy—particularly in their roles as teachers—face an analogous situation. If creative writing in the academy is "in crisis" because (among other possible reasons) one of its originating conditions—that it provided stable employment for writers whose work was successful in literary but not in financial terms—is no longer sustainable, then we must imagine and foster alternative conditions that would allow creative writing not to have to cling to that origin. At the same time, we must attend to some of the pressing questions and friction points that manifest themselves in our classrooms and programs. A deep familiarity with the history of creative writing will help us deal with these questions and friction points, which are too numerous to outline here, so one example will need to suffice: the tension between "literary fiction" and "genre fiction," and the related question of whether the creative writing workshop should allow the latter or focus exclusively on the former, have become persistent recently. Without an understanding of institutional histories, creative writing instructors can have a difficult time examining their own positions on such issues, and an even more difficult time sorting them out for students.

Ultimately, I would like to see creative writers in the academy rally around a redefined purpose—a sense of why we do what we do that differs dramatically from the ways so many of us have thought about this in the past. We need to stop thinking of ourselves as primarily training or producing new writers for the literary marketplace, if we tend to think that way now. Producing new writers for the literary marketplace may remain a major or minor purpose of some MFA programs, especially the oldest and most prestigious ones. But the overall purpose of creative writing instruction should be to provide students with opportunities for experience-based inquiry into the act of writing. There are things that can be learned via the attempt to write a story or a poem or a screenplay or a memoir that cannot be learned via the interpretive analysis of such texts. Creative writing can thus complement traditional interpretive literary study. And it can also complement composition, especially when composition takes the form of a required first-year college class focused on expository or academic writing. We need to stop thinking of our creative writing classrooms or virtual online spaces—especially our undergraduate classrooms, and especially at the introductory level—primarily as improvement zones for student writing, though we should hasten to acknowledge that student writing very often will improve through our efforts. Such improvement in the future, I hope, might be regarded as a by-product of what we do, not its primary purpose. And it will include a sense of what improvement means in the first place. It will highlight that improvement may mean different things in different contexts, and that this has been so throughout the history of creative writing. It will illuminate the contexts and backgrounds that brought (sometimes conflicting) aesthetic doctrines into being. To the extent that creative writing pedagogy continues to make use of lore, it will rely also on critical examinations of where that lore came from. And for such an endeavor, knowledge of institutional histories of the field, as background context, is essential.

References

Bennett, Eric. *Workshops of Empire: Stegner, Engle, and American Creative Writing during the Cold War*. University of Iowa Press, 2015.

Berlin, James A. *Rhetoric and Reality: Writing Instruction in American Colleges, 1900–1985*. Southern Illinois University Press, 1987.

Connors, Robert J. *Composition-Rhetoric: Backgrounds, Theory, and Pedagogy*. University of Pittsburgh Press, 1997.

Crowley, Sharon. *Composition in the University: Historical and Polemical Essays*. University of Pittsburgh Press, 1998.

Dawson, Paul. *Creative Writing and the New Humanities*. Routledge, 2005.

Donnelly, Dianne. *Establishing Creative Writing Studies as an Academic Discipline*. Multilingual Matters, 2011.

Graff, Gerald. (1987) *Professing Literature: An Institutional History*. University of Chicago Press, 2007.

Haake, Katharine. *What Our Speech Disrupts: Feminism and Creative Writing Studies*. NCTE, 2000.

Harkin, Patricia. "The Postdisciplinary Politics of Lore." *Contending with Words: Composition and Rhetoric in a Postmodern Age*. Eds Patricia Harkin and John Schilb. MLA, 1991,. 124–38.

Leahy, Anna, ed. *Power and Identity in the Creative Writing Classroom: The Authority Project*. Multilingual Matters, 2005.

Mayers, Tim. "Figuring the Future: Lore and/in Creative Writing." *Can It Really Be Taught? Resisting Lore in Creative Writing Pedagogy*. Eds Kelly Ritter and Stephanie Vanderslice. Boynton-Cook/Heinemann, 2007. 1–13.

Mayers, Tim. "One Simple Word: From Creative Writing to Creative Writing Studies." *College English* 71:3, 2009. 217–28.

Mayers, Tim. *(Re)Writing Craft: Composition, Creative Writing, and the Future of English Studies*. University of Pittsburgh Press, 2005.

McComiskey, Bruce, ed. *English Studies: An Introduction to the Discipline(s)*. NCTE, 2006.

McCumber, John. *On Philosophy: Notes from a Crisis*. Stanford University Press, 2013.

McGurl, Mark. *The Program Era: Postwar Fiction and the Rise of Creative Writing*. Harvard University Press, 2011.

Miller, Susan. *Textual Carnivals: The Politics of Composition*. Southern Illinois University Press, 1993.

Miller, Thomas P. *The Evolution of College English: Literacy Studies from the Puritans to the Postmoderns*. University of Pittsburgh Press, 2011.

Myers, D.G. *The Elephants Teach: Creative Writing Since 1880*. Prentice Hall, 1996.

Turner, James. *Philology: The Forgotten Origins of the Modern Humanities*. Princeton University Press, 2014.

Wilbers, Stephen. *The Iowa Writers' Workshop: Origins, Emergence, & Growth*. University of Iowa Press, 1980.

2

Against Reading, 2:

Or, Writing Starts Here Reconsidered

Katharine Haake

Just for the record, when I agreed to revisit this essay, "Against reading"—let's call it the precursor essay, or AR_1—I was excited. I'd thought a lot about the subject since; I had more to say. But time is a curious thing, and it's possible that fish and company may have more in common with old writing than we like to think. As well, I did not find the essay I had written to have very much in common with the essay I remembered having written.

AR_1 started off with some stories about how things were still not great in the creative writing world, mainly for reasons that even by then, a decade ago now, had begun to seem tired and old, primary among them, a pervasive top-down star system culture that fetishizes publication normed by market censorship and effectively works to reduce what counts as writing. Not that the culture itself is tired—if anything, it's more vital and entrenched. But our preoccupation with all writing's derivative effects, our incipient careerism, while not without a value of its own, has little to do with the act of writing itself, which, properly speaking, is what we should be teaching students, if we are to ensure it continues in their lives.

I talked about that, and I still consider it a challenge of grave importance to the discipline. But I'd said it a lot, in various ways, for years. Now, another decade later and approaching the end of my teaching career, I'm still saying it, although it's fair to say I am less sure of anything I'm saying these days. We start out with our passions, our convictions, and over an academic lifetime, promote them to countless—in my case, well more than a thousand—students, a staggering number. Sometimes, I can't help but wonder: what if, after all, I turn out to be wrong?

I've spent thirty years, for example, insisting to students that writing proceeds from language, not image, only to discover recently that I am one of an estimated 5–10 percent of people that are affected by aphantasia, a newly named neurological condition in which the mind's eye is blind. I don't *have* any images in my head—it's no wonder I do not write from them.

I don't want to say this—and I know I don't believe it—but in that whole-scale academic move toward pre-professionalization that has taken place in this century, an argument can surely be made that external recognition in the form of publication really is the final goal of teaching writing. Isn't it what students want? Even if only the minutest percentage of them will ever achieve it, even such a premise is sure to embody a pedagogy of monumental failure, getting work somehow into print remains the clearest marker of success we have. Is there really any problem here? Who says there's any problem?

I hedged my bets, too, at the start of AR_1, laying out all that ground work again. In the end, all that hedging didn't get me anywhere. Shortly after that essay was published, I was accosted in the department mail room by our Director of Composition.

"Tell me, Kate," she said, "are you really against students reading."

In 2002, as I began work on AR_1, the NEA had just released its seminal study, "Reading at risk," documenting the decline in literary readership, especially among what was then a new generation of college students, and since, in the precursor edition of this book the subject was lore, I took up the problem of reading. I took lore to mean received wisdom. The received wisdom of reading was that *writers are readers first.*

You and I were, anyway. We grew up immersed in and transported by books. We picked poems to read at our weddings. Some of our most memorable moments grew out of the page, and we became, over time, disciplined disciples of it.

So what were we to do with a generation of students who no longer read, or at least no longer read what we thought they should be reading, what we ourselves had read when we were coming up? For of course our students read all the time, virtually tethered to and remarkably fluent in a wide range of digital discourses well beyond our native ken. Plugged in, addicted to their screens and devices, now that the future is here, our students are already incipient cyborgs, or so Melissa Filbeck argued at the 2015 CSUN Sigma Tau Delta Conference. As for what they might read in a conventional sense on their own—comics, video games, never-ending fan fictions, a few underground texts they pass among themselves with the kind of subversive passion we may only vaguely recall—if we do not dismiss it altogether, we may view it with a kind of tolerant no-nothingness or lukewarm embrace.

That's interesting, we say, tell me more, but most of the time we're not really listening. We have words—real words—on the brain.

I talked about that.

I understood it as a problem.

If I was "against" anything, it was received reading practices, which remained—and remain—largely unexamined, as if reading itself were a "natural" activity to which we all respond as one. I wanted to think not so much about *what* we read—the canon wars already long over by then—as *how,* and what our readerly habits had to say about both our writing and writing lives.

A long time ago, a compositionist in my department wrote a class called "The reading/writing connection," against which she encountered considerable opposition. Not that I or colleagues thought that there was no connection, just that they didn't it as see something you could study.

Years before, my own reading life had evolved under a similar veil of the seemingly natural. To wit, I grew up small town inhaling big books by (male) writers with important-sounding names—*Moby Dick, Crime and Punishment, Magic Mountain*—that gave me what I thought was a kind of cachet, and from which I understood that I was neither smart enough, nor talented enough to be a writer. In college, I discovered nineteenth-century women novelists and Faulkner. I read four Faulkner books in a single weekend. Who could compete with that many words?

All this was good for something, just not the creative writing world as it was shaping up and in which I would soon enough discover the secret shame of having no idea who Raymond Carver was. The single contemporary writer I could name was Robert Coover, whose *Pricksongs and Descants* I'd picked up while traveling in Europe because it was in English and had a cool cover. That book knocked my socks off. I'd never seen anything like that book before. I didn't even know how to *think* about it.

Later, I went to PhD school and read everything else.

Along the way, I'd managed to internalize a strange idea of writing adapted from an inchoate blend of styles, forms, traditions, and intents that took me quite a while to sort out, and that I maybe only recognized when I encountered something like it, and not, in my students. At least my sense of what a story was came from reading other books, but students came to writing with wide-spread exposures to non-prose based narrative texts and not very much experience thinking about language. These days, there's the cyborg thing too. The first challenge, then, of the creative writing classroom is to help take apart the amalgam in their head and examine its inherent assumptions and effects. I've been saying so for years, not just in AR$_1$, but almost anywhere I could, before even *What Our Speech Disrupts*, where I said it most emphatically and most definitively. New technologies and media have changed things in complicated and interesting ways, but all the rest of it is pretty much the same.

Here's a little story I told in AR$_1$ and still tell in my classes.

A long time ago, a close friend, now deceased, observed that the best thing about finishing his PhD prelims was that now *he could read anything he wanted.* He said this with a kind of wonder: *anything at all that he wanted.* Naturally, I thought about this too after my own prelims, almost even before I'd got to my car and started it up to drive home: *anything I want.* But then, almost at once, a terrible sinking feeling. I was thirty-one years old and had been reading *professionally* (as in this was my *job*) for years. A lifelong compliant student, I'd finished (almost) every reading list I'd ever been assigned. Now that I'd never have to read another one *ever again*, in my sudden freedom, I found myself at an inexplicable loss: where, even, to start?

I tell this story to students because they mainly read, like I did, what people tell them to, and, also like me, have given almost no thought to reading as a practice, either theirs or anyone else's, never mind its connection to writing. I call it a practice in the same way we call yoga a practice—a practice and a discipline that can both center and organize our lives, but one we also have to learn through attentive and systematic study.

But that's not really how it works in the world. In the world reading is, among other things: an aspiration (these books will be good for me); an obligation (these books will help me pass my test or be a more scintillating dinner party guest); a materialism of experience (these books will improve me and give me status); and for those purists among us, a pleasure (these books are fun!) sometimes guilty, sometimes not. That is, reading, as an activity, is neither natural nor neutral, but constructed by institutions, forces, and economies that can be said to be, in many ways, peripheral to the essential activities of writing and literature.

I want students to think about this, because I want them to develop autonomous reading practices that proceed from the force of a desire. I want them to *desire* reading.

Ten years ago, in AR$_1$, I went on to discuss at some length the trickiness of reading lists, especially in the context of what Patrick Bizzaro describes as a "...workshop-writing phenomenon (that) no doubt works vertically, where sameness is passed from teacher to student who, in turn, becomes a teacher who passes certain literary biases to yet another generation of students."[1] The problem is a vexed one, exacerbated by the limitations of time in any given class where it falls to us to teach not just reading and writing, but how to think about both, i.e., theory. At some level, I argued in AR$_1$, it hardly matters *what* works we teach; and at some level, and in some ways, I still think that.

Still, I always remember the remark of a mid-career teacher after a first, inflammatory AWP panel on theory (1989). "But how," he said, "can I teach my students if I can't nurture them on the same great writers who nurtured me in my development as a writer?" At the time I was outraged. These were the same writers who'd convinced me to stop writing when I was a girl.

Here is a beautiful poem, we say to our students. Isn't it beautiful?

And even if we do not tell them to, our students think: that's what a beautiful poem is supposed to look like; I will write a poem like that.

If they can. And when they can't, many will, like I did once, just stop writing.

So of course it does matter—it matters a lot—what texts we choose to teach, and every choice is loaded. Whether you teach entirely from the Pushcart Prize Book or the *New Yorker*, the vertical axis prevails, and students figure out what they have to do to climb it. And in AR_1, I mainly argued for a self-reflective practice where reading itself is examined, not just:

> . . . in relation to the particular text – asking what it is, exactly, the writer might be doing, to what effect, and how – that is, questions about *how* to read – but also in relation to larger questions of reading . . . [to] teach, in addition, the dilemma itself, . . . [and to do so in the context of Foucault's famous questions]: "What are the modes of existence of the discourse? Where has it been used, how can it circulate, and who can appropriate it for himself? What are the places in it where there is room for possible subjects? Who can assume these various subject-functions?"[2] [For surely our goal should be not just that students learn to "read," but that they learn also to] think critically about their reading practice, that they learn to identify the kinds of literatures that "speak" to them, that they develop their own bibliographies, and that they articulate the aesthetic principles that underlie these lists as a first, important step in framing and articulating their own poetics – which, as Rachel Blau Duplessis reminds us, "gives permission to continue"[3]. In asking them to do this, we are training them not just to read but also to read as working writers.[4]

I wrote that. I thought that. I'm not taking it back now.

But yet ten years later, we continue to make the untheorized claim that "writers are readers first." Like my colleagues, who saw no real need to actually look at—to examine—the connection between reading and writing, we promote this idea of the former as an essential value and construct our reading lists like little mini canons, giving them to students as they were given us. The texts may be different, but the iconography—its prerogatives and power—persists. You should know this, we are saying: you *should* read it.

Why?

Because *I* say so.

I am almost always late with book orders. I *suffer* over them and find them paralysing: who am I to say what anyone should read? And sure, I know the question is, at least at some level, absurd, because, of course it is my job. But every selection I make is not a selection of something else, and you can make yourself crazy this way.

Looking back, what I might have said to our Composition Director, an avid Rhetorician, who was worried I didn't think students should read, if I weren't so inhibited by her, is: did you even *read* my essay? Or, maybe: have you heard of Susan Sontag? But because such a moment elicits a literal response, I probably just managed, no, no, I am actually *for* reading. One thing I know I did not say: the title was meant to be ironic. Irony, you know, saying something when you mean something else, a *rhetorical* device.

Or, I might actually have had a conversation and tried to explain, as I did in AR$_1$, that what I *am* against is the top-down, whole-scale, unreflective transference of literary standards and aesthetics that persists in the way we promulgate our reading lists, no matter what they look like. And I remain highly interested in and committed to what it means—and what it takes—to guide students toward a lifelong reading practice that is informed, inquisitive, and deliberate. This doesn't happen by osmosis or when we just have them read more; it happens when we give them the tools to think about what they are doing and how they are doing it when they are reading whatever they're reading. And this is important not just for their future lives as readers, but also for their future lives as writers.

Because even though writing is not backwards reading, it *is* a conversation that takes place with other writing. To join the conversation on your own terms, you have to be aware, first, of its very existence, and second, of the terms by which it proceeds, which are as culturally constructed as anything else. "We know now that a text," Barthes wrote half a century ago, "is not a line of words releasing a single 'theological' meaning (the 'message' of the Author-God) but a multi-dimensional space in which a variety of writings, none of them original, blend and clash. The text is a tissue of quotations drawn from the innumerable centers of culture."[5] And so, I might add, are we. These days, David Shields doesn't even use footnotes. But in the midst of all this beautiful noise, surely it is possible—even *necessary*—to clear out some small space where we can hear ourselves speak, and so to begin all over again.

Because this is complicated and takes a lot of time to talk about in class, for a while, I eschewed literary models at all, assuming that students would get enough of those in their other classes. But given what I've just said about the conversation that is writing, this little experiment didn't last long. Because the problem of time persisted—how does one even begin to introduce reading and writing and theory into a single class—I developed a creative writing/literature hybrid selected topics class that I discuss, in more depth, in, among other essays, "To fill with milk," but I want to mention it here because of the way it provided a structure for both *reading* and *thinking* about it: i.e., it wasn't a *literature* class, and it wasn't a *creative writing* class—it was, intentionally, *both*.

And then I took a good look at my own more recent reading practices, those that had evolved from my post-PhD trauma of open-ended reading as both a luxury and onus, every bit as if it marked a grievous absence or a loss at the core of my identity. I knew I would recover; eventually, I did.

Not right away. At first, I just did what I thought I was supposed to do, asking everyone else what they were reading and constructing mental lists by which I figured I could pass for a discerning member of a literate society. I can't say I much enjoyed it, as even though it's not polite to say so, I often found the texts that other people liked vaguely dissatisfying. Not so long before, I'd gone through a similar struggle with movies, which I had always loved. Then, as if overnight, movies failed me, each becoming, in its viewing, and most wretchedly, the "worst movie I had ever seen," or at least among them. I don't think this experience is uncommon, but it was unpleasant, and I didn't much like the person I became when I watched movies this way, no more than I enjoyed the experience of watching them. With movies, the solution was simple: just turn my inner critic off and watch the damned thing.

But reading was different. Reading was my passion and writing, my life. Trapped inside my own experience, all I knew was something was missing, and I wanted it back.

So not right away, but over time, when things settled down after the marriage, the kids, the move to Los Angeles, I found my way back to the public library where I started to indulge what I like to call a "totally random reading practice," described in AR$_1$ as "disorganized, idiosyncratic, and highly generative."[6] I might also have said intuitive, for I was becoming an expert grazer of stacks, which, because they were not subject to such principles of limitation and exclusion as shelf life and/or market censorship, were proving to be much, much richer than anything you've ever find in any bookstore. Libraries just throw all the fiction together, where books can sit happily unread for years until someone comes along and finds them. Today, we can browse even more widely at home with computers, but back then, I liked the feel of the books, their smell, the solid look of the words on the page, even the notes and receipts and shopping lists I'd sometimes find in them, their messy detritus. Today, I also know you can get both book lice and bed bugs from library books. I wish I didn't know this, but I do.

Looking back, this remains among the most engaged reading periods of my life, so much so that it took a while—several years, or more—to notice that almost none of the books that made it from the stacks to my nightstand had originally been written in English. After half a lifetime and three college degrees immersed in Anglo-American literary traditions, I'd discovered a world of living writing beyond our borders, where even if I did not speak the language, I found myself in the company of strangers and improbably at home.

I may not have thought this then (I was just *reading*), but later, I did think about it. Why those books, I wondered, not others? What forces were driving my reading choices, which were central, I know now, to my own evolving poetics? Beyond the lure of the unfamiliar and exotic, what drew me here? By this time in my life I was very comfortable making the claim that my goal as a teacher was to help students frame the guiding questions that would sustain writing for them throughout their lives, but I was just beginning to frame such questions for myself vis-à-vis reading. Students, too, need to learn to think themselves this way—to frame their own questions—to move, in their reading, as in their writing, beyond what they already know.

There are at least two ways to approach what we may call the denaturalization of reading, and the first we take from theory, which I discussed at length in AR_1. It is such familiar territory by now that I find myself reluctant to revisit the tug and pull of it, its promises and limitations, lures and disappointments. Who won the theory wars? a student asked recently. And what you think in such a moment is, you think this: you think, sigh. A sigh is a sound, not something you think, but you know, in such a moment, you really may think it, or, if you weren't affected by aphantasia, see it in fat letters inside a word bubble.

Still, theory remains our most powerful tool for parsing the big questions—questions about language, authorship, power, writing itself— that make writing matter. I love these big questions, which in no small part are what brought me to the page to begin with, and which most surely keep me there. But I was worried in AR_1 about the hyper-specialization of our various disciplines, and no longer as sanguine as I once was about the capacity of theory to set us free—or at least to give us agency in our own work. Here's what I wrote then:

> And even as I lamented certain movements on the part of creative writing toward homogeneity and the privileging of any one particular kind of text over another, theorists were busy concocting their own version of McTheories, screwing their lenses ever closer and tighter to produce such professional myopia as to make at least some of us wonder why we ever looked to them for answers in the first place. There are complex institutional reasons for this too myriad to broach here, but one sad fallout is that we have passed the point for any easy cross-fertilization of discourse and discipline within English studies, which theory might once have supported. Though in some ways it may seem that our work is more complex and specialized, it is also woefully impoverished by our increasing alienations from each other.[7]

What I hoped for—what I still hope for—was a greater spirit of intra-disciplinary collaboration that could move us beyond what Kelly Ritter calls our "markers of professional difference"[8] and enlarge the various projects we all share. In such a view of English Studies, it is easy to imagine that, as I argued in AR_1, what we know about language and literature from being inside it—from producing it—might be of interest and/or value to those who consume it, or who theorize it. We are both the same and different, and for a while—a long time, really—I let myself believe that theory could serve as a means for bringing us together.

But in my own department, a many-years' long project of curriculum revision never mentions creative writing—by the largest option in our major—unless *I* bring it up, and our Composition Director seems susceptible to the suspicion that creative writers don't really even read. Every line we draw between our work and the work of our colleagues, every blinder we let ourselves put on, impoverishes not just us, but the entire discipline. It's shocking to me how little we really do know about the work we do together. Whatever the promise of theory once held for creative writing—or, *unimaginable*, creative writing held for theory—the current climate of careerism that has overtaken our field—maybe all academic fields—is one in which this idea of intra-disciplinarity takes on the feel of fantasy, or worse. For as Ken Burns remarked in his 2016 commencement address, quoting the poet Robert Penn Warren, "Careerism is death."[9]

I haven't stopped using theory to teach creative writing, but I find myself returning, again and again, to the big philosophical breakthroughs of the last century. I have also discovered that the second way to denaturalize reading I referred to above can sometimes do the work of theory, and that is sustained immersion in strange reading. For what happens when you invite students beyond the readily recognizable into a kind of reading they can't immediately make sense of is that they have to step back and consider their own reading habits and assumptions—they have to look at themselves reading, and so look, as well, at the reading/writing connection as a thing that exists in such a way that we can study, or at the very least, be aware of, not just of what it is, but also what it does and how it works.

I had myself inadvertently stumbled upon that same experience when I picked up *Pricksongs and Descants* abroad so long ago, which, because it looked like nothing I had ever read before, made everything I'd read before look different—not inevitable, somehow, or natural, but a thing, a made-thing I had not, quite, been able to see clearly before. No doubt, this happens all the time, at least to writers, probably more than once, arguably often. But I remember the experience as, in no small way, transformative. And from here, it is an easy leap to argue that we can—and, at least some of the time, we *should*—work to create a similar sense of de-familiarization for students with the reading we give them. Teaching new works in translation is one way to do so, although certainly not the only one. When we do, the lens is shifted just enough to produce, like theory "the mechanism through which we [may] frame what writing is and how it is constrained by and moves through the world in such a way as to give our students agency in it."[10]

Take, for example, the practice of modeling I described above, which is so firmly rooted at the heart of our pedagogy, a proven and effective methodology that goes all the way back to our Iowa origins in the art studio workshop. But as someone raised on high minimalism, I remain sensitive to the muting that occurs when we find ourselves adapting to prevalent aesthetics that may not reflect our own. Reading writers whose work proceeds from entirely different literary traditions than our own can highlight and inhibit this process in a positive way. "To study writing," Jonathan Culler argues in "Convention and naturalization," "and especially literary modes of writing, one must concentrate on the conventions which guide the play of differences and the process of constructing meaning."[11] But in the presence of all-new conventions, we can't immediately "naturalize" them in all the old, familiar ways, and because this kind of reading doesn't— it *can't*—disappear into habit, we can talk *about* it—what goes into the reading, what goes into the text.

One of the things that comes up is that it's hard to write like people who do not write like us. So we're not reading this work to learn craft—we are reading this work to learn *writing*. And then there is context.

In AR₁, I described a Linda Nochlin talk in which she observed that "nothing is more interesting, more poignant, or more difficult to seize than the intersection between self and history," an ethos that has become a constant refrain in my classes. This intersection—even just the idea of it— can be an incredibly powerful stimulus for students, once they learn to imagine it. But it's pretty hard to see in the US, where, despite our rich diversity, an overwhelming homogeneity of both information infrastructure works to create the illusion that our ground is neutral. Writing students in Los Angeles write stories that could take place in Kansas, and vice versa; their characters walk through stripped down landscapes that could be *anywhere* at all. And in the midst of more than a decade of world conflict and the most bizarre presidential campaign in the history of this country, students feel detached to the point of passivity and cannot critically imagine an historical moment of their own beyond what they see on TV. But when they read writers whose work engages current political and cultural issues with complexity, urgency, and gravity, something not so subtle shifts in them. These texts reflect worlds that don't look like ours, with very different historical challenges and intellectual traditions. And that, alone, is provocative to students, as they find themselves imagining not just a larger literary world than they are quite familiar with, but also a larger world in general. It is also striking to them that in this larger world, there are places where authors retain a kind of cultural stature as important public intellectuals and influential agents of social change and justice. I do realize how broad an over-generalization that is. Transnational writers are not above career concerns, and US writers are not exclusively driven by them. But at the very least, reading globally creates a pedagogical opportunity to suggest that there is history and that we are in it.

These days, for example, many students want to write anti-realist narratives with fancy fabulist twists and unnatural events, and they call it all Magical Realism. For them, Magical Realism is a kind of free-for-all— sharks for hands, floating ribbons of ladders descending to nowhere in outer space, talking dogs. But when they learn to see the genre as a product of an historical moment of violent repression saturated with political commentary, they develop a more complex understanding not just of what it *looks* like, but *why* it looks like that and what it *does*. In such a context, we can take up problematics of cultural appropriation without opprobrium, and they start to recognize its flourishes in their own work as be little more than what

I once heard described at AWP as "pretty bows and ribbons," they may also begin to wonder what an anti-realist writing that comes from *here*—and *knows* itself as coming from here—might look like. We don't say: write like this. We say: write like you.

I suggested as much in AR$_1$ when I wrote:

> Today [the world of our students] is a vexed and altered one, and though it may not be the job of the creative writing teacher to tell the students how to think about that world, surely it should be to expect them to look at – to 'read' – it. And as they do, they should ask hard questions about the role of writing in the particular world that turns out to be theirs, and how they would have their own work engage and move through it, defining their own intersection with history and what they would have their writing to both *be* and *do* in it.[12]

But what I didn't then go on to talk about explicitly was what was going to happen when I gave myself wholly over to the project of teaching the books I was reading myself, in place of the books I thought I was supposed to teach. What I said was: "there is something generative—and too often overlooked—about the intersection between the local and the global that we should ask students, at the very least, to contemplate."[13] When, perhaps, it might have been more accurate to say what more than one student has: it's like stepping off a cliff.

A lot of the power of those early classes came directly from the texts we were reading, which, with some variation, typically included *Cosmicomics* (Italo Calvino), *Blindness* (Jose Saramago), *The Museum of Unconditional Surre*nder (Dubravka Ugresic), *The Absent City* (Ricardo Piglia), and *The Rings of Saturn* (W.G. Sebald). They were big, complex works, and they were available, and I loved them, and my students did too. In my own earlier encounters with these texts and others like them, I'd responded to cadences and nuances not just of language but also of form, and I found myself thinking about how the aesthetic experience of this reading, even (or especially) in translation, suggested new ways my own writing might respond to the moment of its coming into being. Over and over again it was what I had not seen before that sparked my interest as a reading writer. I hadn't sought to imitate—I couldn't—but to respond, to enter the elusive hum between what I was reading and where it might direct me in my own work, moving beyond—ever beyond—what I already knew how to write toward something I could not quite yet imagine in the borders between what seemed both possible—and *necessary*—and not.

I anticipated that students might have a similar response to this reading, and they did, as intrigued and energized, not so say inspired, by it as I once had been. But in the end, I could only teach these big books for so long, because students liked these books so much they kept repeating my classes. Thus forced by circumstance to step off the same cliff as my students, I had to come up with a new reading list. We all do this, from time to time. It's one of the great things about teaching. But it is also, always, a sobering challenge. I'd gotten good at my old standbys, and could sound at least passably smart about them. There's a certain comfort in that. But in reading, as in writing, it's what you don't know that's compelling and keeps moving you forward, so one semester, I more or less arbitrarily decided to assign a book a week, all recently translated in the last decade and all of them new to me. The "work" in the class wasn't reading, it was writing—the reading was a ground for the writing. In fact, I'm not sure I'd even call it reading, what we did, so much as *encountering*. There was just so much of it that we couldn't even fall back on the old familiar habits of interpretation and analysis. We just read the books, and we talked about them, and all along, we were writing.

Here's what we read:

- *The Literary Conference*, by Cesar Aira (Chile); translated by Katherine Silver, 2010
- *Other City*, by Michal Ajvaz (The Czech Republic); translated by Gerald Turner, 2009
- *Coda: A Novel*, by Rene Belletto (France); translated by Alyson Waters, 2011
- *By Night in Chile*, by Roberto Bolaño (Argentina); translated by Chris Andrews, 2003
- *My Two Worlds*, by Sergio Chejfec, (Argentina); translated by Margaret B. Carson, 2011
- *From the Observatory*, by Julio Cortazar (Argentina), translated by Anne McClean, 2011
- *Against Art: The Notebooks*, by Tomas Espedal (Norway); translated by James Anderson, 2011
- *Too Loud a Solitude*, by Bohumil Hrabal (The Czech Republic); translated by Michael Henry Heim, 1992
- *Animalinside (The Cahiers)*, by László Krasznahorkai (Hungary); translated by Ottilie Mulzet, 2011
- *Dreams and Stones*, by Magdalena Tulli (Poland); translated by Bill John, 2011
- *Bartleby & Co.*, by Enrique Vila-Matas (Spain); translated by Jonathan Dunne, 2007
- *The Private Lives of Trees*, by Alejandro Zambra (Chile); translated by Megan Mcdowell, 2010

At the end of the class, one student (aptly) observed, well, most of the books had either a tree or a walk in them; some of them had both.

At the end of each session of class, I was simultaneously exhausted and exhilarated. Reading those books together, exploring and discovering them along with my students, was a profoundly energizing teaching experience. And as the class progressed, I began to see a serendipitous benefit of modeling a reading practice for my students like one I hope they might develop for themselves and not unlike the writing strategies I also try to promote— exploratory, playful, engaged, self-reflective. As well, it was something we could *talk* about, beginning with the very process I had used in even finding and selecting the works—the presses I'd surveyed, webpages I'd read, places where I'd read reviews, Amazon. And then, because I didn't already know what to think—or say—about these books, my own weekly spectacle of awkwardly moving into a new reading terrain, clearly visible to everyone. There were no experts in this class, only readers reading. So we talked about this too. We observed ourselves reading. In the process, we—all of us— began to develop precisely the kind of meta-cognitive self-awareness vis-à-vis reading and writing—and their interconnectedness—on which sustainable practices in both depend.

This is yet another way of as "reading as a writer," a practice invested not so much in craft (although there is always that), as in larger questions of position (where the writer finds herself), motivation (what the writer aspires to do), convention (what the writing looks like and how it fits into the larger conversation of writing), and circulation (how it moves through the world). That's theory, yes. But let's not call it theory, Wendy Bishop used to say. She said to call it "thinking systematically," a powerful fulcrum for change.

It's been—what, thirty years? since Susan Sontag called for an "erotics" instead of a "hermeneutics" of art. "None of us," she wrote, "can ever retrieve that innocence before all theory when art knew no need to justify itself, when one did not ask of a work of art what it said because one knew (or thought one knew) what it did." [14]True enough. But we can long for it, that innocence, and we can teach it—not the innocence, but the desire for it, and the role that desire must play in the act of writing. Reading work we do not fully understand from unfamiliar places restrains the impulse we all feel—can't not help but feel—toward mastery, which shuts us down, and returns us to the realm of an erotics, where such innocence might still be entertained, even if only in retrospect. I talked more about theory in AR_1 because I worried more about it then. And it remains, in its philosophical tenets, inarguably our ally. But I am by temperament, inclination, and aesthetics drawn more to uncertainty than not. And it is for this reason that I am drawn, as well, to the interstices, which are never as provocative—and inviting—as they are between here and somewhere else.

This model of reading I have continued to develop over the ten years since the publication of the precursor volume of this book is not fixed, but fluid and explorative, and it does not rely on those familiar hallmarks of craft and interpretation, but on something more like curiosity and wonder. And I am pleased to report that things are getting easier as each semester I hole up with my computer and read the blogs and websites—Three Percent,

Words Without Borders, The Quarterly Conversation—and the catalogues—
Open Letters, New Directions, Archipelago, Europa Editions, and now—
and excitingly—having just returned from AWP 2016, New Vessel, New
Vellum, Two Line, three new presses devoted to translation that have opened
in the past several years. Sticking to the principle of discovery and immersion,
I keep finding new books and assigning too may, not really interested in
close reading at all. If there is a guiding principle for all this, David Markson
comes closest to it when he describes just "pouring books over the top of
[his] head." One list I just dug up had more than sixty titles. I got giddy
looking at it.

Sometimes, though, like everyone, I worry: my students are writing short
stories—shouldn't they be reading short stories *if they want to publish*?
Shouldn't they be reading *Americans*? In one class I tried teaching all *New
Yorker* stories from their open database, but even I couldn't finish the
reading that term. Last semester, I taught all recent short story collections in
English, a hit or miss kind of roller-coaster term.

I am forced to conclude that, at least part of the time, some of the reading
we promote to our students should not be the kind of writing we might
ourselves produce and publish—the kind of work they, too, might publish,
one day—but, well, *something else*. Looking at how literature happens, how
it *matters* in the rest of the world, can serve not just as a kind of theorizing
lens, but also as a good reminder that it remains a primary, which is to say
vital, human experience, and that it can still, in its making, record, transcend,
and transform the world. Not that that doesn't happen here, but in the
context of our current and profoundly anti-intellectual presidential politics,
it's impossible not to remember that this country is big and our students
come from all of it. Reading the rest of the world can help them read this
one, and in this unsettling clash of voices, aesthetics, and purpose, in all its
marvelous strangeness, students may begin to clear a space where they might
discover their own voices, aesthetics, and purpose, beginning with the
imperative that writing writing starts here.

Notes

1   Bizzaro, P., "Research and Reflection in English Studies: The Special Case for
    and Creative Writing," *College English* 66.2 (2004), 305.

2   Michel Foucault, "What Is an Author?" in *Textual Strategies: Perspectives in
    Post-Structuralist Criticism*, ed. Josue V. Harari (Ithaca: Cornell University
    Press), 160.

3   Rachel Blau Duplessis, *The Pink Guitar: Writing as Feminist Practice* (New
    York: Routledge, 1990), 156.

4   Katharine Haake, "Against Reading," in *Creative Writing: Can It Be Taught?*
    eds, Kelly Ritter and Stephanie Vanderslice (Portsmouth, NH: Heineman,
    2006), 36.

5   Roland Barthes, "The Death of the Author," in *Modern Criticism and Theory: A Reader*, 2nd edn, eds. David Lodge and Nigel. Wood (New York: Longman, 1968) 149.

6   Haake, "Against Reading," 33.

7   Haake, "Against Reading," 43.

8   Kelly Ritter, "Professional Writers/Writing Professionals: Revamping Teaching Training in PhD Programs," *College English* 64.2 (2001), 208.

9   Ken Burns, Commencement Address, Stanford University's 125th Commencement, June 12, 2016.

10 Haake, "Against Reading," 40.

11 Jonathan Culler, Structuralist Poetics: Structuralism, Linguistics, and the Study of Literature (Ithaca: Cornell University Press, 1976) 156.

12 Haake, "Against Reading," 42.

13 Haake, "Against Reading," 41.

14 Susan Sontag, *Against Interpretation and Other Essays* (New York: Picador, 2001), 4–5.

References

Aira, Cesar. *The Literary Conference*. Translated by Katherine Silver. New York: New Directions, 2010.

Ajvaz, Michal. *Other City*. Translated Gerald Turner. Champaign, IL: Dalkey Archives Press, 2009.

Bakhtin, Mikhail. "Epic and Novel." In *Essentials of the Theory of Fiction*, edited by Michael J. Hoffman and Patrick D. Murphy, 48–69. Durham, NC: Duke University Press, 1988.

Barthes, Roland. "The Death of the Author." In *Modern Criticism and Theory: A Reader*, 2nd edn, edited by David Lodge and Nigel. Wood, 167–72. New York: Longman, 1968.

Belletto, Rene. *Coda: A Novel*. Translated by Alyson Waters. Lincoln, NE: Bison Books, University of Nebraska Press, 2011.

Bizzaro, Patrick. "Research and Reflection in English Studies: The Special Case for and Creative Writing." *College English* 66.2 (2004): 294–309.

Bolaño, Roberto. *By Night in Chile*. Translated Chris Andrews. New York: New Directions, 2003.

Burns, Ken. Commencement Address, Stanford University's 125th Commencement, June 12, 2016. http://news.stanford.edu/2016/06/12/prepared-text-2016-stanford-commencement-address-ken-burns/

Calvino, Italo. *Cosmicomics*. Translated by William Weaver. New York: Harcourt Brace Jovanovich, 1976.

Chejfec, Sergio. *My Two Worlds*. Translated by Margaret Carson. Rochester, NY: Open Letter, 2011.

Coover, Robert. *Pricksongs and Descants*. New York: Plume, 1970.

Cortazar, Julio. *From the Observatory*. Translated by Anne McClean, NY, Brooklyn: Archipelago, 2011.

Culler, Jonathan. *Structuralist Poetics: Structuralism, Linguistics, and the Study of Literature*. Ithaca: Cornell University Press, 1976.

DuPlessis, Rachel Blau. *The Pink Guitar: Writing as Feminist Practice*. New York: Routledge, 1990.

Espedal, Tomas. *Against Art: The Notebooks*. Translated by James Anderson. Chicago: Seagull Books, University of Chicago Press, 2011.

Filbeck, Melissa. AGSE Conference, CSUN, 2015.

Foucault, Michel. "What Is an Author?" In *Textual Strategies: Perspectives in Post-Structuralist Criticism*, edited by Josue V. Harari, 141–60, Ithaca: Cornell University Press, 1979.

Haake, Katharine. "Against Reading." In *Creative Writing: Can It Be Taught?*, edited by Kelly Ritter and Stephanie Vanderslice. Portsmouth, NH: Heineman, 2006.

Haake, Katharine. "To Fill with Milk: Or, The Thing and Itself." In *Key Issues in Creative Writing*, edited by in Dianne. Donnelly and Graeme Harper. Bristol, UK: Multilingual Matters, 2012: 70–102.

Haake, Katharine. *What Our Speech Disrupts: Feminism and Creative Writing Studies*. Urbana, IL: NCTE, 2000.

Hrabal, Bohumil. *Too Loud a Solitude*. Translated by Michael Henry Heim. New York: Mariner Books, 1992.

Krasznahorkai, László and Max Neumann. *Animalinside (The Cahiers)*. Translated by Ottilie Mulzet, New York: New Directions, 2011.

Markson, David. Interviewed by Tayt Halin. *Web Conjunctions*, April 28, 2007. http://www.conjunctions.com/webcon/harlinmarkson07.htm

Nochlin, Linda. "Of Self and History: Exchanges with Linda Nochlin." Interviewed by Moira Roth. *Art Journal*, 59.3 (2000): 18–33.

Piglia, Ricardo. *The Absent City*. Translated by Sergio Waisman. Durham, NC: Duke University Press, 2000.

Ritter, Kelly. "Professional Writers/Writing Professionals: Revamping Teaching Training in PhD Programs." *College English* 64.2 (2001): 205–27.

Saramago, Jose. *Blindness*, trans. Giovanni Pontiero. NY: Harvest Books, 1999.

Sebald, W.G. *The Rings of Saturn*. Translated by Michael Hulse, New York: New Directions, 1999.

Sontag, Susan. *Against Interpretation and Other Essays*. New York: Picador, 2001.

Todorov, Tsvetan. *The Poetics of Prose*. Translated by Richard Howard. Ithaca: Cornell UP, 1977.

Tulli, Magdalena. *Dreams and Stones*. Translated by Bill Johnston. NY, Brooklyn: Archipelago, 2011.

Ugresic, Dubravka. *The Museum of Unconditional Surrender*. Translated by Celia Hawkesworth, NY: New Directions, 2002.

Vila-Matas, Enrique. *Bartleby & Co*. Translated by Jonathan Dunne, NY: New Directions, 2007.

Zambra, Alejandro. *The Private Lives of Trees*. Translated by Megan McDowell. Rochester, NY: Open Letter, 2010.

3

Revisiting Charming Tyrants and Faceless Facilitators:

The Lore of Teaching Identities in Creative Writing

Mary Ann Cain

Roughly ten years after I wrote my quest/romance narrative, the question left on the table is whether and/or how this story has resolved. Is there a way out of the Charming Tyrant/Faceless Facilitator trap described by Kate Haake in her book, *What Our Speech Disrupts: Feminism and Creative Writing Studies*?[1] In that binary, creative writing teachers, particularly women, face the dilemma of two equally bad choices for the persona they can adopt in the classroom. The Charming Tyrant is the "star" writer who, by sheer force of personality, leads the class into becoming reproductions of her- or himself, without the labor of trying to understand students and their needs. The Faceless Facilitator is the caretaker/nurturer whose own personality and identity as a writer, not to mention work hours, takes a back seat to students' endless needs and desires. This gendered binary was one that I saw myself caught in first as a student and then as a teacher of writing. So, I now return to this dilemma to consider: Am I, instead, a Houdini of critical thinking, able to extricate myself from the most impossible of dichotomies? What kind of Face(s) have I since claimed—if I have—as a teacher and a writer? My narrative arc wants to know.

Let me start with a story. In my spring seminar class, How Stories Matter, I diverted unexpectedly into an extended conversation away from the week's assigned texts and into the students' written responses from the previous week. This is a small class full of writers who took a chance following me into a hybrid course, one that is not focused on either workshop or literature and scholarship but instead combines research, theory, and practice that inform stories and storytelling. We address the question of how, in fact, stories matter, not simply as words on the page but as entities that exist in the world.

I was not exactly sure what I wanted to say about their responses, starting with a feeling of discomfort and dis-ease about how they had performed. Why, I wondered, did most of the students not directly engage with the assigned texts? My guidelines did, in fact, allow for alternative responses, and when asked on the first day of class, students were strongly in favor of this less directive approach (i.e., no prompts other than general guidelines). However, I was now facing the questionable results of this "freedom."

I honed in on one student who's been in a number of classes with me and with whom I like to think I share a friendly, even trusting relationship. But now my trust—in him, in the class overall—was suddenly a little shaky. Had I lapsed into fostering a feel-good approach to responding, putting their self-esteem and "freedom" ahead of critical consciousness and creative challenge, as Anna Leahy discusses in her essay, "Creativity, Caring, and the Easy A"?[2] But then, how could I tell them they weren't writing good responses when I was the one who set them up for this "failure"?

In other words, the Faces may have changed, but the dilemma remains. Or maybe they haven't changed. I started to joke about the student's written response for that week by calling it "grumpy."

Sounds a bit like a (maybe Charming) Tyrant.

To be fair, my joking had a context. We had just read Thomas King's performative nonfiction, *The Truth about Stories*, in which he explains, and at the same time demonstrates, how indigenous Americans, of which he includes himself, value humor.[3] And he also performs humor as part of the storytelling posture he adopts at the opening of each chapter, and again at the end, by offering slightly different iterations of the creation story of a flat earth resting on the backs of an infinite number of turtles. The punch line, "It's turtles all the way down," took some members of the class, including me, a while to grasp, let alone appreciate, the humor. Others got it immediately. One or two smiled politely and stayed silent. We talked about the risks one takes when mixing forms and genres, and about the necessity of such mixing to express a complex reality, in King's case, the "Indian" identity he and other North American natives claim. He is, like many fellow natives, also part white/European: mixed. So, humor was his way of bridging the unbridgeable gap between cultural experiences and ontologies.

I am typically not a jokester, in or out of class. I'm usually too careful in my relationships with students to risk a joke gone awry. But I'd come upon a dilemma, namely that I'd offered this "freedom" to respond, only to read responses that I couldn't quite fathom. Not that I literally could not understand them but couldn't quite see what the writers thought they were doing. I didn't recognize their performances, falling outside of the kinds of textual responses I typically expected. Questions surfaced in my mind. Were they doing the reading? Yes, the discussion that week had been vigorous and engaged. Did they understand the reading? I hesitated on this question. Were they veering "off topic" because they didn't quite know how to engage the work? Maybe. But then there was that "grumpy" tone, the I'm-not-crazy-about-reading-this-academic-bs tone, right there on full display.

A tone I had invited. And I admit, one I felt to some extent myself. The other assigned reading, Jerome Bruner's "The Narrative Construction of Reality," was, I told the class, not exactly bedtime reading.[4] I could relate to feeling a little grumpy about reading straight-up theory, especially outside the discipline.

This dilemma of how to respond to "bad" (i.e., work in progress) student writing is, in some respects, part and parcel of teaching writing. To be creative, one purportedly "breaks the rules." The Charming Tyrant, the star who students (should want) to emulate, would consider, in a very charming way, how this work didn't measure up, how it fell short of an implicit standard. The Faceless Facilitator would try to coax the writer into embracing those nasty rules in a cajoling "eat your peas" manner, careful not to break the writer's self-esteem in the process. The problem with both Tyrant and Facilitator is that they are two sides of the same coin—they both are upholding some implicit—or explicit—"standard."

I am both a story writer/teller and, to borrow Wendy Bishop and Alyse Culhane's joking moniker, a theory head, a rhetoric and composition theory head, to be specific. I am a hybrid. I want my students to be hybrids, too. Charming Tyrant?

The discussion moved from joking to more serious topics. The "grumpy" writer explained how in his response he was exploring an ongoing dis-ease he has between "lore" and "canon," between individual works and the scholarly apparatus that surrounds them. The two pieces we'd read—King's nonfiction and Bruner's theory—represented that sort of split-screen focus. Other students chimed in. The whole academic apparatus was cumbersome, difficult, and at times seemingly pointless. Why learn it?

I should add that these are some of the best students I've ever had, not a slacker among them. It might seem shocking that they would be questioning what they have already invested many years, many resources, into studying.

I suppose I could have been hurt, disappointed, even offended (Charming Tyrant) that students didn't like what I had selected, or maybe just hadn't been brilliant enough to teach in a captivating enough way. I suppose I could have switched to self-flagellation (Faceless Facilitator) for not providing students with enough support to find their way to Theory Heaven.

Instead, I got curious. After all these years, I recognize how the lessons of Famous Author, the writer-teacher who showed me a glimpse of how to recast the Tyrant/Facilitator binary, have taken root in some unexpected ways.

The dilemmas that our students and we face as writers and scholars—in my case, to be either Charming Tyrant or Faceless Facilitator—are, of course, quintessential teachable moments. At the time that I wrote the original essay, I was just beginning to grasp what I had learned from Famous Author, namely to focus not on the student's feelings or intentions, or on my intentions and standards, but instead on the writing itself. But not as a throwback to the New Criticism and all its horrors of pseudo-scientific justifications for the importance of literary analysis. Instead, I was understanding writing, in this case stories, as a form that provides what Nancy Welch, borrowing from feminist philosopher Michelle LeDoeuff, calls a "third factor." According to Welch, "[T]he introduction of a third factor to relationships we tend to think of in twos—student and teacher, apprentice and master, scholar and discipline—places particular systems and particular philosophers, mentors, or teachers in historically *interdependent* relationships with others. Third factors ask new questions, reveal unexamined assumptions, and work to deconstruct that myth of the complete and stable model. The third factor redefines philosophy, Le Doeuff writes, 'from the outset as collective,' as 'plural work' in which 'a relationship to the unknown and to the unthought is at every moment reintroduced'" (1997: 62).[5]

The story itself, then, acts as a third factor in transforming these otherwise binary and hierarchical relationships of student-teacher, along with lore-canon, practice-theory, creative writing-academic scholarship into spaces where "*interdependent*" and "collective" "plural" work. Stories provide spaces for negotiation and dialogue between writers and readers, and their identifications.

My now-iconic moment with Famous Author so many years ago recalls her pulling out my novel manuscript and showing me a few red-penned pages. She had agreed to meet me one-on-one in her office for 30 minutes a week before our fiction writing class because I wanted to leave halfway through to attend the second half of my Composition Theory class. I remember breathing deeply, having been persuaded of the evils of red-penning as a writing instructor at Eastern University. I quickly saw how much better those edits made my prose. Having harnessed my knee-jerk reaction for the moment, I prepared myself for the next level of criticism sure to come, the places where I fell short of her Charming Tyrant standards. Famous Author did not fail to deliver. But instead of the usual Tyrant comments ("This character isn't realistic"), Famous Author instead entered the narrative as if putting on a different pair of eyes. She walked around inside and said, Here's what this story is doing and saying. To *her*.

Peter Elbow couldn't have done better himself. Elbow has famously changed the direction of responses to writing by asking those very questions: What is the text saying and doing?[6] Marie Ponsot and Rosemary Deen, in their wonderful guide to first-year writing, *Beat Not the Poor Desk*, similarly ask readers and writers to discuss observations, interpretations, and evaluations of a student draft, in essence to give *readings* of them, to treat student work as literature.[7]

Famous Author read my work as literature. I left her well-appointed office and wept.

So, when confronted with this "grumpy" text, I proceeded to treat it as literature. I did not regard the off-handed tone or the oblique references to the assigned reading as "mistakes." I read them as meaningful and purposeful, or at least potentially so. I did not consider what the student had intended or not. I was interested not only in what the writing was saying, but also what the writing was doing—or in other words, "performing."

This leads to a discussion regarding lore and canon, and the hierarchies that inform it.

In contrast to the "shopping-mall" classes that Leahy (2007) notes we are all too familiar with, this class, with its seven students, provides a refuge, however conditional and fleeting—a "pop-up," if you will—that allows for diversions and "off topic" explorations for which most of my classes don't seem to have time. At any rate, I "allowed" it in ways I have and haven't before. And that's the thing. If we look at such moments in classes and in texts as novel, as fostering "a relationship to the unknown and to the unthought . . . [that] at every moment [is] reintroduced," then we begin to see how the old, familiar ways, the supposedly stable conventions, can only partially and imperfectly inform the tasks before us. It's not about either following the tried and true or rejecting it altogether.

It's about hybridity. It's about improvisation. It's about, to use Welch's term, "remodeling." Things, as it turns out, my students know quite a bit about, and in some ways more than I do.

It's turtles all the way down.

What I learned during this discussion was that I could offer some basic insights into where and how they were currently positioned in their educational arc, basically advanced enough where they stood head and shoulders above most people in the world but also somewhere between novice and expert, that no-person's land of strange Faces and, at times, monstrous insecurities. I could see it, remembering very clearly upon arrival at Eastern University talking to the graduate director about how different being a student this time felt—I had been gainfully employed, was married, and thought I knew something about the world in my late twenties. Going back to being a student ripped away much of my confidence and at the same time made me ask more critical questions about what I was being asked to do as a doctoral student.

I saw these students as unsure about what difference learning "academic discourse" would make, especially since many of them might not go on for more advanced degrees, yet they were committed writers. Ours is a campus that caters to the region, mainly because the students are tied in various ways to this area. I sensed that they had seen some of the damage academic discourse did by way of excluding individuals and identity groups. None of them seemed to feel the excitement and discovery I had when a graduate student at Eastern University, the explanatory power of critical theory at times overwhelming and baffling, but also ultimately empowering.

But then, the tables turned. They started answering their own questions; I became the learner/listener. One student said how having an understanding of the canons of Native American literature gave her insight into King's work. Then there was the question of how theoretical discourse sounds and what a turn-off it is to those outside the academy. In this I heard a reluctance to claim power and authority, not only of the academy, but as writers. They'd seen the damage. They didn't want to reproduce it. Wasn't that, in a sense, what King was showing them by way of Indian schools and the manhandling he'd received at various points in higher ed? But perhaps that last thought was more me than them; why should they want to simply "reproduce" it? These "third factor" moments of reintroducing the "unknown" and "unthought" into our talk and our texts made me trust the class that much more.

I'm risking making this essay seem pointless and without direction to make the point that we can't do without such meanderings. We must look towards the hybridity that is always/already present and all the strangeness of the unknown and unthought that it invites. We can't look only within the conventions, categories, and models we already know. We can't simply throw them out, either—as if that were even possible. But we must do this knowing that whatever we say and write has power, is of consequence, and there's no taking it back. In the age of the Internet, this is abundantly clear. It's not either/or. Not Tyrant or Facilitator. It's both. It's neither. It's what story does so well if we remodel its relationship to the unthought and unknown.

When teaching fiction these days, I pay more attention to narrative arc than I used to. Ironically, early on in my teaching and writing, I resisted that concept. I embraced feminists' critique of its phallocentric structure, the implicit masculinity in the notion of a single climax. In *The Truth about Stories*, Thomas King juxtaposes Western narrative arcs that favor good versus evil plotlines with indigenous stories that are a spectrum of shades of grade, without clear winners or losers, heroes or villains. In my own stories, as well as my scholarly writing, I was only too happy to "experiment" away from narrative arc; I called my stories "blurred" or "mixed" genres. But rejecting the Charming Tyrant plot structure made my work, in some ways, quite Faceless, at least for a while. If you write what is unknown and unthought before, you risk being invisible.

I call attention to narrative arc not because it's a structure I think writers need to follow in a prescriptive way, if at all. Instead, it's because it's been internalized so well by even beginning writers that it becomes a de facto Charming Tyrant, closing down alternatives into what Welch calls a "real tight" structure before the writer even gets started. Welch observes that the problem with how we view student drafts is less about how poorly adapted it is to conventions like narrative arc but rather how overly conscious it is to "fit in," at the expense of alternative perspectives and questions that don't seem to otherwise belong. Her solution? "Getting Restless": using reading (in this case, the story itself) as the "third factor" in how I relate to writers and their intentions. The Charming Tyrant of narrative arc becomes a site where meanings converge and diverge. Instead of flagging a mistake, I get curious. Why does the rising action lead to a plateau, or fizzle out? What else might the story want to do? Where is the unknown, unthought story that writers didn't even know they could write? What choices can I alert them to? In this way, the tyrannical aspects of narrative arc are mitigated, and instead invite an open-ended investigation of form that allows for the hybrid, the never-been-seen before while at the same time maintaining a relationship with what currently exists as convention, models, and forms. If one hews to the plural, the collective, then the relationship between Tyrant and Facilitator shifts. They become visible within a larger web of relationships in which power and identity are interdependent. One does not dominate or submit to the other.

In *Rhetorical Traditions and the Teaching of Writing*, Knoblauch and Brannon contrast directive versus facilitative modes of response. Their arguments for facilitative response had echoed in my ear as Famous Author responded to my novel: "The comments of a facilitative reader are designed to preserve the writer's control of the discourse, while also registering uncertainty about what the writer wishes to communicate" (1984: 128).[8] Was her critique facilitative? Did I care? I mean, it was the word of Famous Author—a rare and precious thing, no matter the mode of response.

For years, I was perhaps too careful as a Facilitator to "preserve the writer's control of the discourse" when responding to drafts, both in writing and in conferences. True, I asked questions, registered places of confusion, engaged with emerging meanings. But I held back my Face, i.e., the person doing the reading, someone who felt and thought and reacted in particular ways, with specific biases, and with some gaps in her knowledge but also some knowledge, experience, and (dare I say) wisdom. But it was clear that students wanted and even needed me to have a Face, to be present in ways that I had been careful not to do. "Facilitative" response was just another way of repackaging the "directive" mode of holding up mythical, unchanging standards.

The energy it took to restrain myself in this way made commenting on student work more and more tedious, more and more of a burden. Of course, few among us look at a pile of student writing and say, Oh goody, I get to comment. But it became difficult to not want to direct—Hey, try this, you missed the boat there, wow, you totally had me there. The Tyrant isn't charming without a reason.

Shifts started while in face-to-face conferences. Like Famous Author, I started imagining along with the story. Since the writer was right with me,

I could ask for meanings and clarifications of intention and still respond fully, in a directive-sounding way but one that ultimately was more of a hybrid of what I had assumed was a binary. Or maybe I had simply not understood the fullest meaning of facilitative response. Regardless, I found myself collaborating more freely, with more enthusiasm, and with better response on the parts of students. I wasn't taking over; I was simply engaging what their texts were saying and doing—to *me*. One has to have not only one Face, not just a Tyrant. One must have many Faces to be the most responsive. Once I started connecting to my multiple faces, I became more attuned to what students and their stories were claiming, or trying to claim in their identifications as well. Precious moments of learning occurred on both sides of the student-teacher divide, however fleeting and imperfect.

The old saw among creative writers who teach is how much they have to protect themselves from being drained by their teaching. While I haven't completely backed away from some protective measures to guard my time to write, I also have found myself learning along with the students, and perhaps more importantly, *from* them as well. I have found profound joy in responding, even in the midst of some spectacular failures.

My narrative arc still wants to know, but not in the "real tight" ways that Nancy Welch claims we internalize "the rules" of writing. Since publishing my original essay, those "rules" have been considerably remodeled, to use Welch's term, because of the vast domain of publication available online. The "rules" as I know them are dramatically and sometimes persuasively "flouted" in favor of emerging forms, genres, and styles. And students don't have to take my word for anything; Google is their muse.

The "grumpy" writer in my seminar had an interview with Facebook for an internship the week after our discussion. Facebook posts, Instagrams, Twitter, and so forth—all these means by which writers express themselves are remodeling our collective understanding of what constitutes publication and how we value such public acts of self-expression. In the past, claiming publication would gain nods of approval and the praise-fear of the Charming Tyrant. Anymore, publication to today's students is more fluid, less driven by status-y publishers and more by followings forged directly with readers. My students already inhabit a future which I may or may not wind up sharing. They have tastes for genre fiction—sci-fi, fantasy, horror, fan fiction—that I doubt I will ever much enjoy. But I can appreciate better the many faces, the many genres that they and their stories contain, the hybridity within us all. To quote Thomas King, It's turtles all the way down.

Notes

1 Haake, Kate. *What Our Speech Disrupts: Feminism and Creative Writing Studies* (Urbana, IL: National Council of Teachers of English, 2000).

2   Leahy, Anna. "Creativity, Caring, and the Easy 'A': Rethinking the Role of Self-Esteem in Creative Writing Pedagogy." In *Can It Really Be Taught? Resisting Lore in Creative Writing Pedagogy*, edited by Kelly Ritter and Stephanie Vanderslice (Portsmouth, NH: Heinemann/Boynton-Cook, 2007): 55–66.

3   King, Thomas. *The Truth about Stories* (Minneapolis, MN: University of Minnesota Press, 2005).

4   Bruner, Jerome. "The Narrative Construction of Reality." *Critical Inquiry* 18:1 (1991): 1–21.

5   Welch, Nancy. *Getting Restless: Rethinking Revision in Writing Instruction* (Portsmouth, NH: Heinemann/Boynton-Cook, 1997): 62.

6   Elbow, Peter. *Embracing Contraries: Explorations in Learning and Teaching* (Oxford, UK: Oxford University Press, 1987).

7   Ponsot, Marie and Rosemary Deen. *Beat Not the Poor Desk* (Portsmouth, NH: Heinemann/Boynton-Cook, 1989).

8   Knoblauch, Cy and Lil Brannon. *Rhetorical Traditions and the Teaching of Writing*. (Portsmouth, NH: Heinemann/Boynton-Cook, 1984): 128.

References

Bruner, Jerome. "The Narrative Construction of Reality." *Critical Inquiry* 18:1 (1991): 1–21.

Elbow, Peter. *Embracing Contraries: Explorations in Learning and Teaching*. Oxford, UK: Oxford University Press, 1987.

Haake, Kate. *What Our Speech Disrupts: Feminism and Creative Writing Studies*. Urbana, IL: National Council of Teachers of English, 2000.

King, Thomas. *The Truth about Stories*. Minneapolis, MN: University of Minnesota Press, 2005.

Knoblauch, Cy and Lil Brannon. *Rhetorical Traditions and the Teaching of Writing*. Portsmouth, NH: Heinemann/Boynton-Cook, 1984.

Leahy, Anna. "Creativity, Caring, and the Easy 'A': Rethinking the Role of Self-Esteem in Creative Writing Pedagogy." In *Can It Really Be Taught? Resisting Lore in Creative Writing Pedagogy*, edited by Kelly Ritter and Stephanie Vanderslice, 55–66. Portsmouth, NH: Heinemann/Boynton-Cook, 2007.

Ponsot, Marie and Rosemary Deen. *Beat Not the Poor Desk*. Portsmouth, NH: Heinemann/Boynton-Cook, 1989.

Welch, Nancy. *Getting Restless: Rethinking Revision in Writing Instruction*. Portsmouth, NH: Heinemann/Boynton-Cook, 1997.

4

"It's such a good feeling":

Self-Esteem, the Growth Mindset, and Creative Writing

Anna Leahy

Ten years ago, I wrote an essay about grading for *Can It Really Be Taught?* that was actually about self-esteem. I asserted then, as I do now, that "our common terminology, the prevalent workshop model, and popular notions of creative writing as unteachable, unacademic, or undisciplined lead to self-esteem in a way that other college classes do not."[1] By that, I meant that the issue of self-esteem is more likely to be evident in the field of creative writing than in other disciplines and to play a discernable role in dynamics and learning in creative writing classrooms, though I now see how my statement might mistakenly be considered as a call to use creative writing classes to boost self-esteem or as a criticism of foundational pedagogical approaches in the field of creative writing.

In other words, what I meant then and still think now is that, while self-esteem may be part of how one understands any learning environment or experience, the position of the self is more apparent in the arts than in the humanities, social sciences, or sciences. The self is always already there in creative writing classrooms, in the process of writing creative work, and in the products of our efforts. The self—the individual writer—cannot be ignored. The word *author,* after all, comes from a Latin verb that means *to originate* and that also means *to increase or grow.* Creative writing is sometimes perceived as or constructed as an environment in which to grow the self or increase self-esteem. In fact, a study in the *Journal of Child and Adolescent Psychiatric Nursing* found that a two-week creative writing program increased the sense of well-being among a group of low-income minority youth,[2] and the ever-popular book *The Artist's Way* involves building confidence and allaying fears.[3] While the self is apparent, it remains, however, only one piece of our pedagogical puzzle and might be seen as beside the point because of its ubiquitous-ness and because, as I pointed out in my chapter ten years ago, high self-esteem carries risks and low self-esteem isn't as bad as we might assume.[4] The self, because it is apparent, can be negotiated, even set aside while—or perhaps because—it remains part and parcel of what we do in creative writing.

Since that earlier essay, I have come to more fully understand the workshop as varied in practice. As such, the workshop plays an integral part in how the field of creative writing allows for wide and deep learning—for a writing life, for a reading life, for transferable skills, for curiosity—even when a particular class doesn't follow the traditional model. Adaptations of the workshop sometimes shift the position of author and of response, may include seemingly more objective tasks such as critical writing or quizzes, and, ultimately, can allow an instructor to use the self to help students get away from or around the self, to position the self as means (doing) rather than goal (being). As a result, creative writing courses encourage varied ways to understand the relationship between self-esteem and accomplishment.

In addition, over the last decade, the discipline's terminology and approaches, including the workshop model, have been critiqued in many ways or, to use the recently trendy expression for sorting through parts of complex ideas, have been unpacked. While some who've unpacked this discipline through explanation and analysis have called for a reconfiguration of what we do so that it is more recognizably teachable, academic, and traditionally disciplinary, I'm not one of those advocates. I'd rather get a bigger suitcase than throw out clothes that are in good shape and that I might wear (or, in another trendy phrase for such decision-making, that bring me joy). In fact, rethinking self-esteem ten years later makes me more attached to the strengths of creative writing as a discipline distinct from the traditionally academic. I see greater possibilities and a longer view than I could ten years ago.

Both sides of the desk

Also in *Can It Really Be Taught?* was an essay by Priscila Uppal called "Both Sides of the Desk," that, in some ways, works as a companion to my contribution and a touchstone for issues related to self-esteem. Uppal points out that Donald Hall's so-called McPoem syndrome exists only in workshops that encourage writers to write more like each other and to replicate models (like a copy machine?) rather than seek distinctive voices.[5] She argues that this syndrome and related problems in the workshop are the responsibility of the instructor, not the students or the workshop format.[6] If the students are not producing innovative work, experimenting with language and form, or risking originality, the instructor likely has not designed and implemented the class toward those goals. It's not an inherent flaw in the discipline or in the workshop model but in the teaching of creative writing, in the individual implementation or iteration. Uppal goes on to point out examples of poems that might be doomed in certain kinds of workshops, poems such as those by Allen Ginsberg or Langston Hughes. If poems full of creative risk and imagination fail, we're all in trouble. In that case, the very concept of *author* is withering and students wilt right along with it. Uppal asserts, "If this is the case, the fault rests primarily with the instructor."[7]

imp

The issue of self-esteem, then, is one for instructors as much as it is for students. When I walked into the classroom ten years ago, I was well aware of how I would be orchestrating my classroom with students' self-esteem in mind: "[. . .] every teacher in every creative writing class has to spend a fair amount of time, sometimes most of her time, showing students how to become teachable, that is, how to listen to what others are saying about their stories and how not to resist but to receive."[8] Jane Smiley's definition of teaching creative writing is among the best I've heard, and showing students how to become teachable, how not to resist but to receive, remains an important broad-based goal for me as a creative writing instructor. I stand by what I wrote ten years ago: "Our first duty, then, is not to our students' desire to feel good, not to self-esteem, whether ours or theirs. Instead, we must negotiate self-esteem to enrich the writing process of and possibilities for students."[9] In that statement, I was clearly focusing on students but instructors—*our* self-esteem—snuck into my sentences.

To be sure, I addressed in that essay complications of self-esteem for instructors, including the role of student evaluations and other pressure we are under, including larger cultural forces (such as the so-called crisis in the humanities or decreased funding in the arts, including for the National Endowment for the Arts[10]), to help students feel good about themselves. In hindsight, however, I didn't grapple fully with negotiating one's own self-esteem as a crucial responsibility for the creative writing instructor. Uppal's bluntness—*the fault rests primarily with the instructor, she's not fulfilling her responsibility*—is something I admire and did not muster myself in my scholarship a decade ago.

Not too long before *Can It Really Be Taught?* was published, I began to more consciously grapple with this relationship between responsibility and self-esteem. I'd never bought into the notion that students needed to like me in order for me to feel successful as a teacher, but it was another thing entirely to have my teacherly confidence shaken anyway. In a literature class (in a job previous to the one I have now), I'd assigned *Jane Eyre*, a favorite book of mine, a book I assumed every student would deeply appreciate as an exploration of coming of age—they were in the midst of coming of age themselves—and as a captivating story of how we negotiate ambitions and constraints as human beings. I thought they'd relish the sentences as well as the story. But most students in the class didn't like the novel, found it boring, or thought it too depressing. That the students didn't like *Jane Eyre* took me by surprise, but what really shocked me was how immediately judgmental of them I became. We slogged through the discussions, and I worked hard—

too obviously hard—to convince students to appreciate, if not actually like or enjoy, the language and story-telling as writers and literary scholars.

Now, of course, I would orchestrate the reading, discussion, and writing assignments differently. I'd do a better job now, and students would learn more. But back then, my initial reaction to this teaching experience was that I would never again teach a book that I liked as much as I liked *Jane Eyre*, which cut out a lot of options in the subsequent couple of years. I backed off; I hunkered down. *If that's the way you want it, I'll take my toys and go home.* That initial response emerged from a blow to self-esteem and led me to shirk my responsibility, to deny my own failure to teach an amazing novel, and to avoid risking failure in the future by lowering the bar. My self-esteem temporarily led me to limit my options, reduce my risks, and make decisions based on what was easiest not on what would lead to the greatest accomplishment. My reaction was the opposite of the habits of mind I work to cultivate in my students. That decision to not teach favorites temporarily robbed me of a certain level of investment and enthusiasm that ends up glistening in the classroom air and sparking ideas. I felt crushed and looked for an excuse; I had, as Stanford University psychologist Carol Dweck would say, a typical fixed mindset reaction even though I was a growth mindset teacher.

All instructors have an off-the-rails discussion or a less-than-stellar semester now and then. Kendall Dunkelberg writes with candor, "As a teacher, I have experienced many unproductive workshops over the years! They come with the territory, and there is always next time. I no longer see workshops as individual learning experiences, but rather as an ongoing learning process."[11] It's our responsibility to get ourselves and our students through those rough times, even when they have a lot to do with circumstances beyond our control, like classroom configuration or a mentally ill student. It's our responsibility to take the long view, which is especially difficult when we are learning the ropes in the early years of our careers.

I do not always succeed in the classroom; not every moment of my teaching is momentous to me or to my students. My students do not always write stellar work; not every exercise leads to brilliance expressed originally and authentically. Whether teaching or writing, failure—obstacles—is part of the creative process; missteps are opportunities. Had I never had my *Jane Eyre* moment, I may not have become the teacher I am now, for my initial reaction and its repercussions taught me valuable lessons and made me more aware of my responsibilities more quickly than any other way I can imagine.

I still agree with what I said ten years ago: "If we redefine self-esteem, we can relocate the responsibility for having it: The student who uses the learning process to accomplish goals within an environment the teacher creates is able to build confidence."[12] Now, though, I'd rewrite that sentence with the teacher—or our responsibility—as the subject: The teacher's responsibility is to create a learning environment in which students are encouraged to reach for goals beyond what they can do easily and are able to build their confidence through accomplishment. I see self-esteem more clearly through the lens of

ility, both students' responsibility as active participants in their
and my own responsibility as creator and orchestrator of the
ent that fosters—even demands—students' responsibility.

Of course, an odd thing about this responsibility of the creative writing
instructor is that it must remain mostly hidden in the classroom in order for
the students to recognize their accomplishments as their own, even as those
accomplishments emerge out of the orchestrated learning environment.
Part of the difficulty of teaching creative writing is making the teaching
look easy. It's the writing that must look hard, worthy of accomplishing—
self-esteem is, then, a by-product of the accomplishment of writing.

The growth mindset

It seems no coincidence that Carol Dweck's *Mindset: The New Psychology
of Success* is also celebrating its tenth anniversary. In that book, Dweck
discusses research that indicates students' perceptions of their abilities plays
an important role in how motivated they are and how much they achieve.[13]
Importantly, this work is distinct from numerous and long-standing studies
that reveal that American students tend to over-estimate their abilities and
from newer research that indicates gender and other factors play a role in
perceptions about relative ability.[14] Ten years ago, I touched upon the ways
American culture reifies high self-esteem and the potential effect it has in
creative writing classrooms. Dweck focuses on issues more directly related
to learning and creative thinking and, therefore, more directly relevant to
creative writing pedagogy.

Early on, she explains that children who were excited to tackle a
challenging task inspired her research. Of these children, she writes, "They
knew that human qualities, such as intellectual skills, could be cultivated
through effort. [...] Not only weren't they discouraged by failure, they
didn't even think they were failing."[15] These children were immersed in
problem solving, complex tasks, and creative thinking for its own sake and
for their own development as much as for the right solution. The main point
of her work is that students who understand that their intelligence and
abilities can grow tend to achieve more, whereas students who understand
their mindset as fixed tend to be less motivated, less accomplished, and more
likely to take their toys and go home when faced with an obstacle.

Over the last decade, readers and educators oversimplified these claims,
and the lore that proliferated suggested that greater self-esteem—feeling
good about any energy expended, regardless of outcome—led to greater
success. Even though Dweck clearly states that those with a growth mindset
do not believe anyone can be anything,[16] interpretation and application of
the term trended toward notions that there existed no limits and all that
mattered was trying. Anyone who reads the book itself will see its strengths,
but the ideas there quickly became lore less connected to that original

research. Suddenly, everyone wanted to have growth mindset. Learning and accomplishment fell by the wayside, while confidence and effort became goals in and of themselves instead of means to goals.

So, as I am revisiting the topic of self-esteem in creative writing ten years hence, it seems no coincidence that, in an article in *Education Week* in 2015, Dweck writes, "as we've watched the growth mindset become more popular, we've become much wiser about how to implement it."[17] In other words, we got the implementation wrong; we liked the term *growth mindset* but didn't do the hard work of figuring out what it really meant to practice growth mindset.

According to Dweck, another researcher, Kathy Liu Sun, "found that there were many math teachers who endorsed a growth mindset and even said the words 'growth mindset' in their middle school math classes, but did not follow through in their classroom practices."[18] Dweck herself, along with her collaborator Kyla Haimovitz, started "finding many parents who endorse a growth mindset, but react to their children's mistakes as though they are problematic or harmful, rather than helpful."[19] *Growth mindset* quickly became trendy lingo but doesn't describe actual practice in classrooms. We need to refocus and make adjustments, Dweck asserts now, in order to take advantage of the approach, which has everything to do with building confidence through learning and accomplishment and recognizing that learning and accomplishment involve risk, failure, and perseverance.

I grew up with Mr. Rogers, who told children in song, "You are special."[20] On its surface, that sounds like a version of the empty ego-boosting that Dweck is concerned emerged as her research was put inadequately into practice. That you-are-special attitude could explain why every kid on every team gets a trophy, no matter the win-loss record, no matter the individual performance. Some soccer leagues don't even keep score, as if not counting goals will prevent children from noticing who achieves them, as if achievement of goals is unimportant.

Parents have become so concerned about protecting their children's self-esteem and ensuring their children's success that the term *helicopter parent*, coined in the late 1960s by teenage kids to describe their hovering parents in a negative light, is now common parlance. Recent research, interestingly, suggests that a high level of individual attention and assistance, especially when parents step in to solve a problem or handle a crisis, leads to a lower sense of self-worth in undergraduate students.[21] The same research suggests, surprisingly, that helicopter parenting, which has long been assumed to develop from parents' concern for their children, "in and of itself is not inherently warm."[22] Though the research has just begun, parents may hover, at least in part, to feel better about themselves, and over-parenting, especially when not coupled with actual warmth, may lead to more narcissistic, anxious, depressed, underprepared, or grumpy young adults—the opposite of what these parents are trying to ensure. And what happens when over-parented young adults filled with confidence and unused to coping with failure walk into our creative writing classrooms, participate in workshop critique, or are asked to revise?

As I pointed out in a convocation speech a few years ago, after quoting that Mr. Rogers song to incoming students and their parents, "Each of us is a unique, original iteration of what it means to exist as a human being. But when you think about it, if each of us is special, then being special isn't, in and of itself, very special at all."[23] Anyone who was raised in part by Mr. Rogers (as I clearly was) will know that his overarching ethos is about responsibility and the benefits we reap individually and collectively through taking responsibility. *You are special* is a starting point, a foundation for responsibility, not a goal in itself. Or, as Mr. Rogers puts it, "As human beings, our job in life is to help people realize how rare and valuable each one of us really is, that each of us has something that no one else has— or ever will have—something inside that is unique to all time. It's our job to encourage each other to discover that uniqueness and to provide ways of developing its expression."[24] Whatever is special about an individual, therefore, becomes responsibility to do something with that quality. For a creative writing professor, that means presenting students with challenges and opportunities to fail and encouraging them to learn from failure by revising—and orchestrating the process so that they have a sense of accomplishment at the end of fifteen weeks. Creative writing is an immersive, practice-based discipline, and teaching it carries a lot of responsibility.

As Dweck says, "we're all a mixture of fixed and growth mindsets."[25] Learning this about myself has made me a better teacher, a teacher who embraces what Dweck calls a wider "repertoire of approaches—not just sheer effort—to learn and improve" and to create an environment in which students do the same. Another researcher, Angela Duckworth, says in her TED Talk, "Having perseverance in the face of adversity [. . .] setbacks, failures, that's important."[26] It's not easy to set students up to fail, but that's what creative writing really is: an always striving. I've learned, through practice, to get students excited about considering weaknesses in what they write and feeling better about themselves for being able to see and address alternatives through workshop discussion and revision.

Duckworth says, "There is no domain of expertise that has been studied where the world-class performers have put in fewer than ten years of consistent, deliberate practice to get to where they are."[27] I'm thinking more now than I did a decade ago about the long haul of which each fifteen-week semester is only a small stint and how I can orchestrate tasks and conversations in that short timeframe to foster perseverance over the long haul and, as a welcome by-product, foster self-esteem. My class will not transform any student into a great poet, but students do learn what it might take if they stick with creative writing or, for that matter, any serious pursuit. And this focus on students reverts back to me—to creative writing instructors—because the long view, facing pedagogical weaknesses, trying new things, and sticking with it works for teaching in similar ways as it does for writing, for both are creative practices.

Larger responsibilities

As a creative writing professor, I'm a poet and creative nonfiction writer, a scholar, a teacher, an administrator, and an editor—all those roles intersect and inform each other as the whole of my career. Some combination of these roles seems relatively common in the discipline of creative writing, and that offers us both opportunity and responsibility. It also means that our self-esteem is tied to numerous roles and various types of accomplishment.

Ten years ago, I was a more traditional creative writing teacher, though I was already loosening up. I'd begun experimenting, for instance, with when to employ or relinquish the (uncomfortably named) gag rule that prevents the author from participating in workshop discussion (and I continue to consider how who has a voice and is permitted a voice matters). Shortly after *Can It Really Be Taught?* was published, I started a new job and decided to teach the multi-genre, introductory creative writing course with a focus on point of view and perspective. Next, I developed a graduate poetry course focused on chapbooks that I now teach every spring. I teach books I adore and books I don't much like. In fact, last year, an MFA student latched onto a chapbook filled with gritty prose poems that was not my cup of tea but that I'd included in the syllabus because of the relationship of its form and content and its relationship to other chapbooks on the list. That student re-envisioned her thesis as a result; she didn't replicate what she'd read but, instead, was motivated by the possibilities it suggested to her and ended up with a stronger thesis (and stronger work than that which had inspired her).

In other words, I now more consciously treat teaching as a creative practice and as a dynamic, teacher-orchestrated exchange among teacher, students, published texts, and student writing. I'd probably known these things all along and even written about them in one way or another over the years. But it's one thing to say *growth mindset* and another to practice it, to feel immersed day to day in what you're doing. Some days, of course, I still have a fixed mindset to manage. It takes time and patience—at least it did for me—to cultivate a growth mindset for teaching.

Ten years ago, I was more traditional in my scholarly role, too, working to establish myself as an academic pursuing tenure and to establish—or solidify—a then-precarious aspect of the discipline of creative writing, an area that explored creativity, pedagogy, and the profession. Back then, though I tested some boundaries, I was not bold enough to quote Mr. Rogers in a scholarly essay. I see my responsibility as a scholar differently now.

Katharine Haake has written about Marjorie Perloff's argument in 1987 that the separation between *poet* and *professor* is phony, and Haake herself asserts, "Between the entrenched anti-intellectualism that infects a large number of us and the self-abnegation endemic in the rush to scholarship (and respectability) that has left a good number of the rest of us sounding weirdly more like theorists than writers, there has to be a fruitful middle ground—a suture."[28] I'd like my scholarly work now to work at that suture, to stitch together my thinking as both poet and professor. That possibility is one of the amazing aspects of creative writing.

I want my academic writing to be useful, and I'm willing to risk being less traditionally academic—to express my uniqueness and this discipline's uniqueness—in order that my scholarly work becomes more useful both inside creative writing and as a way to expand the possibilities in academia generally. This approach, one that is undoubtedly easier to take after tenure (and one for which I feel more responsible after tenure), seems crucial if scholars of creative writing are to take full advantage of the field's underlying strengths and use them to shape the larger academic environment. As scholars, creative writers have a responsibility to our discipline of creative writing—to its specialness-ness—and also to the knowledge creation for which academia as a whole is responsible.

So, do we still have a responsibility to be creative writers? Our students are right there waiting for us, in our email inbox and in the next class meeting. The scholarly essay has a deadline and length limit and adds a line to the CV. I'm an administrator, too, now (I direct undergraduate research and creative activity for my university), so not a day goes by that I don't address a problem or an individual's question or idea and feel good that I've contributed to my institution and to the work of faculty and students there. A literary journal produces tangible evidence of my editorial efforts every other month. Almost every Friday is a celebration of having not only survived but having accomplished something specific and meaningful. Overall, the combination of these roles is great for my self-esteem. I've built a career—not just a job—in which I could probably get by in the eyes of my institution without writing any more poems. In fact, it will be a decade between my first and second full-length poetry collections.

Though I've been writing regularly and publishing during this last decade, I cringed while typing that last sentence. (I erased it because I didn't want to admit that information publicly, and then I retyped it because I want this essay to be useful.) I didn't get into the field of creative writing so that I could reach a point when I no longer had to do creative writing. I didn't get into creative writing so that I could substitute asking students to write poems for writing poems myself. My teaching is an offshoot of or a complement to my immersion as a writer, and my students are better off for it. That's a fundamental *both/and* in my career. I didn't get into creative writing so that I could substitute running a summer research program for writing a book about the space shuttle. These substitutions are tempting, as administrative and teaching tasks usually don't put my self-esteem at risk in the same way as does writing and they often provide relatively immediate validation that makes me feel satisfied. It's not that I don't think these other roles are important; it's not that I don't take my responsibility seriously when I accept these roles. The word *responsibility* comes from the Latin meaning *to answer or promise in return*. In fact, the growth mindset demands that I answer to each role with attention and skills—the repertoire of approaches—it deserves. Admittedly, that demand sometimes seems impossible to meet on a given day of multitasking, and sometimes, therefore, the writing appears to be a luxury I can't afford.

I look back at the essay I wrote ten years ago and wonder where the poet was then. I wrote, "Moreover, when we see ourselves as responsible for our students' self-worth, we exhibit a kind of hubris; our generous compassion reveals an unreasonable sense of our own power and control that ultimately diminishes students, their achievement, and their empowerment."[29] When the creative writing professor stops writing, she may be tempted to substitute the student's growth as a writer for her own. The *yes!* a teacher says, perhaps only in her own head, in response to the student's revised poem may well be self-congratulatory. I must write to stay humble as a teacher.

There exist many good reasons for creative writing professors to be creative writers, and the Association of Writers and Writing Programs encourages this as a best practice (though does not claim that every good writer is a good teacher).[30] Ultimately, a creative writing professor who has no inclination to write or spends no time writing makes as much sense to me as if we changed our pedagogy to what Maureen Freely suggests as an outrageous alternative: "My colleagues and I could stop reading student work tomorrow and no one in the university hierarchy would notice, let alone complain. We could offer lectures on writing instead of looking at what they write."[31] If one sees one's responsibility as a professor mainly as "conforming to standards that were designed for a very different kind of teaching,"[32] then the choice a creative writing professor might make to do other important tasks instead of writing is understandable. But Freely points out that creative writing programs in the United Kingdom survive because their faculty "are hybrid creatures who move between two cultures, and who insist on the importance of doing so, even when those who run universities fail to see the point."[33] Self-esteem, of course, is at risk when we resist bureaucratic pressure. The balance between disciplinary and university conventions is tricky for each of us to maintain, as is the balance between writing and teaching.

Perhaps, it's my responsibility to write because it's my responsibility to not choose only those roles that boost my self-esteem most easily, to keep my hubris in check, to keep growing. Or maybe, like Shonda Rhimes (if you thought Mr. Rogers wasn't scholarly, here's a bonus) in her *Year of Yes*, I admit, "Writing and I are MFEO. [Made For Each Other . . .] And I have no ability to downgrade my creativity in my soul. I have no desire to do so either."[34] That creativity in my own soul—or personality or core consciousness—is something I want to cultivate in others who have some creativity in their souls too. As humans, we each have at least a spark of creativity glistening, if not heaps bursting forth. That's why I teach.

Even if it's only for fifteen weeks, I ask my students to accept the responsibility of being a creative writer, to share in this making, this doing, this practice of craft and expression. I cannot, in good conscience, ask them to accept that responsibility—and risk their self-esteem as they do so—if it's a responsibility that I am shirking, either as a teacher or as a writer. And so I close here so that I can return to writing that book about the space shuttle.

Notes

1   Anna Leahy, "Creativity, Caring, and The Easy 'A': Rethinking the Role of Self-Esteem in Creative Writing Pedagogy," *Can It Really Be Taught? Resisting Lore in Creative Writing Pedagogy*, eds Kelly Ritter and Stephanie Vanderslice (Portsmouth, NH: Boynton-Cook, 2007), 57–8.

2   G.E. Chandler, "A Creative Writing Program to Enhance Self-Esteem and Self-Efficacy in Adolescents," *Journal of Child and Adolescent Psychiatric Nursing* 12, no. 2 (1999), 70–8.

3   Julia Cameron, *The Artist's Way* (New York: Putnam, 2002).

4   Lauren Slater, "The Trouble with Self-Esteem." *New York Times Magazine* 151 (February 3, 2002), 46.

5   Priscila Uppal, "Both Sides of the Desk: Experiencing Creative Writing Lore as a Student and as a Professor," *Can It Really Be Taught? Resisting Lore in Creative Writing Pedagogy*, eds Kelly Ritter and Stephanie Vanderslice (Portsmouth, NH: Boynton-Cook, 2007), 46–54.

6   Uppal, "Both Sides of the Desk," 49.

7   Uppal, "Both Sides of the Desk," 50.

8   Jane Smiley, "What Stories Teach Their Writers: The Purpose and Practice of Revision," *Creating Fiction: Instruction and Insights from the Teachers of the Associated Writing Programs*, ed. Julie Checkoway (Cincinnati: Story P, 1999), 244.

9   Anna Leahy, "Creativity, Caring, and The Easy 'A'," 59.

10 "National Endowment for the Arts Appropriation History," National Endowment for the Arts, https://www.arts.gov/open-government/national-endowment-arts-appropriations-history [accessed July 17, 2016].

11 Kendall Dunkelberg, "Creative Writers Respond," *Teaching Creative Writing to Undergraduates: A Practical Guide and Sourcebook*, eds. Stephanie Vanderslice and Kelly Ritter (Southlake, TX: Fountainhead Press, 2011), 75.

12 Anna Leahy, "Creativity, Caring, and The Easy 'A'," 64.

13 Carol Dweck, *Mindset: The New Psychology of Success* (New York: Ballantine, 2007).

14 Daniel Z. Grunspan., Sarah L. Eddy, Sara E. Brownell, Bejamin L. Wiggins, Allison J. Crowe, and Steven M. Goodreau, "Males Underestimate Performance of Their Female Peers in Undergraduate Biology Classrooms," *PLoS ONE*, 11, no. 2, http://journals.plos.org/plosone/article?id=10.1371/journal.pone.0148405 [accessed February 28, 2016].

15 Dweck, *Mindset*, 4.

16 Dweck, *Mindset*, 7.

17 Carol Dweck, "Carol Dweck Revisits the 'Growth Mindset,'" *Education Week* (23 September 2015) http://www.edweek.org/ew/articles/2015/09/23/carol-dweck-revisits-the-growth-mindset.html [accessed January 12, 2016].

18 Dweck, "Carol Dweck Revisits the 'Growth Mindset.'"

19 Dweck, "Carol Dweck Revisits the 'Growth Mindset.'"

20 Fred Rogers, "You Are Special," first sung on *Mr. Rogers' Neighborhood*, 1968.

21 Larry J. Nelson, Laura M. Padilla-Walker, and Matthew G. Nielson, "Is Hovering Smothering or Loving? An Examination of Parental Warmth as a Moderator of Relations between Helicopter Parenting and Emerging Adults' Indices of Adjustment," *Emerging Adulthood*, 3, no. 4, *Sage Premier*, 283–4.

22 Nelson et al., "Is Hovering Smothering or Loving?", 284.

23 Anna Leahy, "To find, to create, to remake," Opening Convocation Speech, Chapman University, Orange, CA, August 24, 2011.

24 Fred Rogers, *The World According to Mister Rogers: Important Things to Remember* (New York: MJF Books, 2003), 137.

25 Dweck, "Carol Dweck Revisits the 'Growth Mindset'.'"

26 Angela Duckworth, "True Grit; Can Perseverance Be Taught?" TEDTalk, https://www.ted.com/talks/angela_lee_duckworth_the_key_to_success_grit [accessed October 17, 2015].

27 Duckworth, "True Grit."

28 Katharine Haake, "Thinking Systematically About What We Do," *Teaching Creative Writing*, ed. Heather Beck (New York: Palgrave MacMillan, 2012), 134.

29 Anna Leahy, "Creativity, Caring, and The Easy 'A'," 64.

30 "AWP Hallmarks of a Successful MFA Program in Creative Writing," Association of Writers and Writing Programs, https://www.awpwriter.org/guide/directors_handbook_hallmarks_of_a_successful_mfa_program_in_creative_writing [accessed February 28, 2016].

31 Maureen Freely, "No Factories, Please—We're Writers," *Teaching Creative Writing*, ed. Heather Beck (New York: Palgrave MacMillan, 2012), 89.

32 Freely, 89–90.

33 Freely, 90–1.

34 Shonda Rhimes, *Year of Yes: How to Dance It Out, Stand in the Sun and Be Your Own Person* (New York: Simon & Schuster, 2015), 281.

References

"AWP Hallmarks of a Successful MFA Program in Creative Writing." *Association of Writers and Writing Programs*. https://www.awpwriter.org/guide/directors_handbook_hallmarks_of_a_successful_mfa_program_in_creative_writing

Cameron, Julia. *The Artist's Way*. New York: Putnam, 2002.

Chandler, G.E. "A Creative Writing Program to Enhance Self-Esteem and Self-Efficacy in Adolescents." *Journal of Child and Adolescent Psychiatric Nursing* 12.2 (1999): 70–8.

Duckworth, Angela. "True Grit; Can Perseverance Be Taught?" TEDTalk. https://www.ted.com/talks/angela_lee_duckworth_the_key_to_success_grit

Dunkelberg, Kendall. "Creative Writers Respond." In *Teaching Creative Writing to Undergraduates: A Practical Guide and Sourcebook*, edited by Stephanie Vanderslice and Kelly Ritter. Southlake, TX: Fountainhead Press, 2011.

Dweck, Carol. "Carol Dweck Revisits the 'Growth Mindset.'" *Education Week*. September 23, 2015. http://www.edweek.org/ew/articles/2015/09/23/carol-dweck-revisits-the-growth-mindset.html

Freely, Maureen. "No Factories, Please—We're Writers." In *Teaching Creative Writing*, edited by Heather Beck, 86–92. New York: Palgrave MacMillan, 2012.

Grunspan, Daniel Z., Sarah L. Eddy, Sara E. Brownell, Bejamin L. Wiggins, Allison J. Crowe, and Steven M. Goodreau. "Males Underestimate Performance of Their Female Peers in Undergraduate Biology Classrooms." *PLoS ONE*, 11.2. http://journals.plos.org/plosone/article?id=10.1371/journal.pone.0148405

Haake, Katharine. "Thinking Systematically About What We Do." In *Teaching Creative Writing*, edited by Heather Beck, 131–135. New York: Palgrave MacMillan, 2012.

Leahy, Anna. "Creativity, Caring, and The Easy 'A': Rethinking the Role of Self-Esteem in Creative Writing Pedagogy." In *Can It Really Be Taught? Resisting Lore in Creative Writing Pedagogy*, edited by Kelly Ritter and Stephanie Vanderslice, 55–66. Portsmouth, NH: Boynton-Cook, 2007.

Leahy, Anna. "To find, to create, to remake." Opening Convocation Speech. Chapman University, Orange, CA. August 24, 2011.

"National Endowment for the Arts Appropriation History." *National Endowment for the Arts*. https://www.arts.gov/open-government/national-endowment-arts-appropriations-history

Nelson, Larry J., Laura M. Padilla-Walker, and Matthew G. Nielson. "Is Hovering Smothering or Loving? An Examination of Parental Warmth as a Moderator of Relations between Helicopter Parenting and Emerging Adults' Indices of Adjustment." *Emerging Adulthood*, 3.4 (2015): 282–5.

Rhimes, Shonda. *Year of Yes: How to Dance It Out, Stand in the Sun and Be Your Own Person*. New York: Simon & Schuster, 2015.

Rogers, Fred. *The World According to Mister Rogers: Important Things to Remember*. New York: MJF Books, 2003.

Slater, Lauren. "The Trouble with Self-Esteem." *New York Times Magazine* 151 (February 3, 2002): 44–7.

Smiley, Jane. "What Stories Teach Their Writers: The Purpose and Practice of Revision." In *Creating Fiction: Instruction and Insights from the Teachers of the Associated Writing Programs*, edited by Julie Checkoway, 244–55. Cincinnati: Story P, 1999.

Uppal, Priscila. "Both Sides of the Desk: Experiencing Creative Writing Lore as a Student and as a Professor." In *Can It Really Be Taught? Resisting Lore in Creative Writing Pedagogy*, edited by Kelly Ritter and Stephanie Vanderslice, 46–54. Portsmouth, NH: Boynton-Cook, 2007.

5

Finding Truth in the Gaps:

A Hybrid Text

Patrick Bizzaro

. . . [I]t is imperative that I tell you what I want from you creative writing professors, from writing teachers of any writing course where serious, committed students can be found: . . . I want you to show me how to see[1]

We must question those ready-made syntheses, those groupings that we normally accept before any examinations, those links whose validity is recognized from the outset; we must oust those forms and obscure forces by which we usually link the discourse of one man with that of another; they must be driven out from the darkness in which they reign.[2]

. . . [A] hybrid text is one that brings together elements from disparate discourses, traditions, or conventions that would not ordinarily be found together to create either a new form or a kind of stitched together text so as to express something that cannot be expressed in other ways.[3]

My former student, Michael McClanahan, in an essay we co-authored a decade ago, made a request on behalf of other "serious, committed students" that I have waited until now to address. Mike wrote, "I want you to show me how to *see*. . . ." This is a risky proposition, to be sure, to try to show someone else how (or what) to see. It is no wonder, then, that I've put it off until after I've retired.

Something that Needs to be Done

Something that needs to be done
walks ahead of me. I'm walking fast,
trying to catch up. Its footprints,
once hard in the earth, are soft
and fresh as I get closer.

This thing that needs to be done
waits ahead of me, now turns
and walks back to where I push against
the ground with my worn and tired feet.

Its sockets are empty. Its nostrils
flare at my scent. When we meet,
we embrace like distant relatives.
I give it my eyes and help it to
the end of this long, unfamiliar road.[4]

I'm still not sure it's ethical or even possible to teach someone how to "see." Nonetheless Mike's request has led me to take this opportunity to address the issues he raises in the ways I am able to because we were perfectly comfortable with that request all those years ago. But now it's "see what?" and "see how?" So, I have taken the liberty here of slightly altering Mike's request, so I can focus on the related emphases of genre and vision rather than on how students perceive the world. Here is a poem I wrote originally for a special issue of *Making Connections* devoted to the work of playwright August Wilson. It, too, says something about vision in a way I'd be hard-pressed to duplicate in academic prose. It shows a poetic rendering of the subject of vision that Mike's use of the term *see* brings to mind for me as I consider in this poem the related notions of "sight" and "vision."

Light, if
for August Wilson

Light, if
anything at all,
is "the radiation visible
to the human eye."

We don't see anything
except light
when we look from here
to whatever's out there
within the spectrum
of what we can know.

If color is light, it is also sight.
But it is not
vision. We know
because light
and the spectrum
are science's admission
that it might be wrong.

Light has wavelengths
which are not absolute,
but science treats spectrum
as universal,
as all we need
if we want to know
the deep universe,
the colors of different planets,
the elements on Saturn,
chemicals of its rings
and stones of its moons.

Light moves us
toward August
who moved us toward
light, both particle and wave,
a vision we were blind to
in July.

There are bodies in the universe,
physicists say, that absorb
all light. But the August
light radiating
on the Hill
seems to be the vision
knowledge makes possible,
once we look beyond the spectrum.

Vision permits us
to see all things

we can know and even those
we can't.
It is the light that fills gaps
between the decades, separations
in our knowledge filled
dramatically by light,
the theatrical successes
and failures of our time
on this planet, safe
and content in the knowledge
we can only know what enters
our spectrum

and what art understands
to be true for now
on this planet
and on the next.[5]

What's this? A poem sent to do the work of academic prose? Not quite.

By juxtaposing academic prose with poetry in this way, I hope to explore questions that seem to include the one Mike wants answered when he says he believes teachers of creative writing should teach their students how to see. Do we see differently when we write a composition than we do when we make a poem? Are vision and sight the same thing to writers? These questions avoid the ethical conundrum of teacher appropriation—that is, of the teacher telling the student to "do it like this"—and gives me license to make a poem alongside a composition to demonstrate the differences and similarities between the two genres in addressing the same topics. In doing so, I will address the place of composition in Creative Writing Studies in a kind of mixed response to Douglas Hesse's discipline-defining essay, "The Place of Creative Writing in Composition Studies."[6]

The goal of a hybrid essay, as the quote from Katherine Haake that introduces this essay suggests, is not only to bring "together elements from disparate discourses, traditions, or conventions" but also "to express something that cannot be expressed in other ways." In short, I have held the position, increasingly unpopular at Conference on College Composition and Communication (CCCC) and in most of our composition journals, that creative writing and composition are not the same thing. I have argued in panels and in print for the contrasting views of plagiarism in the two disciplines and concluded that they are different at the level of epistemology.[7,8] I have further called for the scrutiny of our research methods to honor the differences in what we call evidence in the two. In short, I have attempted to trace the root of the "ready-made synthesis" we have constructed of composition and creative writing, to use Foucault's apt language in describing the forced connections between the two. In this essay, I want to return to what many consider the source of the thinking that has grown into Creative Writing Studies, Wendy Bishop's seminal *Released Into Language*.

Houses of History
for Wendy Bishop

In the lot
across the street, four men enter
my vision, all doing almost
what I think they're doing,

all building a house
cooperating in the movement of dirt
to a designated spot across the yard,
all building one house
from a single plan.

But as I watch, I see
ahead of their weary motions
the house of our understanding
and the house of theirs
though all the while
they ignore me

as if the structures we live by
differ at the brick foundation,
and the house this will become
is finished as they begin it,
stretched to its imaginary posts,
so people we have never seen
can enter and make it
a house of their own.[9]

Bishop worked skillfully and perceptively around the difficulties she found in advocating for a synthesis of composition and creative writing. To do so, she wisely studied "writing" and "writers at work." In the first chapter of her remarkable book, Bishop whets our appetites by drawing our attention to "*Writers*' Self-Reports" and "Research on *Writing*" in order to set up the influential, lasting, but ultimately confusing work of "Combining *Writers*' Self-Reports and Research on *Writing*" (my emphases).[10] Lest we allow these headings to lead us astray—because they suggest that composition and creative writing (and technical writing and scientific writing and business writing . . .) are intrinsically connected—we must acknowledge that Bishop was able to make the moves she makes so smartly by talking inclusively about writing in general, not specifically about creative writing or specifically about composition. Her effort, of course, changed the thinking of many (this author, included) who then came to CCCC to deepen their thinking about this new synthesis and to find support they would ultimately not find at the meeting of any other organization, including Association of Writers and Writing Programs (AWP). My ongoing concern since then is a natural one (and personal) because it applied to my career path as well as to the trajectory of other people's academic lives: the lure of CCCC has been so great many would-be poets, novelists, and creative essayists have given up the vision that propelled them into university creative writing programs to think and publish instead almost exclusively as compositionists. By doing so, I fear, students like my friend Mike have, indeed, been shown a way to see. But they come to *see* in a creative writing class through the eyes of compositionists. Again, these seem the wrong glasses to use for focusing on the road ahead— unless, of course, the road to heaven is paved with freshman themes . . . as it probably should be! Or unless the arguments of scholars like D.G. Myers in *The Elephants Teach* and Tim Mayers in *(Re)writing Craft* are heard.[11, 12] In those books Myers and Mayers agree that a third "idea" be admitted into conceptions of the way modern English Studies is constructed, an idea they call creative writing, to go along with the bipartite division most often assumed to exist, the poetic and the rhetoric, literary study and composition.

To dig deeper into the issue that arises when we treat composition and creative writing as one and the same, I bring poetry together with academic prose in this alternative text because some work, mostly outside English departments, has already shown the value of doing so.[13, 14] Some scholars nowadays believe those poetic reports provide us with insights we cannot have any other way.[15]

Let me briefly justify the use of poetry in this essay, though I contend, as others have, that this contextualization of knowledge-making in English Studies could be done equally well using fiction and clearly borders on what has been called fictocriticism.[16] Because I am more comfortable amplifying ideas using poetry than any other genre, in this text I want to exemplify what Elliot Eisner says when he writes about poetry, that "The open texture of the form increases the probability that multiple perspectives will emerge. Multiple perspectives make our engagement with the phenomena more complex. Ironically, good research often complicates our lives."[17]

In a more succinct fashion, William Wordsworth says much the same in "Tintern Abbey" when he writes, "We see into the life of things."[18]

We get additional support for this view of poetry's potential from Furman and his colleagues in Social Work at University of Washington, Tacoma. They extend the argument that poets have been making for hundreds of years by identifying poetry as a genre well suited to relaying the human experience. To be clear, when I discuss the discipline of Composition Studies and its place in creative writing in this essay, a topic that has been mostly avoided for three decades—because young scholars have preferred to see creative writing as a subdiscipline of Composition Studies, as Douglas Hesse does in the essay cited above—I use poems to see the "multiple perspectives" that emerge and thereby deepen our understandings of the ways occurrences in the field impact the lives of individuals like myself who teach in it. For one, I believe we should not pass up the opportunity to see the human consequences of our research. Why through poetry? As Furman et al. state:

> As a document of social phenomena, poetry can be viewed as a vehicle through which to communicate powerful and multiple "truths" about the human experience. While poetry may not commonly be thought of as a source of knowledge, poems are powerful documents that possess the capacity to capture the contextual and psychological worlds of both poet and subject.[19]

With much the same perspective on poetry in mind, poet Melisa Cahnmann-Taylor writes, "if poetry is to have a greater impact on research, those engaged in poetic practices need to share our processes and products with the entire research community, and the terms of its use must be clearly defined."[20] Poems of my own that I have selected for this text from an array of published sources reflect, as a starting point, what David Hanauer describes as "the experiences, thoughts and feelings of the writer through a self-referential use of language that creates for the reader and writer a new understanding of the experience, thought or feeling expressed in the text."[21] My poems hopefully convey the personal reactions of a poet to the living and working issues current in the synthesis we have made of composition and creative writing. I don't think these issues can be presented more personally than in poems I have placed alongside my academic inquiry into English Studies.

Exactly for the reasons Furman and his colleagues offer and Hanauer echoes, my goal is to use a hybrid text in order to demonstrate the unique perspectives on generating knowledge the essay and the poetic form offer us. They also enable us to reconsider Mike's difficult question. Are composition and creative writing the same discipline? Should they be treated as though they are?

At the 2012 CCCC in St. Louis, I was on a panel with three colleagues in what has come to be called "Creative Writing Studies," Dianne Donnelly, Mary Ann Cain, and Stephanie Vanderslice. Over coffee after our session, we all agreed that creative writing had taken the social turn, and our papers were proof of that fact. I argued in my paper that because creative writing as a college course had become democratized by becoming available to a wider range of students than ever before, the tenets of critical pedagogy that we apply in our composition classes apply equally well in our creative writing classes.[22] The possibility that students in creative writing are similar to those in first year composition supports the view forwarded by advocates of the writing about writing pedagogy,[23] Douglas Downs and Elizabeth

Wardle, who have noted that there is little if any carryover from first year writing to other writing courses our students might take. Ironically, even in an age marked by increased complication of the notion of genre but widespread use of multi-genre writing in composition classes, we cannot anticipate that students taking an introductory creative writing class will know much about creative writing based upon what they learned in first year composition. In fact, we might argue, as Donald Murray did nearly twenty-five years ago, that some students may need to unlearn some of what they learned in composition class if they hope to succeed in creative writing.[24] The tools they have been given just aren't the right ones for creative writing.

Repairing the Car

Some days I search
through the car's engine
for the source of the hiss
I hear as I drive.
I search foreign places—
carburetor, distributor—
for air, for a leak
the size of my pupil,
seeing its way into sound,
into life. I worry all day
that this hiss will expand
into a line of hisses
and stand along some belt or hose
like a police barricade
preventing my travels home.

Sometimes I reach for a tool,
a hammer usually or a saw,
and place it beside my car
as I unlatch the hood,
lift it in the air,
and lean over into something
stinking of rubber,
something futureless as grease.
I squeeze with thumb and forefinger
anything that smokes,
any signal that gambles
with travels I am yet to make,
that gambles with its own
well-being, as I reach down
for the hammer
to set myself free.[25]

I felt some uneasiness when I walked back to my hotel that day in St. Louis, thinking about creative writing and the social turn it seemed to be taking at CCCC. I have long been troubled by the different emphases of CCCC and AWP in their views of what constitutes instruction in creative writing. That is not to say that I have considered giving up on my efforts to better understand academic creative writing, how it gets taught, why it attracts so many students, and what it might contribute to literacy studies. But I do think we have made a wrong turn in creative writing, not that the social turn is necessarily the wrong one. But making that turn *because Composition Studies has* may very well be the wrong reason for making it in Creative Writing Studies. What will that turn mean in terms of the ways we instruct students in our creative writing classes, and will such a turn further distance AWP from CCCC? Will it further distance established programs from smaller, less-ambitious ones? These questions are especially perplexing at a time when Composition Studies has so clearly articulated its dismissal of expressivism.[26]

No doubt, it is as difficult to theorize academic creative writing using composition as a model nowadays as it was some thirty-five years ago to model the theorization of composition after literary theory. And it is misleading to do so. James Zebroski asserted his belief, in advocating for composition's independence from literature "[i]n the mid-1980s," that "Compositionists now must pursue their own kind of theory which arises from the grassroots of composition, rather than submitting to what amounts to re-colonization once again from literati."[27] What makes the theorization of creative writing so difficult for me is that I must now separate myself from those, including my much-respected mentor, Wendy Bishop, who assert the belief that writing is writing, that we as creative writing teachers can learn how to teach our courses by studying what gets done in composition. I think this view has left many of us confused for years, including people who select papers for CCCC. I have written elsewhere, based on my understanding of papers on creative writing given between 1995 and 2009 at CCCC, that for a paper on creative writing to be accepted for presentation at CCCC it must demonstrate ways that creative writing has learned from composition or, to use the title of Hesse's essay, it must articulate "The Place of Creative Writing in Composition Studies."[28] I call this imposition (colonization, some might call it) by the term (com) positioning: "the (com)positioning of creative writing." What's more, the belief that the place of creative writing is *in* Composition Studies has made many of us, as creative writers, try to fit into a place where we don't fit comfortably

Tailor

I am looking for the tailor
who sewed this dark suit,

who forgot to tuck
black threads into cloth,

who invented the pattern
for a jacket so tight
eyes echo in their sockets,
winter weeps

against the weight
of its dead fabric.
I am looking for a needle
to stitch back together

pieces of cloth from a jacket
no one can live in
long, a coat
I will gladly give to you.[29]

Nonetheless, I urge young scholars who are theorizing academic creative writing—and especially those who are planning to do so—to do what Zebroski urged composition theorists to do back in the early 1980s: to pursue their own theory from the grassroots of Creative Writing Studies. What does this mean? Ironically, to me it means claiming as its own elements of writing instruction rejected by those who have theorized Composition Studies in its post-process phase, including reliance on expressions of feeling typical of personal writing as well as adaptation of writer's self-reports to the purposes of classroom instruction. This seems a shameful actualization of the cliché, one man's garbage is another man's gold. But let me be specific.

We need to understand why it is that the elements of writing instruction that have fallen to the wayside in the theorizing of Composition Studies with the emergence of post-process theory are the ones that have proven to be quite useful in contemplating a theory for teaching creative writing in the academy. They seem to me to constitute creative writing's "grassroots." So, we need to address the plight of personal writing in composition and then say something about writers' self-reports as a way of beginning the development of a theory of creative writing using creative writing's grassroots as a basis. Clearly, my effort takes me into the realm of feeling because I am a practitioner whose chief professional life has been in the classroom. It makes me wonder why the emphases of CCCC and AWP appear to be so far apart and, in the end, one must wonder who's in control here and what's at stake.

As is well known, expressivism absorbed rough treatment in the 1980s and 1990s due, at least in part, to composition study's growing social self-awareness. Deborah Mutnick,[30] for one, connects expressivism to personal writing, a connection that makes sense to many who continue to use expressivist practices on all grade levels. Mutnick summarizes six ways of rejecting expressivism, including attacks by Bartholomae, Berlin, Bizzell, and Faigley (quoted in Mutnick), to be strictly alphabetical about it. I want to be clear: no one in this group singled out creative writing. My point is simply that what they wanted deleted from composition's emphases were the things fundamental at the time to the way we thought about teaching creative writing, and that includes personal writing. In reality, creative writing never had a relationship with Composition Studies that could last for long. What does that mean in human terms?

As a creative writer who taught composition but still advocates for literacy, I am feeling now, at the end of my teaching career, a sense of urgency. I understand this much: like composition, creative writing had to find its way into English Studies where, like composition, it found itself serving literature for over 100 years. I believe Composition Studies found its way out from under the jurisdiction of literature by enacting its democratic ideals. Nearly everyone who goes to college must take composition. So it is in that class that we have access to them, and many of us can assert our longing for social justice. We have not only tried to make composition courses relevant for most of them, but we have used our theories of composition to save the world, one literate student at a time, as many in the profession like to say.

Creative writing, too, has become democratized, causing more than a bit of confusion among creative writers who teach in the academy. To explain what I mean, let me focus for a moment on an interesting but thus far mostly neglected moment in the history of composition's relationship with creative writing. Within months of each other in 1981 and 1982, compositionist Art Young and poet Donald Hall remarked on a change in English departments both had noticed but described differently, tellingly. Young advocated for the potential of what he and later Bishop called poetry (by which Young clearly meant Britton's "poetic function of language").[31] Young, in that essay, argues that the poetic function of language could be called upon to help students become better learners in all disciplines. Hall, at about the same time in his famous essay "Poetry and Ambition," complained that university creative writing programs were producing poets with little ambition as poets.[32] Hall called the poems students wrote for their workshops by the catchy but misleading term "McPoems" and argued for abolishing MFA programs entirely from academe. In remarking on the poetry being written by students in the academy, I believe Young and Hall were talking about the same thing, the hallmark of the democratized creative writing course in its most intimate relation to literary studies, the making of knowledge in a previously excluded genre.

Subsequently, post-process composition theorists have, by and large, rejected the use of personal writing in composition classes, as noted earlier in this essay and in ways clearly articulated by Mutnick. Because there are large ideological issues at stake, I want to be very careful here. No doubt, either side of issues related to the democratization of creative writing might be reasonably argued. For instance, just a short while ago I argued for the relevance of critical pedagogy in a creative writing class. And now I seem to be taking back my commitment to that position. Composition and creative writing are not the same thing. As creative writers, we have been only short-term visitors to the land of Composition Studies, just passing through really.

Wind Homes

There are ways of entering homes
I had not imagined.
Last night wind slashed through my yard,
and I heard metal
strike metal, sheets of air rising
in my house like panic.

From bed, my eyes fluttering
and aroused by curtains
sailing into my room,
I ran
to my children
and tucked them back
beneath layers of sleep.

Across the street, the sounds
of others, awakened, slamming
wooden windows. One window screamed.
Even now I hear it
in fire alarms
and promises of catastrophes to come.
Later I dreamed my neighbors
rose to sleepwalk
as though they own some portion of the wind,
as though everywhere the wind dropped
it set up a home of its own
and let us live there
for a while.[33]

The social-epistemic view of "expressionistic rhetoric," as voiced with great resolve and unprecedented influence by James Berlin, is that the emphasis on the individual subject depoliticizes resistance to oppressive social structures, and its practitioners (Berlin cites Macrorie, Gibson, Coles, Murray, and Elbow) "continued the ideological critique of the dominant culture while avoiding the overt politicizing of the classroom."[34] In short, composition in its post-process phase privileges pedagogy for social change, Berlin's "social epistemic rhetoric." This view of writing as politicized is of less concern in creative writing where self-reports form the basis for teaching the kind of writing that gets done. W.H. Auden, for one, laments that "poetry makes nothing happen."[35] The object of poetry is aligned more with the goals of the rejected expressionistic rhetoric, which Berlin describes as "an art of which all are capable" but which values as most important "the presence of originality in expression."[36] But the self-reports of folks such as Auden are most often of greatest relevance to teachers of creative writing because self-reports provide data directly relevant to the way creative writing has been taught.

Yet when Flower and Hayes used the thinking-aloud protocol to better understand what writers do when they compose,[37] they too came under attack for their methodology because the writers they studied validate the class system: "it is clear that the rationality of the universe is more readily detected by a certain group of individuals" (Berlin, 724). While Berlin did not mandate that we remove writers' self-reports from our development of writing pedagogy, we dismissed such reports nonetheless as a by-product of our rejection of the thinking-aloud protocol. Bishop's theorizing in *Released Into Language* was challenged too by the dismissal of cognitivist protocols when she wrote, "Useful sources for thinking about curricular change can be found in professional writer's stories, anecdotes, aphorisms, and other forms of self-report . . .". But in the very next paragraph, Bishop recants these statements, saying writers' self-reports constitute, at best, "a wealth of unsubstantiated yet intuitively accurate knowledge" (Bishop, 1990, 17). I believe one task in the future of Creative Writing Studies is to develop ways these reports may be substantiated. But I also want to resist the claim that we should use tools of research employed in Composition Studies to do so. Right now we in Creative Writing Studies have only wind homes.

But I believe we have misspoken about writer's self-reports. We must wear our crap detectors and pull on our boots when we listen to most writers, of course. But some statements should provide the foundation for a theory of Creative Writing Studies because writers' self-reports constitute the grassroots of creative writing, and I believe Zebroski is correct in his notion that we should start with the very foundations of our disciplines when we attempt to theorize them. To the end of making writers' self-reports a valuable guide to how to teach creative writing, I advocate developing research methods in creative writing that will verify the usefulness of what we do in academic creative writing.

I want to end by being clear on my position in this: I don't believe anyone ever intended to diminish the importance of literary writing, as Hall seems to have feared. But most of us who have connected composition to creative writing over the years had hoped to assist creative writing in finding its place in the academy and, thereby, to help students become better writers and learners. These goals are praiseworthy, if somewhat confusing. Like Bishop before me, I do not merge the genres to show the superiority of the poem. I do, however, as William Stafford intimates, believe poems are accessible to more people than we might ordinarily assume.[38] They are nothing special, just "a truth that has learned jujitsu."

The Australian Crawl

"Poems are nothing special," Stafford claims.
They are "the kind of thing"
the kind of thing you have to see
from "the corner of your eye."
Like a very faint
star, Stafford says, if you look straight
at it, you can't see it. Teachers of young poets

are not astronomers, though maybe they should be.
But "no interest" in this vision of the stars
is better than the "conscientious interest" of a scientist.
That's why conscientious, even learn'd
astronomers are most often failed poets.
A poem is a joke, a very serious joke,
"a truth that has learned jujitsu."[39]

There is much work to do in deepening and broadening what we know about creative writing as an academic discipline. We have been cautioned, on the one side, that to explore this subject in depth means we cannot be counted among the creative writers. On the other, we're told we must argue that creative writing is a subdiscipline of Composition Studies and use research methods usually employed in Composition Studies to do so or we cannot be counted among the compositionists. Those who will continue to explore this field must do so with courage enough to withstand attacks from those who will resist change and the loss of writing students more committed to creative writing than to English Studies.

For better or worse, right or wrong, composition has valued writing as a process, and we have adapted that pedagogy to creative writing, as Bishop encouraged. As I see it, this is the view of CCCC. AWP values most the finished and published product. Yet the following poem, with which I end this journey, first appeared in *College English*.

The Product

The product is always in a hurry
to be sold. Maybe it tries too hard.
A salesman can sense this

in the way cloth rubs between his fingers.
Maybe a stitch is poorly sewn.
Maybe a string circles his palm.

The woman who shops carefully knows
a salesman's shaking hands,
the way cloth folds around his fingers.
The man who shops carefully learns the shaking
light of a salesman's eyes, the movement of cloth
between counters where flesh may be knit back to bone.

I have held the product so near
I could feel its lashes rub my cheek,
and I have not known its flaws.
At night, standing in front of blue-lit
stores, I have covered the product
where it rests inside its window.

And I've stood there alone, watching until
the sun has dragged its nylon legs
over tall buildings across the street,
and have not learned a thing.[40]

For reasons that might seem obvious, it is difficult to wrap up this essay. Nonetheless, decorum and academic convention require something be said. The problem is this: these two tracks could go on indefinitely into the future, never making contact with one another. They are parallel. Their parallelism as academic disciplines might be best demonstrated in the relationship between the academic prose and the poems in this hybrid text. But let me explain as best I can.

The concern here goes beyond textual preferences and into epistemology, so I must go there as well in this ending to my text. We are asking, in a sense, which way of seeing should be privileged as knowledge? We cannot argue which one is more truthful, necessarily. But we might argue which provides reasons that are most compelling, so compelling that they can be considered knowledge. Do we, then, believe in one way of knowing or the other (understandings rendered by the academic essay or by the poetry) or, possibly, even in both as a kind of Keatsian "negative capability"? Remember it was Keats who, in a letter to his brothers, privileged beauty over Coleridgean knowledge, and praised the human condition "when man is capable of being in uncertainties."[41] Forgive me, then, if this essay ends in uncertainties.

As a result, my inability in this essay to find a conclusion that serves all purposes reinforces for me that composition and creative writing provide parallel strategies for reaching understandings and need not make the points of contact the scholarly work of the past thirty years has seemed to insist upon. Keats again: "O for a Life of Sensations rather than of Thoughts!"[42]

Kierkegaard Explains Geometry to My Son

Tell your math teacher
You believe
In the theorem.
What more proof
Does she need?[43]

For many, no doubt, hybrid texts should be banned from scholarly conversations, at least until the texts figure out what they want to be. From this perspective, the poem and the argumentative essay should be kept apart. There are good reasons for segregating them. In "The Uses of Argument," Stephen Toulmin helps us understand their relationship in his discussion of "a field of arguments."[44] In it he offers insight into why the poem and the argumentative essay should not meet in a hybrid text because they do not "Belong to the same field," as he explains in the following passage:

> Two arguments will be said to belong to the same field when the data and conclusions in each of the two arguments are, respectively, of the same logical type: they will be said to come from different fields when the backing or the conclusions in each of the two arguments are not of the same logical type.[45]

We find that the essay and the poems "see" differently because, as Toulmin continues, some aspects of their "form and merits" are *field-invariant* and others are *field dependent*—that is, some ways of assessing the truthfulness of a proposition are the same because they are participants in the same field while others vary when we move from one field to another, as we do from essay to poem.[46]

Determinism at the Outer Banks
for Antonio

After it's done,
it always seems as if
it was meant to be.
The child at the beach
taking his mother's hand
to avoid the jelly
fish he does not want
to step on because
"mom told me."

She later at the computer screen
in our cottage two blocks from jelly fish
and the thump of waves reads
"they may sting
even after they're dead."
They don't mean any harm to you,
we explain to our son. It's just
inevitable
and in their futures
and probably in yours
unless these are just
"gelatinous organisms"
and not jelly fish at all.[47]

Does it, then, even make sense to compare the argument in academic prose to an argument in a poem? The safest conclusion is to say academic prose and poetry constitute two fields, but fields nonetheless in contact with each other in their inclusion in English Studies in the academy. Now, what did Mike want? He asked that teachers of all writing courses "where serious, committed students can be found" be shown by their teachers "how to *see*." The academic prose and the accompanying poems develop general patterns of persuasion, one under the guise of scientific objectivity and the other under the umbrella of creative imagining. Aristotle helps us understand these two ways of thinking and resolves that thinking for us when he says: "Rhetoric may be defined as the faculty of observing in any given case the available means of persuasion."[48] In this hybrid text, academic prose argues rhetorically—that is, by enthymeme and syllogism—for a view of the profession while poetry used in the text simultaneously comments on the human consequences of implementing aspects of the rhetorical argument—that is, imagines individual responses to a world of changes beyond our ability to control them.

Writers of compositions and poems see differently, following the demands of their texts to reach certain kinds of insights. We might add to this argument the proposition that all genres, if we follow their conventions, will offer different ways of seeing and, thereby, lead us to different knowledge. Truth is in the gaps.

Notes

1   Patrick Bizzaro and Michael McClanahan, "Putting Wings on the Invisible: Voice, Authorship and the Authentic Self," in *Can It Really Be Taught: Resisting Lore in Creative Writing Pedagogy*, eds Kelly Ritter and Stephanie Vanderslice (Portsmouth, NH: Boynton/Cook, 2007), 78.

2   Foucault, *The Archeology of Knowledge* (New York: Vintage, 2010), 22.

3   Katherine Haake, "Re-envisioning the Workshop: Hybrid Classrooms, Hybrid Texts," *Can It Really Be Taught?*, 188.

4   Patrick Bizzaro, *Undressing the Mannequin* (Conover, NC: Third Lung Press, 1989), 12.

5   Bizzaro, *Interruptions* (Georgetown, KY: Finishing Line Press, 2014), 4–6.

6   Douglas Hesse, "The Place of Creative Writing in Composition Studies," *College Composition and Communication*, September 2010, 31.

7   Bizzaro, "Weiner Shrapnel, the Poem, and Weiner Shrapnel, the News Article," Panel, Conference on College Composition and Communication, New Orleans, March 2011.

8   Bizzaro, "Research and Reflection in English Studies: The Special Case of Creative Writing," *College English*, January 2004, 294–309.

9   Bizzaro, "Houses of History," *September 11, 2001: American Writers Respond*, ed. William Heyen (Etruscan Press, 2004). 37.

10 Wendy Bishop, *Released Into Language* (Urbana: NCTE, 1990). Bishop keenly argues for a view of writing as writing in the first three chapters of this book, enabling herself to adapt research in composition to the teaching of creative writing, stressing teaching writing as a process.

11 D.G. Meyers, *The Elephants Teach: Creative Writing Since 1880* (Englewood Cliffs, NJ: Prentice-Hall, 1996). This remarkable history of creative writing in America fills in many of the gaps concerning the evolution of creative writing in American universities.

12 Tim Mayers, *(Re)Writing Craft: Composition, Creative Writing, and the Future of English Studies* (Pittsburgh: University of Pittsburgh Press, 2005). Mayers, in this book, importantly opens conversation concerning what constitutes English Studies and deliberates creative writing's place in English Studies.

13 E.W. Eisner, "The Promise and Perils of Alternative Forms of Data Representation," *Educational Researcher*, October 1997, 4–10.

14 Rich Furman, C.L. Langer, C.S. Davis, H.P. Gallardo and S. Kulkarni, "Expressive, Research and Reflective Poetry as Qualitative Inquiry: A Study of Adolescent Identity," *Qualitative Research*, March, 2007, 301–15.

15 Monica Prendergast, Carl Leggo and Pauline Sameshima, eds. *Poetic Inquiry: Vibrant Voices in the Social Sciences* (Rotterdam: Sense Publishers, 2009).

16 For the details of this argument and an excellent demonstration, please see Patricia Leavy, *Fiction as Research Practice: Short Stories, Novellas, and Novels*, Walnut Creek, CA: Left Coast Press, Inc., 2013 as well as both C. Ellis, *The ethnographic I: A methodological novel about autoethnography*. Walnut Creek, CA: Alta Mira Press, 2004 and *Revision: Autoethnographic reflections on life and work*. Walnut Creek, CA: Left Coast Press, 2009.

17 Eisner, "The Promise and Perils," 8.

18 William Wordsworth, "Lines Composed a Few Miles Above Tintern Abbey," l. 49, in David Perkins, *English Romantic Writers* (New York: Harcourt Brace Jovanovich, Publishers, 1967), 209.

19 Furman et al. "Expressive Research," 302.

20 Melisa Cahnmann-Taylor, "The Craft, Practice and Possibility of Poetry in Educational Research," in *Poetic Inquiry*, eds Prendergast, Leggo and Sameshima, (Rotterdam: Sense Publishers, 2009), 16.

21 David Hanauer, *Poetry as Research: Exploring Second Language Poetry Writing* (Philadelphia: John Benjamins Publishing Company, 2010), 10.

22 Bizzaro, "Mutuality in the Creative Writing Classroom," in Peary, A. and Hunley, T.C., eds *Creative Writing Pedagogies for the Twenty-first Century* (Carbondale, IL: Southern Illinois University Press, 2015).

23 See Wardle, Elizabeth and Douglas Downs, *Writing About Writing*, second edition (New York: Bedford, 2014).

24 See Donald M. Murray, "Unlearning to Write," in *Creative Writing in America: Theory and Pedagogy*, ed. Joseph M. Moxley (Urbana: NCTE, 1989), 103–14.

25 Bizzaro, "Repairing the Car," in *Undressing the Mannequin*, 20.

26 For an early articulation of this position, see James Berlin, "Rhetoric and Ideology in the Writing Class," *College English* (fall 1988), 477–93.

27 James Zebroski, "Toward a Theory of Theory for Composition Studies," in *Under Construction: Working at the Intersections of Composition Theory, Research, and Practice*, eds Christine Farris and Chris M. Anson (Logan, UT: Utah State University Press, 1998), 30–50.

28 Bizzaro, "Writers' Self-Reports, (Com)positioning, and the Recent History of Academic Creative Writing," in *Composing Ourselves as Writer-Teacher-Writers: Starting with Wendy Bishop*, eds Patrick Bizzaro, Alys Culhane, and Devan Cook (New York: Hampton Press, 2001), 119–32.

29 Bizzaro, "Tailor," in *Every Insomniac Has a Story to Tell* (Greenville, NC: independent press, 2004), 15.

30 Deborah Mutnick, "Rethinking the Personal Narrative: Life-Writing and Composition Pedagogy," in Farris and Anson *Under Construction*, 79–92.

31 Arthur Young, "Considering Values: The Poetic Function of Language," in *Language Connections: Writing and Reading Across the Curriculum* (Urbana: NCTE, 1982), eds Arthur Young and Toby Fulwiler. 77–98.

32 Donald Hall, "Poetry and Ambition." *Poetry and Ambition: Essays 1982–88* (Ann Arbor: University of Michigan Press, 1988), 154–70.

33 Bizzaro, "Wind Homes," in *Fear of the Coming Drought* (Mount Olive, NC: Mount Olive College Press, 2001), 62.

34 Berlin, "Ideology," 477.

35 W.H. Auden. "In Memory of W.B. Yeats." in *Another Time* (New York: Random House, 1940), l. 36.

36 Berlin, "Ideology," 426.

37 Linda Flower and John R. Hayes, "A Cognitive Process Theory of Writing," in *Cross-Talk in Comp Theory: A Reader*, ed. Victor Villanueva (Urbana: NCTE, 1997), 251–75.

38 See William Stafford, "Writing the Australian Crawl," in *Writing the Australian Crawl: Views on the Writer's Vocation* (Ann Arbor: University of Michigan Press, 1978).

39 Bizzaro, "The Australian Crawl," in *Creative Writing Pedagogies for the Twenty-First Century*, eds, Alexandria Peary and Tom C. Hunley, (Carbondale: Southern Illinois University Press, 2015), 52–3.

40 Bizzaro, "The Product," in *Every Insomniac*, 59.

41 Keats, "Letter To George and Tom Keats," in *English Romantic Writers*, 1209.

42 Keats, 1206.

43 Bizzaro, "Kierkegaard Explains Geometry to My Son," in *Interruptions*, 15.

44 Stephen Toulmin, "The Uses of Argument," in *The Rhetorical Tradition: Readings from Classical Times to the Present*, eds Patricia Bizzell and Bruce Herzberg, (New York: Bedford/St. Martins, 2001), 1413.

45 Toulmin, "The Uses of Argument," 1413.

46 Toulmin, "The Uses of Argument," 1413.

47 Bizzaro, "Determinism at the Outer Banks," in *Interruptions*, 6.

48 Aristotle, "Rhetoric," in *The Rhetorical Tradition*, 181.

References

Auden, W.H. "In Memory of W.B. Yeats." *Another Time*. NY: Random House, 1940. L. 36.

Berlin, James. "Rhetoric and Ideology in the Writing Class." *College English* 50.5 (1988): 477–93.

Bishop, Wendy. *Released Into Language*. Urbana: NCTE, 1990.

Bizzaro, Patrick. "The Future of Graduate Studies in Creative Writing: Institutionalizing Literary Writing." *Key Issues in Creative Writing*. Dianne Donnelly and Graeme Harper, eds Bristol, UK: Multilingual Matters, 2013: 169–78.

Bizzaro, Patrick. "Research and Reflection in English Studies: The Special Case of Creative Writing." *College English* 66.3 (January 2004): 294–309.

Bizzaro, Patrick. "Mutuality and the Teaching of the Introductory Creative Writing Course." *Creative Writing Pedagogies for the Twenty-First Century*. Alexandria Peary and Tom C. Hunley, eds Carbondale: Southern Illinois University Press, 2015: 52–77.

Bizzaro, Patrick. "Weiner Shrapnel the Poem and Weiner Shrapnel, the News Article: The Limits of Plagiarism." Panel presentation, CCCC, New Orleans, March 2011.

Bizzaro, Patrick. "Writers' Self-Reports, (Com)positioning, and the Recent History of Academic Creative Writing." *Composing Ourselves as Writer-Teacher-Writers: Starting with Wendy Bishop*. Patrick Bizzaro, Alys Culhane and Devan Cook, eds. NY: Hampton Press, 2011: 119–32.

Bizzaro, Patrick and Michael McClanahan. "Putting Wings on the Invisible: Voice, Authorship and the Authentic Self." *Can It Really Be Taught?: Resisting Lore in*

Creative Writing Pedagogy. Kelly Ritter and Stephanie Vanderslice, eds. Portsmouth, NH: Boynton/Cook, 2007: 77–90.

Britton, James, et al. *The Development of Writing Abilities (11–18).* London: Macmillan Education, 1975.

Cahnmann-Taylor, Melisa. "The Craft, Practice and Possibility of Poetry in Educational Research." *Poetic Inquiry: Vibrant Voices in the Social Sciences.* Monica Prendergast, Carl Leggo, and Pauline Sameshima, eds. Rotterdam: Sense Publishers, 2009: 13–30.

Eisner, E.W. "The promise and perils of alternative forms of data representation." *Educational Researcher* 26(6), (1997): 4–10.

Flower, Linda and John R. Hayes. "A Cognitive Process Theory of Writing." *Cross-Talk in Comp Theory: A Reader.* Victor Villanueva, Jr., ed. Urbana: NCTE, 1997: 251–75.

Foucault, Michel. *The Archeology of Knowledge.* New York: Vintage, 2010.

Furman, Rich, Langer, C.L. Davis, C.S. Gallardo, H.P. and S. Kulkarni. "Expressive, Research and Reflective Poetry as Qualitative Inquiry: A Study of Adolescent Identity." *Qualitative Research* 7.3: (2007): 301–15.

Haake, Katherine. "Against Reading." *Can It Really Be Taught? Resisting Lore in Creative Writing Pedagogy.* Kelly Ritter and Stephanie Vanderslice, eds. Portsmouth, NH: Boynton/Cook Heinemann, 2007: 14–27.

Hall, Donald. "Poetry and Ambition." *Poetry and Ambition: Essays 1982–88.* Ann Arbor: University of Michigan Press, 1988: 154–70.

Hanauer, David. *Poetry as Research: Exploring Second Language Poetry Writing.* Philadelphia: John Benjamins Publishing Company, 2010.

Hesse, Douglas. "The Place of Creative Writing in Composition Studies." *College Composition and Communication* 62.1 (September 2010): 31–52.

Keats, John. "Letter to George and Tom Keats, December 21–27." *English Romantic Writers.* David Perkins, ed. NY: Harcourt Brace Jovanovich, Publishers, 1967: 1209–10.

Leavy, Patricia. *Fiction as Research Practice: Short Stories, Novellas, and Novels.* Walnut Creek, CA: Left Coast Press, Inc., 2013.

Mayers, Tim. *(Re)Writing Craft: Composition, Creative Writing, and the Future of English Studies.* Pittsburgh: University of Pittsburgh Press, 2005.

Murray, Donald. "Unlearning to Write." *Creative Writing in America: Theory and Pedagogy.* Joseph M. Moxley, ed. Urbana: NCTE, 1989: 103–14.

Mutnick, Deborah. "Rethinking the Personal Narrative: Life-Writing and Composition Pedagogy." *Under Construction: Working at the Intersections of Composition Theory, Research, and Practice.* Christine Farris and Chris M. Anson, eds. Logan: Utah State University Press, 1998.

Myers, D.G. *The Elephants Teach: Creative Writing Since 1880.* Englewood Cliffs, NJ: Prentice-Hall, Inc., 1996.

Prendergast, Monica, Carl Leggo, and Pauline Sameshima, eds. *Poetic Inquiry: Vibrant Voices in the Social Sciences.* Rotterdam: Sense Publishers, 2009.

Stafford, William. *Writing the Australian Crawl: Views on the Writer's Vocation.* Ann Arbor: The University of Michigan Press, 1978.

Toulmin, Stephen. "The Uses of Argument." *The Rhetorical Tradition: Readings from Classical Times to the Present.* Patricia Bizzell and Bruce Herzberg, eds. NY: Bedford/St. Martins, 2001: 1413–28.

Wardle, Elizabeth and Douglas Downs. *Writing about Writing, second edition.* NY: Bedford, 2014.

Young, Arthur. "Considering Values: The Poetic Function of Language." *Language Connections: Writing and Reading Across the Curriculum.* Urbana: NCTE, 1982. 77/98.

Zebroski, James. "Toward a Theory of Theory for Composition Studies *Under Construction: Working at the Intersections of Composition Theory, Research, and Practice*, eds Christine Farris and Chris M. Anson. Logan, UT: Utah State University Press, 1998: 30–50.

6

Box Office Poison:

The Influence of Writers in Films on Writers (in Graduate Programs)

Wendy Bishop and Stephen B. Armstrong

It's a tossup as to which film type is more boring—movies about writers or movies about drunks and drug addicts. The former films try to dramatize what it's like to be creative on paper, while the latter try to analyze the self-destruction of losers.
JOE BALTAKE, *SACRAMENTO BEE* MOVIE CRITIC, ON *BIG BAD LOVE*[1]

When I picture writing, I often see a solitary writer alone in a cold garret working into the small hours of the morning by the thin light of a candle. It seems a curious image to conjure, for I am absent from this scene in which the writer is an Author and the writing is Literature. In fact it is not my scene at all.
LINDA BRODKEY.[2]

We both write, teach writing and gravitate toward films about writers, fully aware that critics often disdain these cinematic works, general audiences tend to ignore them and producers consider them box office poison.

Nevertheless, some of these films have been hits—*Misery*, *Almost Famous* and *Finding Forrester*—while others have become cult favorites, especially with academics—*His Girl Friday*, *Citizen Kane*, *Barton Fink*, *Henry Fool*. The ubiquity of cinematic portrayals of the writing life, including life in college writing programs (consider *Wonder Boys*, *Storytelling* and *Orange County*), has prompted us to wonder how someone new to the writing profession, as well as the writing instruction profession, picks up pointers from watching them. In fact, we believe it is beneficial for writers and instructors to consider the likely influence these movies have had on them as they enter a graduate program and participate in or conduct a writing workshop.

Having conducted a substantive search for cinematic images and stories that reflect our own experiences and profession, we feel comfortable asserting that writers in films regularly receive heroic and romantic treatments. The entertainment industry has long compensated for the challenge of depicting cognition and text-production with narratives designed to entertain ticket buyers, typically (re)creating writers as tough guys, war correspondents, investigative reporters, beautiful losers and male geniuses. As a result, these movies are box office poison in another, new sense, functioning—tacitly or explicitly—as examples of creative and pedagogic behavior that we might adopt as our own. Movies about writers, we contend, can therefore adversely influence the classroom and writing community with their often inauthentic depictions of how writers live and work.

Our search prompted us to craft a list of titles in which writers are showcased and the writing process is rendered and commented upon by the filmmakers; and we have used these groupings to help us with our analysis of writer types, writer roles and writer practices (see groupings in next section). In this chapter, we look at how these character types and narrative scenarios may be informing the graduate curriculum; and after considering the most commonly circulated of these "received" constructions, we submit for consideration some of the pedagogical problems they can foster and offer ideas for using these constructions more productively. By asking what it means to teach—or "unteach"—motion pictures about writers and their thematic implications, in short, we aim to (re)construct better, more useful, accounts of the writing life.

Writing as film and cultural figuration

Everyone's a film critic, particularly when it comes to movies depicting writers, and it does not take long to unearth a multitude of negative opinions about such films. We found several reviews, for example, like the one about *Big Bad Love* written by the *Sacramento Bee*'s Joe Baltake, whose quote opens this chapter. Baltake suggests enough is enough, that no one needs movies about writers because these pictures forfeit the truth and yield a distorted—and tedious—impression of writerly activity. Yet after enjoying such films as *Misery* and *Adaptation*, after encountering a writing student's claim that *Wonder Boys* propelled him to enroll in a writing course and after swapping names of films about writers with friends and peers, our interest in this genre increased. We proceeded from there to more systematically seek recommendations from colleagues and searched collections available to us through video stores and libraries. Next, we journaled collaboratively, developing our thoughts over several weeks, discussing our frustrations with the depictions of writers as we found them, wondering all the while about the likely influence these depictions have on writers and writing teachers in the classroom.

Eventually, we constructed an alphabetical list of well-known movies in which writer-characters appear and from this, we noted oft-recurring character types and traits and narrative scenarios. For instance, we found that male writers in film tend to uphold the stereotype of the "macho hero," while most females exemplify the "cute nuisance" or "sheep in wolf's clothing"; and minorities and members of the LGBTQIA community are rarely portrayed. Then we grouped films by these characteristics their writer protagonists exhibit, from which we developed typological groupings of the following kind:

- The Action Hero: *Blood on the Sun, Julia, Foreign Correspondent, The Battle of Anzio, True Crime*
- The Disoriented Woman: *Absence of Malice, Lifeboat, The Legend of Lylah Clare, Romancing the Stone, Iris, Not for Publication*
- The Mad Man: *Sweet Smell of Success, The Shining, Big Bad Love, Beyond a Reasonable Doubt, The Lost Weekend, Laura*
- The Master Writer: *Misery, Wilde, Kafka, F for Fake, As Good as it Gets, Papa; Hemingway in Cuba, Capote*
- The Male Ingénue: *Almost Famous, Finding Forrester, The Basketball Diaries*
- The Reporter: *Citizen Kane, The Front Page, Absence of Malice, His Girl Friday, Lifeboat, Meet John Doe*
- The Screenwriter and The Playwright: *Sunset Boulevard, All About Eve, Sudden Fear, Adaptation, Barton Fink, Midnight in Paris*
- The Writer Who Doesn't Write: *Under the Volcano, The Royal Tenenbaums, All the King's Men, The Third Man, The Ghost Writer*
- The Writing Program: *Wonder Boys, Storytelling, Orange County*

The "typical" writer, we found, presents a dramatized version of compositionist Linda Brodkey's "solitary writer" in that he is male. "In much of literary modernism," she explains, "solitude is at once inevitable and consequential, the irremediable human condition from which there is no escape. And whenever writers are pictured there, as they so often are, the writer-writes-alone is a narrative of irreconcilable alienation, a vicarious narrative told by an outsider who observes rather than witnesses life."[3] The typical film writer differs from Brodkey's modernist literary writer, however, in that he dominates his films. We rarely see him writing, but we often see him as a successful *character*, brawling, drinking, a creative and self-destructive genius, a lone wolf who enjoys a surprisingly robust social life.

Meanwhile, the manual act of writing by persons labeled as writers rarely appears on the screen. Instead, these characters spend the bulk of their time conducting research (*Citizen Kane*, *Beyond a Reasonable Doubt*) or experiencing (frequently) the negative consequences that result from the publication of their work (*The Ring*). While writers are presented as professionals, usually affiliated with newspapers (*Call Northside777*, *Blood on the Sun*), the "show-don't-tell" requirement of cinematic storytelling entails putting them into situations that cannot occur at or near the place where they actually work—the desk or table.

In order to keep their writer-characters true to type, if not to reality, filmmakers customarily displace the act of writing and substitute imagined impressions of the writing process in which there is more likely to be action. Usually this means emphasizing the activities that occur before the act of writing. *Citizen Kane* features a reporter who sets out to discover the meaning of the eponymous publishing magnate's cryptic last word, "Rosebud." Less often, filmmakers focus on the consequences of the writing act. In *Absence of Malice*, a reporter attempts to correct the problems she's created for an innocent man by writing an unintentionally libelous article.

Filmmaker-critic Ivor Montagu explains why in movies this departure from the real action to the fanciful undertaking occurs.

> "Moving picture" or "motion picture"—the significance of this term is that it implies that the object (process or experience) described has two aspects, both equally essential. It is a *picture*, that is, it is a representation, not actual, not real and it conveys *the appearance of motion*.[4]

The depiction of the writer on film, engaged in the act of writing, that is, is intrinsically nondramatic. An authentic onscreen rendering of a writer at work would give us a person hunched over a desk, moving her or his fingers. To sidestep visually uninteresting material of this sort, films with writers in them thus keep the depiction of *the act of writing* to a minimum. For, say, a writer experiencing writer's block—an inward conflict—a filmmaker cannot render the struggle in a fashion that is both dramatic and realistic because the true location of the conflict is within in the mind and the hands can only move after the conflict, at least temporarily, has been resolved. Nor can filmmakers treat writers writing in the ways they most often write—alone, placing words on paper or computer screen. Instead, they put their characters into situations in which action and movement occur vividly, constantly. The writer-writes-alone simply resists representation on commercially-oriented film

The most artful (and pleasing) films, according to Montagu, are those that encourage viewers to associate themselves with the story's characters— those in which the filmmakers rely on *pictorial* rendering, a strategy that minimizes the use of verbal elements: dialogue, verbal commentary, the depiction of text-production.[5] And because the act of writing itself entails little movement from the human figure—in contrast, say, to a martial arts melee or lovers ballroom dancing or a chariot race—the filmmaker will resort to non-cinematic efforts when she attempts to portray writing, using, for instance, voiceover readings of texts as they are being written—or symbolic, abstract representations of "creative breakthroughs," as we find in *Wonder Boys*, when the master writer character *imagines* his troubling manuscript stack disappearing.

Choosing our poison

To begin to understand how movies may influence writers and writing teachers, it will help us to examine some paradigmatic examples of the writer film genre. We might start with the first important film about the writing life, *The Front Page*. Originally a stage play written by Ben Hecht and Charles MacArthur, this story of a love-hate relationship between a distracted crime reporter and his megalomaniac editor was first adapted for the screen in 1931. Directed by Lewis Milestone and starring Pat O'Brien and Adolphe Menjou, *The Front Page* uses ironic scenarios, witty dialogue and gallows humor to critique big-city government as well as big-city papers. Nearly every character is a scoundrel, prone to sarcasm, cigars and hard liquor; and the reporters in the newsroom, arguably the meanest members in this gallery of rogues, more often use their desks for playing cards and trading insults than writing.

Frequently the crime reporter, Hildy (O'Brien), opines in hard-boiled fashion about his profession and his peers. Upon deciding to quit his job, for instance, he exclaims:

> Journalists! Peeking through keyholes. Running after fire engines. . . . Waking up people in the middle of the night to ask them what they think of Mussolini. Stealing pictures off of old ladies of their daughters who got attacked in Grove Park. . . . For what? So a million hired girls and motormen's wives can know what's going on.

Obscure as the picture may be now, according to Joseph Millichap, it's "mood of tough, seedy masculinity" connected with audiences, scoring well in the box office. More significantly, it gained quasi-immortality by receiving an Academy Award nomination for Best Picture in 1931. These factors, Millichap suggests, made the film influential: it generated so many copycat newspaper movies that "the type became almost a genre during the 1930s,"[6] a genre that, to a large extent, has persisted up to the present.

In addition to its imitators, which codified the image of the tough, beat reporter, *The Front Page* inspired several remakes, including Howard Hawks's *His Girl Friday* (1940). Here, the jaded reporter, Hildy, now played by Rosalind Russell, wishes to leave her career behind for a new life with a new husband. Her ex-husband, played by Cary Grant, happens to be her old boss, the uncompromising editor Walter Burns. Once again, in this film the depiction of the writer-who-doesn't-write materializes as Hildy and Walter spend the majority of their time on the screen arguing and trying to outsmart each other, feigning they are no longer in love. Hawks's decision to change Hildy's sex might be interpreted as an endorsement of the egalitarian workplace. Hawks's biographer Todd McCarthy explains how Hildy appears as

> a smart working woman torn between her professional talent and her domestic inclinations. . . . On the surface, of course, Hildy comes off as exceedingly modern, a sharp-dressed feminist before her time who can out-think, out-write and out-talk any of her male colleagues, an unusual woman even in Hawks's world in that she long ago proved herself worthy of inclusion in the otherwise all-male group.[7]

Yet as Robin Wood has pointed out, Hildy, by film's end, is forced into choosing between her ex-husband and her future husband—between the writing life and the domestic one—and her decision to return to the paper is not a victory, but a capitulation.[8]

The third remake of *The Front Page*, directed by Billy Wilder in 1973, retains the original's title and storyline, casting Jack Lemmon as Hildy and Walter Matthau as his double-dealing boss. This version—much like *The World According to Garp* and *In a Lonely Place*—portrays women as angels and slices of cheesecake, as lovers who either serve their male writer companions or distract them. Simultaneously, Wilder's movie restores the tough veneer to the journalist character, depicting him again as a creature who becomes interesting only when he leaves his desk. Though a minor production, the movie reveals the staying power of the original stage story's scenarios and characterizations. And so does the fourth remake of the film, *Switching Channels*, which appeared in 1988.

How much, we wonder, have these portraits—of tyrants and weaklings, sour pusses and cynics—colored cultural attitudes in general and students' attitudes in particular toward not only writing but also writing teachers, who, in their positions of authority (and occasional bad moods) might now and then share more than a little likeness with the films' unattractive editor figure?

More recently Hollywood has turned its attention to the writing classroom, an inevitable development, perhaps, given the movement of literary writers into the academic workforce and the rise of creative writing graduate degree programs. Featuring the depiction of "normal people" learning the skills necessary for literary success and the collective involvement engendered by the workshop, these films ostensibly demystify the writing process by reducing its romantic dimensions. "The teacher," explains Dale Bauer, "is the center of a vast amount of attention and students are often attracted to, or repulsed by, the display of a teacher's power, knowledge, self." Bauer also suggests that "If the culture didn't project so much onto English professors, they wouldn't have to be so systematically trivialized and parodied, on the one hand, or revered and sentimentalized, on the other hand. Contemporary movies about teaching seem to be hypothesizing the very source of this fascination."[9]

We find that these polarizations seem greater when the teacher is an instructor of creative arts. An essential tension exists between students who seek to emulate master-teachers as they strive to form singular writing identities; and maturation often includes elements of transference or resistance. The process both is and is not about control. There is often a Frankenstein element present, that of creation taking over from creator. Compositionist Robert Brooke suggests that "The teacher, no matter how exciting a model she presents, just isn't in control of the identity the student will develop. Students are not as tractable as that—the identities they negotiate in any class are the result, to a large extent, of the identities they already have."[10] If novice writers seek to measure against or up to the writers/teachers/mentors they admire, if they move into the profession of writing, striving to establish writers' identities for themselves, then the images of authorship and authors they receive are of enormous importance. Yet films about writers in writing programs tend to misrepresent the experience they attempt to describe, too. For instance, in *Finding Forrester*, the master writer character appears most often in the context of home or community, rarely at the desk or table.

Even when these films reach for authenticity—by introducing workshop discussions, pedagogical demonstrations and the like—they magnify some aspects of the creative process over others, reifying (and reinforcing) the perception of the writing community as a social snake pit, where masculine personalities overwhelm feminine ones. *Wonder Boys*, which directs much of its attention to the relationship between a creative writing instructor and his students, underscores the merit of this claim. Fulfilling popular clichés about English teachers, the instructor-novelist Grady Tripp (Michael Douglas), is a fatuous person whose interest in writing has developed into a self-centered obsession that impairs his professional and personal lives. Grady's protégée, a student writer named James Leer (Tobey Maguire), shapes his identity by refusing to completely accept the professor as a model, ignoring Grady's practical advice, for instance, as well as countering the elder's heterosexual prowess by engaging in a gay tryst (a rare instance in this genre that challenges heteronormative codes). We can discern that Leer's refusal to mimic his mentor contributes to his own renewal as a writer and a person. He gains self-knowledge through the process of accepting and rejecting his, at first reluctant, mentor's suggestions.

The same cannot be said for Hannah Green (Katie Holmes), a student who lives with Grady—and adores him. Like Grady's wife and his girlfriend, Hannah can't fully connect with the teacher—creatively or spiritually. (In this environment, hot-shot male writers interact best with other males and rivalry and competition are the norm.) Of course we don't assume that female viewers identify with Hannah—they may already read against the movie's grain but they might be wise to do so actively when viewing such a conventional film representation of the writing life and writers' communities. Viewers like our student who cited this as his favorite representation of writers may be tempted to say, "It's so accurate" rather than "Why should it be this way?"

Todd Solondz's *Storytelling* also addresses the relationships between writing teachers and their students. In it, however, the students and instructors have physical relationships with one another. The film's first section, "Fiction," narrows on a college creative writing class, where the instructor Mr. Scott (Robert Wisdom), a parody of the workshop despot, rewards students who talk and think like him and punishes those who don't. Disturbingly, "Fiction" presents the workshop as a place occupied by angry, self-pitying wretches who shred one another and their stories. As Wisdom explains in the film's press notes, his character is

> a Pulitzer Prize-winning writer who teaches at a second or third rate university. He is on the outside in every sense. The Pulitzer Prize doesn't open any doors for him. He is resentful, angry and bitter. And he expresses his anger by seducing his female students and destroying them in the process. There is a very S&M take that develops, but from a very cool distance. He knows exactly what he is doing and in the process, he projects the worst prejudices on his students. In a way, it is revenge.[11]

These two films—as well as *Orange County*, a story about trying to secure admission into a writing program—portray their characters as neurotics with terrible habits and foggy ethics, who entertain the myth that writers need to experience over-the-top situations in order to generate compelling material for their writing. Do students accept these scenarios as examples of cinematic realism? Do they begin to expect and prepare themselves to encounter similar mayhem and cruelty? Do they approach the screen depictions like diners in a cafeteria line, selecting some items and ignoring others? Or do they accept these aspects as not only real, but permanent and condition themselves to expect the best anyway? From our own experience— as writers whose professional positions depend on publication—we know that histrionic adventures—in the classroom and away from the desk—occur less frequently than long hours spent in research, in drafting, in working with and for readers.

Life inside and outside the frame

The student of writing, we suspect, will arrive in the graduate workshop influenced not only by the texts she has read for the previous eight years—texts by modernist authors such as Hemingway or Conrad or Cummings continue to shape the required canon (*writer-writes-alone*) in high school and in undergraduate English courses—but also writers in films (*writer-as-dynamic-hero*). As it dawns on developing readers that they too might want to become authors, they may match their prose against the texts they read and their lives against the lives they watch in movie theaters.

Inevitably, novice writers are encouraged to join their individual talents to tradition through extensive reading and emulation and to participate in the writing communities that surround academic writing programs. Live readings at local bars and workshops with visiting writers represent just a small portion of an identifiable process of enculturation to an entire aesthetic lifestyle that can also include haunting used bookstores to fill out one's collection of literature with the right texts and spending writing hours in coffee shops to see and be seen. In these locales, writers gain experience, collect characters and form their own character and always they talk about getting more "time for their writing." They learn the images and to live the image. As writers-as-dynamic-heroes on a small academic scale, they are living the life they have seen depicted in countless films held up to them as mirrors for manners. This is true, of course, not only for images of writers but for images of teachers in general: Dale Bauer claims that "Hollywood eventually misrepresents all professions and all vocations are ultimately sexualized."[12] And Robert Brooke throws this sort of modeling into relief when he explains

> [W]hen a student (or any writer) successfully learns something about writing by imitation, it is by imitating another *person* and not a text or a process. Writers learn to write by imitating other writers, by trying to act like writers they respect. The forms, the processes, the texts are themselves less important as models to be imitated than the personalities, or identities, of the writers who produce them. Imitation, so the saying goes, is a form of flattery: we imitate because we respect the people we imitate and because we want to be like them.[13]

Certainly, this mix is unpredictable. There is no canon of writer movies. One of us hadn't seen *Wonder Boys* until it was suggested to her by an excited writing student and that same student had yet to view one of our influences,

His Girl Friday. We do note, however, that every writer we asked was able to name at least one film image of a writer at work when they listed for us upon request a list of published authors who had influenced them (and sometimes film images came more readily than real authors). It is at just this juncture that transference may begin. Again, Brooke reminds us that "Students don't come into classroom as blank slates. They come with a wealth of past experience and, by the time they reach college, a fairly well-defined sense of the kinds of persons they are. Their interaction with any attempt to model an identity for them, then, must take into account the identities they have already developed for themselves."[14]

Bauer argues that images of teachers in movies help sexualize and contain teachers and that these images (to the teachers who view them) often define what teachers are *not* while failing to define teachers as they really are.[15] In a similar manner, the image of the writer in film leads the writing student to fail to define herself in a way that aids her craft. Speaking of identity formation, particularly for a woman-who-writes, Katharine Haake suggests,

> There is nothing "natural" about who we are as writers. We turn out the way we are by virtue of our experience in culture, in class, in gender, in race, in family, in history, in being. There is nothing new in saying so, but when we say so to novice writers, they feel—as I once felt, so passionately—*what about ME? Myself. My expression. My being. . . . Accommodating my own "voices" to received ideas of what "good writing" was, I became more absence than presence.* When I learned to name the things—what I was trying to produce as well as who I felt myself to be in some relation to those modes of production and their products—then I could hear myself speak.[16]

Writers in graduate programs

While images of writers in films are changing, the focus still falls on the "glamour" myth of sex and adventure—and again dominant males sit on top of the heap (*I Love Trouble, As Good as it Gets, Big Bad Love*)—or is galvanized into dramatic nonwriting action (*Vanilla Sky, The Ring*). From our list of films, only a slight number depict writers who produce Literature (*Iris, Kafka, Shakespeare in Love*). The normalized workshop-leading academic writer, the winner of awards and producer of a dying art form, "the book," represents a type of person who thwarts normalcy, a man gifted with powers of thought and expression that may alienate average viewers. This possibility seems to be confirmed by the frequency of pictures in which writing is presented as a professional occupation. Indeed, the professional writer most often writes articles and features (*Almost Famous, All the President's Men, The Man Who Shot Liberty Valance*) rather than fiction and poetry (*Henry and June, Tom and Viv*).

Our study of films that circulate images of writers suggests that teachers and students should be alerted to their potential influence—as we have attempted to do in this chapter. The limits of film roles and film images should be acknowledged, interrogated and taught. In general, these cinematic constructions are seductive. They present glamorous/glamorized personae who resemble the viewer in several aspects: gender, race, occupation, education, class. That is, the screen image is enough like the viewer to establish identification. The screen, however, must present these images in a manner that exaggerates and distorts positive aspects of them, so that what is offered is an improved (fantastic/fantasized) version of the viewer. Presumably, pleasure results because the viewer sees the best of what she is/ does (the romantic ideal) and not the worst (the nonromantic real).

But the screen image delivers an enhanced "reflection" of the self. Unless we can recognize this tendency, we remain at the mercy of our culture at large. As Siegfried Kracauer writes, "American audiences receive what Hollywood wants them to want; but in the long run public desires determine the nature of Hollywood films."[17] And Haake reinforces the problem at the more local, workshop level: "The irony is that until we can see ourselves clearly in relation to the discourse that frames us, whatever discourse that might be, we continue to reflect it back, unchallenged and unchanged."[18] We do not presume to think that this chapter and our suggestion for unteaching or teaching against images will reform the entire film industry. Far from it, since the requirements of the medium militate against the writing process ever being well-represented in film for reasons we have already laid out.

However, we do suggest that audiences' attitudes toward a profession will be influenced by film depictions of these professions and that in some sense we have ourselves to thank, at least in part, for the circulation of available images and the views of contemporary writers as they are maintained by contemporary students of writing. The degree to which these depictions of writers will influence the ways in which writing is taught and learned are unclear, but the images we have analysed are certainly part of the mix. The writing classroom may be by means of film complicit in an imposition of dominant social codes. If we seek to change that expression, we must begin with a pedagogy that interrogates received images. "[T]he success of curriculum reform movements initiated in the field of composition will depend on disrupting the scene of writing through acts of the imagination that revise the scene to accommodate our students and ourselves,"[19] Brodkey maintains and we would extend that argument to the curriculum of graduate writing workshops.

Depictions such as those found in *Storytelling*, *Wonderboys* and *Orange County* are still limiting. As long as the mentor in film partakes of the qualities we've discussed, contemporary evocations of the workshop milieu will mirror the old values. To unteach and interrogate these images is not to purge them—for they do reflect certain realities—but to broaden them. Neither do we want to insult our reader/viewer and assume each buys into these images without reflection and resistance.

We can learn from women viewers who have long had to resist mainstream cinematic values. In studying the responses of her students to film images, Winifred Wood notes

> Other feminists would argue that there are other forms of non-passive participation available for this woman [as critical spectator]: reading against the grain, for example (Basinger), or humorous reappropriation of dominant cultural messages (Rich). "There is a lot that we don't know about the audiences of the past," acknowledges Jenine Basinger. But: "What we do know is that women did not surrender their brains, or their prior experiences, when they entered a movie theater. Rather, they used them both to understand and to respond to what was on the screen . . ."[20]

We realize writers (especially women who write) do not surrender their brains and prior experiences when they enter movie theaters or writing workshops. Nevertheless, they might benefit from the support of the sorts of discussions raised here. For a classroom exercise, we suggest Haake's scene-of-writing exercise, where peers are encouraged to collaborate on new images of writers and writing spaces.[21] We also find that watching more movies about writers has taught us to cast a more critical eye on the genre even as we continue to enjoy and study it. We now take an alternate route to the theater, considering how we can teach against the grain, subvert these images with humor and analysis, create exercises that broaden our understandings of lifestyles and options? In doing this, we seek to balance these predominately male depictions, to counterbalance the mainstream films' tendency to engender the oppressive conditions set by the status quo. We ask, as well, along with Foucault

> "What are the modes of existence of this discourse? Where has it been used, how can it circulate and who can appropriate it for himself? What are the places in it where there is room for possible subjects? Who can assume these various subject-functions?" And behind all these questions, we would hear hardly anything but the stirring of an indifference: "What difference does it make who is speaking?"[22]

We feel it makes a great deal of difference. To acknowledge that we are all evolving *versions* of our writer-selves is to suggest that a closer examination of how film images of writers works for and against us is inevitably in order.

Notes

1   "*Big Bad Love* Wastes Its One Asset–Winger," *Sacramento Bee*, March 29, 2002.
2   "Modernism and the Scene(s) of Writing," *College English* 49, no. 4 1987: 396.

3   "Modernism and the Scene(s) of Writing," *College English* 49, no. 4 1987: 398.

4   *Film World* (Baltimore: Penguin, 1964), 13.

5   *Film World* (Baltimore: Penguin, 1964), 114.

6   *Lewis Milestone* (Boston: Twayne, 1981), 56, 60.

7   *Howard Hawks* (New York: Grove, 1997), 286.

8   *Howard Hawks* (New York: Grove, 1997), 287; cited by McCarthy.

9   "Indecent Proposals: Teachers in the Movies," *College English* 60, no. 3 1998: 302–303

10 "Modeling a Writer's Identity." *College Composition and Communication* 39, no.1 1988: 38.

11 Press materials for *Storytelling*.

12 Bauer, 301.

13 Brooke, 23.

14 Brooke, 26.

15 Bauer, 313.

16 *What Our Speech Disrupts: Feminism and Creative Writing Studies* (Urbana, IL: NCTE, 2000), 191.

17 *From Caligari to Hitler* (Princeton, NJ: Princeton University Press, 1974), 14.

18 Haake, 191.

19 Brodkey, 397.

20 "Double Desire: Overlapping Discourses in a Film Writing Course." *College English* 60, no.3 (1998): 289.

21 Haake, 188–202.

22 "What Is an Author?" *Modern Criticism and Theory: A Reader*. 2nd edition. David Lodge with Nigel Wood, eds, (New York: Longman, 2000), 187.

References

Baltake, Joe. "'Big Bad Love' Wastes Its One Asset–Winger." *Sacramento Bee*, March 29, 2002.

Bauer, Dale M. "Indecent Proposals: Teachers in the Movies." *College English* 60, no. 3 (1998): 301–17.

Brodkey, Linda. "Modernism and the Scene(s) of Writing." *College English* 49, no. 4 (1987): 396–418.

Brooke, Robert. "Modeling a Writer's Identity." *College Composition and Communication* 39, no. 1 (1988): 23–41.

Foucault, Michel. "What Is an Author?" In *Modern Criticism and Theory: A Reader*. 2nd edition. Edited by David Lodge with Nigel Wood. New York: Longman, 2000.

Haake, Katharine. *What Our Speech Disrupts: Feminism and Creative Writing Studies*. Urbana, IL: NCTE, 2000.

Kracauer, Siegfried. *From Caligari to Hitler*. Princeton, NJ: Princeton University Press, 1974.
McCarthy, Todd. *Howard Hawks*. New York: Grove, 1997.
Millichap, Joseph R. *Lewis Milestone*. Boston: Twayne, 1981.
Montagu, Ivor. *Film World*. Baltimore: Penguin, 1964.
Wood, Winifred J. "Double Desire: Overlapping Discourses in a Film Writing Course." *College English* 60, no. 3 (1998): 278–300.

The Future of Creative Writing Lore: New Voices, New Challenges

7

The Traces of Certain Collisions:

Contemporary Writing and Old Tropes

Jen Webb

Introduction

I was a sickly child, and spent long winters shut away, bed-bound, in a heated room. What could I do but read? And top of my reading list, each year, were collections of myths; the myths of the ancient world; of my own home continent, Africa; and those of the Middle East, India, the Americas, the Pacific. I lived for gods and monsters, for impossible transformations and improbable choices, for the heartbreaks, and triumphs, and uncertainties of those tales. Literary scholars, mythographers, and narratologists identify patterns and processes across stories; as do children. I noticed, for instance, that no matter the origin of the story, gods were likely to be capricious and heroes to be trammeled by character flaws; old women could be relied on to make mischief; and death was rarely the end of the tale.

As I grew older, my reading expanded from myths into accounts of myths and, later, theories of myth-making. Robert Graves was an obvious early source; later came Joseph Campbell, and later still Claude Lévi-Strauss, Vladimir Propp, et al. I read on, into the scholarly literature and the creative re-inventions of those old takes. The more I read, the more I observed the extraordinary extent to which myth, and its close cousin lore, have penetrated even the most contemporary societies, the most sophisticated thought.

In this chapter I draw on this mode of thinking and knowing as way into considering aspects of creative writing within universities, and the mobilizing forces that can direct the actions of creative writing professors. In doing so, I revisit a landmark essay published over a decade ago, Kelly Ritter and Stephanie Vanderslice's "Teaching Lore: Creative Writers and the University" (2005), which depicts US creative writing teachers operating at the margins of the academy: a "self-marginalization"[1] adopted, I suspect, in the interests of establishing what Bourdieu termed distinction through social distance.[2]

Lore vs logic?

Myth and lore are closely related, observes the nineteenth-century antiquarian William Thoms,[3] in that each relies on story and custom rather than evidence. This is not to dismiss their social value. Both lore and myth originated in antiquity, and thus possess a sort of ecological validity; each has enduring attraction for human beings; either has stood up well to the test of time. Both are modes of knowledge—the etymology of *lore*, for example, stems from the Germanic/Old English *lar*, meaning *instruction*— but their epistemological basis, and their relationship to instruction, operate according to a very different logic from that valued in the higher education sector.

The contemporary university community, necessarily, treats myth and lore as interesting cultural and social artifacts, but not as modes of truth, not least perhaps because the use of the narrative mode, writes Haydon White, is considered evidence of "methodologically unsound" science.[4] We don't want stories; we want cold facts: "Enlightenment's program was the disenchantment of the world. It wanted to dispel myths, to overthrow fantasy with knowledge."[5] We contemporary academics are committed to knowledge that is *won* through the pursuit of rational, systematic investigation. Myth and lore, by contrast, are *given*: they are the sum of accumulated knowledge: folk wisdom, rather than tested and contested evidence.

And yet it is rare that reason, logic, or evidentiary knowledge truly dominate human thought or academic practice. Story, and the enchanted thought that is a part of story, remain central to the ways in which humans make sense of the world and conduct their professional practices, because the technical and the instrumental cannot alone operate as affordances for knowledge. Even a mode as positivist and objective as investigative science is driven, in no small part, by hunches and intuition:[6] by the stuff of myth; by the application of lore. This does not mean that lore should be valorized as the basis for professional practice, and it is a problem if, as Ritter and Vanderslice explain, teachers in the university system remain attached to lore, and eschew reason. The concern is that if teachers rely on customary practices, and don't expose their assumptions or techniques to critical testing, they risk introducing real problems into the curriculum, not least by failing to accommodate and account for cultural and technological change.

The worrying portrait presented by Ritter and Vanderslice in their 2005 article was of creative writing courses in the US university system. It is less evident in Australian or UK creative writing courses, largely because government initiatives and related institutional demands have propelled writing teachers into the logic of the academy. The requirement of the Australian government that universities deliver good citizens and good professionals as graduates means that in all subject areas there needs to be a focus on generic skills.[7] That means we must train students not only in the specifics of their chosen discipline area, but also in people skills (collaboration; communication); thinking skills (problem solving; decision making); and personal skills (self-direction; integrity). As a consequence, the free-range, idiosyncratic, "seat of the pants" pedagogies depicted by Ritter and Vanderslice are less likely to occur, and certainly less likely to be tolerated, in Australian creative writing classes. What we lose in individual creative individuality we gain, perhaps, in a more examined, more defensible approach to our students. What we lose in a representation of creative writing as being somehow above, or beside, the other university disciplines we gain in graduating significant numbers of writers who are likely to be able to find employment and support both themselves and their creative practice.

As a consequence, most writing teachers in Australian universities are at home in the work of researching pedagogy, interrogating traditions and truisms, producing analyses of process, and developing arguments about research in practice. It is a long time since anyone seriously wondered, for example, whether it is possible to teach creative writing, as is clear in the index of the journal *TEXT* (www.textjournal.com.au). But this does not mean that Australian writer-academics are truly integrated into the academy. Although on the one hand they are committed to the professional and intellectual mode, they tend nonetheless, like the US-based teachers described by Ritter and Vanderslice, to identify themselves first as writers and next as teachers or academics. They are writers; they therefore write; but they often describe this almost as a guilty secret, as the something that can be done only in the interstices, rather than being an integral part of their role as scholars. They may not cling to the lore of the teacher as described by Ritter and Vanderslice, but they remain attached to the myth of the distanced and disinterested writer.

In this they follow a long tradition: as I discuss elsewhere,[8] many writers, whether within the academy or in other professions, have kept their writing identity distinct from their income-earning identity. And this is as much a virtue of necessity as a considered choice. Writers in Australia earn, on average, somewhere between $9,000 and $15,000 for their writing.[9] It is not feasible to make a living as a writer, and so writers need to find either a generous patron or another source of income. For many writers, the best solution is to teach their craft at university level. Consequently, as (Australian novelist) Frank Moorhouse writes:

> never has the writing community been so closely integrated into the universities. . . . Some academics and some university students, of course, were sometimes also writers but even they felt some discomfort about their position at the university. Now the joke goes that when someone says they're a writer the next question is, 'Where do you teach?'[10]

Many writers find employment in universities as casual teachers, a position that allows them to commit to teaching their craft and art to students who are pleased to be in the presence of a "real writer." Their role is to transmit enthusiasm and technical knowledge, while the tenured writing academics take on the responsibility, or perhaps the burden, of satisfying their institution's requirements for engagement, entrepreneurship, research, and service, as well as teaching and pedagogy. While the casual teachers can remain to some extent guided by customary knowledge, or lore—that is, as long as they follow the curriculum set out by the academic responsible for that course—the academics on permanent contract have to demonstrate a commitment to contemporary scholastic values, and to deliver on the best practice standards of the time.

Of course, those teachers, the writer-academics on contract, are still *writers*, and however committed they are to their jobs and to the policy and regulatory expectations of their institution, they are likely still to orient themselves at least in their creative practice to the logic and lore of the creative domain. This means that unarticulated magical thinking still exists, even in the academy. We may accept the disenchantment of the world that was initiated by the Enlightenment, but we have probably at some point experienced the donnée: that unsought gift of idea or image, which is described by Henry James (1884), F.E. Sparshott (1977), and many other writers, and which exceeds the parameters of scientific knowledge. So, we hold simultaneously to two quite distinct paradigms: lore, in relation to our own writing and the magic of that domain; and logic in relation to curriculum design and pedagogical practice.

Between lore and logic

It need not be a surprise that any individual can juggle two contradictory modes of practice; lived experience is, after all, complex and often under-determined, and few people are able to conduct their lives on the basis of reason alone. While academics are trained and practiced in looking to research literature and working papers, and in adjusting our own teaching to what stands as established and evidentiary knowledge, we are also human beings who throughout our lives have relied on emotional or habituated responses, protecting ourselves from complexity and discomfort by attending not to rational processes, but to what is familiar.[11] Myth and lore are important bridges between informed and automatic ways of being and thinking, because they are expressions of millennia of human experience and emotions associated with such experience. Myth is not concerned with empirical reality, but with story; indeed, the word itself comes from the Greek *mythos*, meaning *speech, thought, story*. A myth, then, can be understood as something that generates ways of saying and thinking, and consequently provides spaces in which cultural experiences can be portrayed and explored. Giambattisto Vico implies this, arguing that myth offers "true and trustworthy histories of the customs of the most ancient peoples of Greece . . . stories of the times."[12] He is echoed by Michel de Certeau who writes, centuries later, that the contemporary novel acts as "the zoo of everyday practices"[13]—a place to visit, a place in which to experience, within the safe domain of story, the sorts of things that matter to contemporary readers, or to the ancients, each of us bound within the ethical and epistemological frameworks of our cultures.

Viewed in this way, it is possible to discount the Enlightenment rejection of enchantment, and instead perceive myth as a discourse that is directed toward knowledge. August Schlegel suggested this, writing that myth is "a universal and necessary product of human poetic power . . . a metaphorical language of reason."[14] Schlegel's view is supported by twentieth-century mythologists who likewise argue that myth constitutes a knowledge framework. Joseph Campbell, for example, takes this position on the basis that myth is capable of "seizing the idea and facilitating its epiphany."[15] Myths are not merely stories or works of imagination; they are also vehicles for the *speech, thought, story* we use at moments of reflection and analysis, and that make visible the limits of cultural knowing. They allow writers to look directly at the chaos and the contradictory elements of everyday life, and to take up those tools for thought that have been circulating in our cultures for millennia.

Myth also comprises stories that "embod[y] a people's deepest insights into its origins and destiny";[16] and not only its insights, but also its anxieties. We cannot know precisely what our origins were or our destiny might be, but we can tell and retell stories in an attempt to accommodate what we can never really know or control. And creative writing teachers can certainly convey this very long body of thinking, dreaming, and imagining as grist to the writer's mill, as consolation in trying times, and as confirmation that the sheer weight of cultural history supports a more imaginative, less evidence-driven, approach to practice.

Lore also provides the freedom to get things done without over-thinking it, as Donald Schön observes. "Our knowing," he writes, 'is ordinarily tacit, implicit in our patterns of action and in our feel for the stuff with which we are dealing."[17] In the everyday activities of our lives, we operate according to tacit knowledge—implicit, unarticulated, and internalized ways of being, ways of doing. When we know our field very well, we effectively embody and then forget that knowledge. Pierre Bourdieu explains this by reference to professional football players, of whom he says: "Nothing is simultaneously freer and more constrained than the action of the good player. He quite naturally materializes at just the place the ball is about to fall, as if the ball were in command of him—but by that very fact, he is in command of the ball."[18] This is tacit knowledge working very well: it is knowing by doing; and this is what teachers of writing who are first and foremost writers are likely to do: rely on that deeply embodied knowledge of their field, and the unarticulated "lore" of how to teach this practice, as though it were second nature.

Unfortunately, tacit knowledge, and lore, only take us a certain distance along the path of functioning effectively as creative and intellectual members of the community of practice. They only work when everything is going well, and there are no new issues that rattle the familiar ways of teaching. Relying on the confirmations of lore, or the consolations of myth, really only serve when everything is going well. Neither lore nor tacit knowledge offer the flexibility and reflection that allow people to deal genuinely with the exigencies of the lived—the physical and the social—world. So, when the context changes, the mode of operation, and the logic, must also change.

We live in an era when professionals are under conditions of constant change, and face constant demands for innovation. To deal effectively with this context, it is vital that we cease to rely on lore—however good a starting point it may have been—and turn toward a more thoughtful and engaged stance. For Donald Schön this means adopting reflective practice, which he describes as "the capacity to reflect on action so as to engage in a process of continuous learning," and "one of the defining characteristics of professional practice."[19] To do this, we first recognize a problem, and then generate and test suggestions for how to approach it. Lore will not answer the demands of a rapidly changing situation; it does not keep up, because it relies on the long slow burn of accumulated community knowing. Instead we need to apply concentration, creative thinking, evaluation, and attention to the situation. We do not need to set aside our love of the enchanted world, or our commitment to imagination and to the established ways of doing; we simply need to take our field, the teaching of creative writing, more seriously.

And it is not just writers; all professional fields face the same problem of shifting between the conventional ways of teaching/doing and the demands of the new, and for all their practitioners, reflective practice allows the embodied, tacit knowledge to interact with professional actions and thus come up with novel and productive ways of doing.[20] Being a professional, reflective practitioner does not come with the demand that we set aside all that we already know, all that we value or love; the pleasure in professional practice remains an important motivating force. We simply need to add to the established ways a willingness to test the things we do, the things we take for granted, and to incorporate changes where appropriate.

The trace

Pleasure; *delight*; *enchantment*; *desire*. These do not sound like the sorts of terms that any serious academic would deploy in discussing better modes of teaching. But they are at the heart of what we do. Creative writing students typically enter their studies because they are attached to the domain of myth, story, imagination: they are not usually captivated by instrumental logic, or motivated by career prospects. Rather, the "truths" and motivations found in myth and lore are in their bones. And why not?—myths allow us to trace our way through the dark. They deliver form within the chaos of everyday life[21] and, by filling our imaginations, they fit us for our cultural contexts.[22] Knowledge and reason are important; but it is emotion or affect—the product of story, of the imagination, of the felt world—that literally and figuratively move us.[23]

But they do not provide stability—oddly, given their enduring character and presence. Though they remain, a constant thread in culture, they change as the contexts change. Each time we read and reread or tell and retell the myths, the content of those stories changes—sometimes subtly, sometimes more radically. Each new reader and each new (re)writer of those tales leaves on them what Italo Calvino calls "the traces of readings previous to ours," and the myths themselves "bring in their wake the traces they themselves have left on the culture or cultures they have passed through."[24] The very passage of myth through our culture informs us that relying on a fixed way of teaching is inappropriate for a creative writer, for someone committed to story and to the domain of enchantment and imagination.

In an attempt to extend the notion of reflectivity and flexibility in my teaching and research, I have recently been tracing a path through a small collection of ancient stories, adding my own traces to them as I rewrite them; changing them, and changing myself, at the same time. The mythological situation that has captured me is the one that deals with Icarus, Daedalus, and the royal family of Crete. At the heart of these tales is the labyrinth, and in attempting to craft my own sense of that environment, I find myself wandering through a new kind of labyrinth, one whose corridors lead to other cultures, other historical epochs. The residents of Crete reappear in North American antiquity, in Indonesian myth and in the stories of ancient Sumer. The trickster, the goddess, the fecund mother, the ill-fated lover, the boy who tried to fly to the sun: all occupy parts of the labyrinth, playing similar but different roles. Their appearance and reappearance across time and cultures almost give credence to the insistence of mythologists like Joseph Campbell that myths are a biological feature.[25]

But this plurality stymies my efforts to build contemporary versions of the myths. I cannot find a path through all the possibilities; the story is never there, or not reliably there; and as I trace the possibilities, I find myself lost. I should have known; there is no Ur-version of any myth, writes Marina Warner;[26] there is no beginning, writes Jacques Derrida. All we have are variants, or possibilities, and the trace I think I see is only a presence in absence, "presence-absence,"[27] an origin that *is-not*, a space that presents itself as the starting point when in fact it is only a point on the journey.

The effect is a concatenation of voices, a tangled ball of narrative threads. And they are usually threads of story rather than a completed tale. Many of the myths that have come down through the centuries exist only as fragments, told by many different authors. The story of Icarus and Crete, for instance, is told as both story and history by (among others) Ovid, Apollodorus, Pausanius, Euripides, Catullus, Severus, Libanius, Herodotus, Strabo, Philostratus, and Pliny. And that is just in the classical period. Icarus has returned consistently throughout the millennia that followed. Brueghel's famous painting, "Landscape with the Fall of Icarus" (*c.* 1555), and two poems it sparked—William Carlos Williams's "Landscape with the Fall of Icarus" (1962) and W.H. Auden's "Musee de Beaux Arts" (1976)—are among the better-known creative retellings of the boy who flew and fell. But major and minor practitioners have returned to this story for the past 2,000 years.

One significant aspect of its enchantment, for me and perhaps for others, is the fragmentary nature of its being. There are gaps I can fill. There are ways of seeing, thinking, and telling that have not been done, or not quite in that way, before. I have been captivated by the women in the story, and it has generated a sustained series of poems and short fictions. Key among those women is Icarus's mother—who is she? His father appears everywhere in the Greek accounts, but only one writer (Apollodorus, in *The Library*) mentions his mother by name. She is absent from the scene.

This absence, viewed through a lens that is willing to suspend science (in its broadest sense) and to engage story as though it might be true, is generative of thought and practice. I have spent many hours combing through translations of the ancient texts, looking for his mother; reflecting on the position of women in story per se, and myth in particular; reviewing the historical and political context of Crete and Athens in the period in which this story is set; reading alternative creative accounts and analyses by narratologists and mythologists; and considering the capacity of myth to generate axiological and ontological reflection. However slight the data that are the fragments of this narrative, and however impossible the leap from reason and logic into story, it offers a powerful stage on which to think as a writer, and as a scholar. It is not surprising, then, that I have seen so many creative doctoral theses emerge, in the past decade or so, that begin with myth. It gives us tools to think with, to analyse critically, and to create.

And so, the contemporary university re-invigorates these stories that will not die; the story of Icarus and Daedalus, and of others too. Prometheus, the bringer of fire; Herakles who continues to appear in film and television; the Trojan War and its aftermath, which has spun out stories, poems, film, theater, philosophy, and psychology ever since. In each case, what we have in the twenty-first century is a series of palimpsests: stories told and retold by the ancients, relayed to the present by way of the artists and writers of the Renaissance, the baroque, the neoclassical, the Romantic, the modern, and the postmodern periods. Layer upon layer of story, a concretion building across history.

Roger Caillois describes myth as comprising "two converging strands of determinations"[28] operating according to "a form of vertical integration" and "a form of horizontal integration."[29] Both depictions suggest the warp and weft of a piece of fabric, fabric that provides a canvas on which to express enduring questions of human being and of cultural formations. But pick at that weaving, and it may disintegrate into a handful of threads: it is a work of human creativity and not a natural phenomenon. It has no Ur-form, no fundamental being; it is only "one of the representatives of the trace in general," writes Derrida, "it is not the trace itself. *The trace itself does not exist.*"[30]

Bronislaw Malinowski's anthropological explanation of the role of myth provides a way of thinking through what we can do, as teachers of writing, as writers:

> Myth, as a statement of primeval reality which still lives in present-day life and as a justification by precedent, supplies a retrospective pattern of moral values, sociological order, and magical belief . . . The function of myth, briefly, is to strengthen tradition and endow it with a greater value and prestige by tracing it back to a higher, better, more supernatural reality of initial events.[31]

The ancient versions typically present their characters and events according to what we now read as stereotypes; contemporary writers can upend the old traditions and all their imperfections, and overlay the earlier narrative threads with contemporary values and beliefs, more suited to the sort of communicative, ethical, and reflexive modes that are expected of graduates, at least in the Australian tradition.

A conclusion

So, is it reasonable to take a story that emerged in a very different episteme and a very different ethical context, and apply a twenty-first-century framework to it? Is it possible to retell ancient stories without sanitizing them, colonizing them, and taming them? Is it possible to reject the folkloric knowledges about how the world is, and how we should live in it? Perhaps. But I am not sure these are the right questions to ask. If myth is indeed "a metaphorical language of reason" (August Schlegel) and an exploration of "a people's deepest insights into its origins and destiny" (J. Hillis Miller); and if there is in fact no point of origin (Marina Warner, Jacques Derrida), then perhaps we owe no debt to earlier iterations of the tales, and can do them no harm.

Perhaps what matters more than an attempt to identify and preserve an origin, or to honor collective understandings, is a commitment to a continual re-exploration of the possibilities offered by chaos, by catachresis, and of the poetry that resides at the heart of language. Perhaps what will be achieved is a productive collision between different sets of values and aesthetics, and explorations of relationality or what the Greeks called the *ontoglial*, "the glue of being."[32] Tracing the lines that flow and ebb across cultures and centuries, it may prove possible to exploit that relational glue in the interests of building not just story, but also knowledge about the quality of being, and the interrelationships in and beyond the writing classroom. As Foucault observes:

> the poet is he who, beneath the named, constantly expected differences, rediscovers the buried kinships between things, their scattered resemblances. Beneath the established signs . . . He hears another, deeper discourse, which recalls the time when words sparkled in the universal resemblance of things: the Sovereignty of the Same, so difficult to express, effaces in its language the distinction between signs.[33]

Acknowledgments

I acknowledge the support of the Australian Research Council, which has provided support for my investigations of creative practice through the Discovery project "Understanding creative excellence: A case study in poetry" (DP130100402).

Notes

1   K. Ritter and S. Vanderslice, "Teaching Lore: Creative Writers and the University," *Profession* (2005), 103.

2   P. Bourdieu, *Distinction: A Social Critique of the Judgement of Taste* (London: Routledge, 1984).

3   Cited in D. Emrich, "'Folk-Lore': William John Thoms," *California Folklore Quarterly* 5, no. 4 (October 1946): 355–74 (The original is not accessible.)

4   See H. White, "The Question of Narrative in Contemporary Historical Theory," *History and Theory* 23, no. 1 (February 1984): 1–33.

5   T. Adorno and M. Horkheimer, *Dialectic of Enlightenment: Philosophical Fragments* (Palo Alto: Stanford University Press, 2002), 1.

6   A. Seago, "Research Methods for MPhil & PhD Students in Art and Design: Contrasts and Conflicts," *Royal College of Art Research Papers* 1, no. 3 (1994/95), 5.

7   Australian Qualifications Framework Council, Australian Qualifications Framework (second edition, 2013).

8   J. Webb, *Researching Creative Writing* (Frontinus Press: Cambridge, 2015), 115.

9   D. Throsby, J. Zwar and T. Longden, *Book Authors and their Changing Circumstances: Survey Method and Results* (Sydney: Macquarie Economics Research Papers, 2015), 21.

10   F. Moorhouse, "The Forum," *The Australian* (23 October 2004), B02.

11   W. James, *The Principles of Psychology 1* (New York: Cosimo Press, 2007), 402.

12   G. Vico, *The New Science*, 3rd edn (New York: Cornell University Press, 1948), 6.

13   M. de Certeau, *The Practice of Everyday Life* (Berkeley: University of California Press, 1984), 78.

14   Cited in E. Behler, "On Truth and Lie in an Aesthetic Sense," in *Revenge of the Aesthetic*, ed. M.P. Clark (Berkeley and LA: University of California Press, 2000), 81. Note that I cite Schlegel via Behler because I cannot access a copy of the original in English, and my German is too poor to provide a reliable English version.

15   J. Campbell, *The Flight of the Wild Gander: Explorations in the Mythological Dimension* (New York: HarperCollins, 1951), 48.

16   J.H. Miller, *Others* (Princeton NJ: Princeton University Press, 2001), 5.

17   D. Schön, *The Reflective Practitioner: How Professionals Think in Action* (New York: Basic Books, 1983), 49.

18   P. Bourdieu, *In Other Words*: *Essays Towards a Reflexive Sociology* (Stanford, CA: Stanford University Press, 1990), 63.

19   Schön, *The Reflective Practitioner*, 102, 104.

20   G. Bolton, *Reflective Practice: Writing and Professional Development*, 3rd edn (London: Sage, 2010).

21   Miller, *Others*, 64.

22   M. Foucault, "The Imagination of the Nineteenth Century," in *Aesthetics, Method, and Epistemology: Essential Works 1954–84* (New York: New Press, 1998), 239.

23   See H. Scheub, *Story* (Madison: University of Wisconsin Press, 1998).

24   I. Calvino, *The Literature Machine: Essays* (London: Vintage, 1986), 128.

25   J. Campbell, *The Flight of the Wild Gander: Explorations in the Mythological Dimension* (New York: HarperCollins, 1951), 55.

26   M. Warner, *Managing Monsters: Six Myths of Our Time* (London: Random House, 1994), 8.

27   J. Derrida, *Of Grammatology* (Baltimore: Johns Hopkins University Press, 1976), 71.

28   R. Caillois, *The Edge of Surrealism* (Durham: Duke University Press, 2003), 116.

29 Caillois, *Edge of Surrealism*, 118.

30 Derrida, *Of Grammatology*, 167.

31 B. Malinowski, *Magic, Science and Religion and Other Essays 1948* (Whitefish: Kessinger Publishing, 2004), 122.

32 D. Mertz, *Moderate Realism and its Logic* (New Haven: Yale University Press, 1996), 25.

33 M. Foucault, *The Order of Things: An Archaeology of the Human Sciences* (London: Routledge, 2002), 49.

References

Adorno, T. and M. Horkheimer. *Dialectic of Enlightenment: Philosophical Fragments*, trans. E. Jephcott. Palo Alto: Stanford University Press, 2002.

AQF: Australian Qualifications Framework Council. Australian Qualifications Framework (second edition, 2013), http://www.aqf.edu.au/wp-content/uploads/2013/05/AQF-2nd-Edition-January-2013.pdf [accessed December 12, 2014].

Behler, E. "On Truth and Lie in an Aesthetic Sense," in *Revenge of the Aesthetic*, edited by M.P. Clark. Berkeley and LA: University of California Press, 2000: 76–92.

Bolton, G. *Reflective Practice: Writing and Professional Development*, 3rd edn. London: Sage, 2010.

Bourdieu, P. *Distinction: a Social Critique of the Judgement of Taste*, trans. Richard Nice. London: Routledge, 1984.

Bourdieu, P. *In Other Words: Essays Towards a Reflexive Sociology*, trans. Matthew Adamson. Stanford, CA: Stanford University Press, 1990.

Caillois, R. *The Edge of Surrealism*, trans. C. Naish. Durham: Duke University Press, 2003.

Calvino, I. *The Literature Machine: Essays*, trans. P. Creagh. London: Vintage, 1986.

Campbell, J. *The Flight of the Wild Gander: Explorations in the Mythological Dimension*. New York: HarperCollins, 1951.

Certeau, M, de. *The Practice of Everyday Life*. Berkeley: University of California Press, 1984.

Derrida, J. *Of Grammatology*, trans. G.C. Spivak. Baltimore: Johns Hopkins University Press, 1976.

Emrich, D. "'Folk-Lore': William John Thoms," *California Folklore Quarterly* 5.4 (October 1946): 355–74.

Foucault, M. *Aesthetics, Method, and Epistemology: Essential Works 1954–84*, edited by P. Rabinow, trans. R. Hurley. New York: New Press, 1998.

Foucault, M. *The Order of Things: An Archaeology of the Human Sciences*, trans. A.M. Sheridan Smith. London: Routledge, 2002.

James, H. "The Art of Fiction," in *The Victorian Art of Fiction: Nineteenth-Century Essays on the Novel*, edited by Rohan Maitzen, 317–32. Toronto: Broadview Press, 2009.

James, W. *The Principles of Psychology 1*. New York: Cosimo Press, 2007.

Malinowski, B. *Magic, Science and Religion and Other Essays 1948*. Whitefish: Kessinger Publishing, 2004.

Mertz, D. *Moderate Realism and its Logic*. New Haven: Yale University Press, 1996.

Miller, J.H. *Others*. Princeton NJ: Princeton University Press, 2001.

Moorhouse, F. 'The Forum," *The Australian* (23 October 2004), B02.

Ritter, K. and Vanderslice, S. "Teaching Lore: Creative Writers and the University." *Profession* (2005): 102–12.

Scheub, H. *Story*. Madison: University of Wisconsin Press, 1998.

Schön, D. *The Reflective Practitioner: How Professionals Think in Action*. New York: Basic Books, 1983.

Seago, A. "Research Methods for MPhil & PhD Students in Art and Design: Contrasts and Conflicts." *Royal College of Art Research Papers* 1, no. 3 (1994–5).

Sparshott, F.E. "Every Horse has a Mouth: A Personal Poetics." *Philosophy and Literature* 1, no. 2 (Spring 1977): 147–69.

Throsby, D., Zwar, J. and Longden, T. *Book Authors and their Changing Circumstances: Survey Method and Results*. Sydney: Macquarie Economics Research Papers, 2015.

Vico, G. *The New Science*, 3rd edn, trans. T.H. Bergin and M.H. Fisch. New York: Cornell University Press, 1948.

Warner, M. *Managing Monsters: Six Myths of Our Time*. London: Random House, 1994.

Webb, J. *Researching Creative Writing*. Frontinus Press: Cambridge, 2015.

White, H. "The Question of Narrative in Contemporary Historical Theory." *History and Theory* 23, no. 1 (February 1984): 1–33.

8

Lore 2.0:

Creative Writing as History

Phil Sandick

Any pedagogical maneuver that relies on a logic of "try it this way, it works" is in danger of falling into that large, troubling category of "lore."[1] Lore-based writing pedagogies can give off an impression of softness, of lacking in intellectual rigor; they can signal an isolated discipline guilty of mindless traditionalism or, at the very least, one that refuses to actively keep its teaching practices in check. Our dependence on lore-based pedagogies has opened the door for various indictments, the most pointed of which come from practitioners working in creative writing studies. The charges include a critique of lore's properties of mystification, a critique of teachers who often reinforce a sense of writing's "unteachability," as well as a critique of lore that characterizes creative writing as ultimately a "romantic process that exists outside the boundaries of the classroom."[2] And yet, even as the field expands and diversifies, lore, which is "embod[ied]" in "ritual, writing, and talk,"[3] has sustained its central role in our pedagogical practices.

Today much of the lore perpetuated in creative writing classrooms has become so ingrained that it might even ring familiar to those outside of the field. For example, there is Hemingway's decree that "writers write," Woolf's call for "A Room of One's Own," Forster's "only connect," Lamott's "bird by bird," and that type of iconic guidance. The workshop itself has also become a form of lore, carrying its own particular aura of prestige and historical significance. In lore, we find pithy (and contradictory) truisms like "write what you know" or "use your imagination." In what Stephen North has called the unfinished House of Lore, we discover, among other things, adages and fragments of writerly advice that often have an unclear origin: write 500 words per day, write two hours each day, or don't take days off; type out sentences or verses of literary greats in order to see them from the

inside; recapture a childlike state of seeing; pretend you're explaining
_____ to a visitor from a distant planet who has never seen or heard of it
before; you can create any world you want, as long as your rules are
consistent; and of course there is the ubiquitous "Show, don't tell."

While lore-based pedagogy in creative writing studies has isolated our
field from more research-based disciplines, it is potentially hazardous to be
too hasty in looking for ways to dismiss lore from our pedagogical
frameworks. A dip into most creative writing classrooms will, on any given
day, almost certainly reveal a kind of referential, contextual educational
frame—a frame that an instructor has set up in order to help to facilitate
discussion and encourage student learning. For instance, we might encounter
the transmission of practical "advice" or literary tidbits and/or experience-
based anecdotes in response to student ideas or to student work. Over the
course of a semester, the students and the instructor often informally build
this a unique web of references. For example, as an undergraduate, my
creative writing professor used to emphasize the way stories often benefit
from unexpected, or even whimsical turns of plot. This professor described
such a turn from an obscure Victorian novel he had read in graduate school,
and repeatedly came back to this text in future workshops, using this
author's work as shorthand for a reminder about striving for dynamic
pacing and plotting.

Another major source for these classroom conversations is the canon of
creative writing craft books, which exists within a larger continuum of texts
that I will refer to here as "the archive of writers on writing." This group of
texts exerts considerable influence over the teaching of creative writing, and
in many ways is the engine of the field's sociality. The little tidbits, or
fragments that comprise the House of Lore can often be the discussion
starters or discussion extenders that serve to cement affective bonds within
the creative writing classroom. This capacious archive serves as a kind of
universal source text or dataset for what becomes creative writing lore, and
embodies a diverse spread in terms of genre, intended function, and
consideration of audience. Most are popular texts, intended for aspiring or
established writers, or those with an interest in language, literature, cultural
studies, literary culture, and/or literary history. In the classroom, all of this
information is up for grabs and units of lore are continuously being
borrowed and re-borrowed and sometimes repurposed by students and
teachers to fit various exigencies: structuring a workshop, leading a
discussion, offering feedback, revising a poem. This seemingly haphazard
method of instruction has proven to be steadily persistent, even as writing
theorists continue to note both its drawbacks and the field's overdependence
on, what Mayers has termed, "institutional-conventional wisdom."

But why?

To address this question, I believe we must delve deeper into the nature
of lore, and consider how the anecdotes, myths, conventional wisdom, and
bits of advice present in our classrooms possess a value to practitioners

beyond obvious or superficial meanings. The very nature of "process" (as a series of actions, both conscious and unconscious) makes it impossible to discuss an act of composing with complete thoroughness; there are bound to be omissions and elisions as writers reconstruct narratives of how texts come into being. As Paul Prior discusses in his analysis of writing as a practice: "A text does not fully or unambiguously display its history—even the most insightful of interpretation and analyses are only likely to recover some elements of its fuller history . . . ."[4] Likewise, Graeme Harper points out that the "evidence trail of writerly action" does not rely solely on the finished work.[5] And yet, through lore, we may be able to gather clues. In other words, lore can point toward a history of writing processes and thoughts—and a history of creative writing instruction—and say, "I can't show you the whole process of writing or teaching, but I can show you what's recoverable." Lore's productive value might be elucidated if we can refocus our attention on relational and history-specific contexts that shape its new encounters—as well as the role of those who come in contact with fragments of processes and pedagogies and recombine/remake/remix them to meet new needs.

Seen through this lens, I would like to engage with the idea of lore as a form of historical discourse: specifically, the history of how creative writing texts come into existence. In this framework, each unit of lore is not necessarily prescriptive or proscriptive in and of itself, but rather represents a *topos* within a larger, more expansive, socially contingent, and potentially chaotic system of knowledge-making. Particular units of lore, then, serve as signposts toward even deeper and more complicated histories of both teaching and composing in the literary arts. Lore is unofficial, unvetted, fairly chaotic, and even teetering on irrationality, yet still it remains significant in its accumulation of past practices, traditions, and beliefs regarding writing process.

We can imagine this phenomenon through the metaphor of Hemingway's iceberg. While Hemingway was using the iceberg in a different context, to discuss subtext, we may use it to consider the way a unit of lore—like a visible peak—indicates a submerged and massive and unrecoverable history. All of the material located below the waterline is that which is not able to be re-collected: it is the unrecorded work of writing and revision. We know that this history is there—it must be because the creative texts themselves exist—but lore is currently our best and only access to that history.

Much as historical writing often seeks to recreate the layers and complexities of lived experience with the positivist aim of "getting things right," so too do our pedagogies, then, seek to carve up the morass of shoptalk and lore. Together this creative writing lore helps apprentice writers read themselves into literary history and encourages students to see themselves in dialogue with writers, teachers, and fellow students. Analysing tidbits of lore—in class discussions or in workshop practice—might uncover various writing habits and beliefs that students find useful and necessary to fueling their own creative production. Lore, to put it differently, speaks to the psyche of writers by encompassing a more complete version of the writing process (i.e., one that is messy and serendipitous), in which students are free agents, forming affective bonds with teachers, writers, fellow students, and dare I say it, with writing, reading, daydreaming, and social engagement as well.

Why history?

As Andrew Pickering uncovers in his analysis of scientific study, most creative acts and discoveries come about through manifestations of a surprisingly large set of prior actions and thoughts.[6] In this "mangle of practice," as he calls it, prior traditions, acts, and beliefs are tested, embraced, or rejected through the machine of creation and experiment. I believe we can use the concept of "the mangle of practice," derived in part from Actor-network theory, in describing how creative works come into existence. For just as in North's original description of lore as a form of knowledge-making: "The communal lore offers options, resources, and perhaps some directional pressure; but the individual, finally, decides what to do and whether (or how) it has worked—decides, in short, what counts as knowledge."[7] Here practitioners have a heightened degree of agency[8] which coincides with the recent prosumer turn in creative literacy.[9] Meanwhile, lore gives us an account of the composing process—this complicated mangle—and also provides a component in future composing practices for others. Or as Patricia Harkin pointed out in the context of composition research, lore tells us "what practitioners do" instead of offering "abstract accounts" of process.[10]

The mythologies that inevitably stem from writer accounts and the "cyclical" use of lore in the classroom are indeed complex, but they are still, I would argue, analysable, particularly in their nature as a "collective history."[11] Each unit of lore carries a historical trace, and in its deployment, leaves a historical trace. As Ritter and Vanderslice have said: "Behind our collective pedagogies as teachers of creative writing lies a collective history of learning fueled by lore." And, "to ignore this history and its deceptively simple construction does a great disservice to the field." Instructors are constantly doing the work of historical writing when we categorize structures and processes of the past into our own pedagogical narratives. For instance, imagine a college student attending a reading where a poet instructs the audience to "write into the dark," and twenty years later, this same student, now an assistant professor, makes the same claim in a graduate poetry workshop. If we take a step back and consider the discursive nature of lore, perhaps we can learn more about how individual writers are actually interacting with some amount of process-based knowledge that precedes them.

Lore, in this understanding, does not exist in a vacuum, but functions as both a historical entity (existing in time) and as a rhetorical entity, meant for both primary audiences and in many cases second and tertiary audiences. It comes to us slantwise: through a capacious archive of beliefs and customs that stems from our collective activities and processes of writing, and is passed from generation to generation through spoken, written, audiovisual transmission and even interactions with materials: visual art; new media objects; writing tools; writing spaces; and even Hesse's mention of the best kind of tea for writers to drink.[12] Our first instinct may be to laugh or shrug shoulders at this sort of advice, but is that really fair? For instance, what have cognitivists said about caffeine, creativity, and the flow state? How does the scene of writing (in a café, at home, at the library, in writers' spaces or writing colonies, on the subway, in a car, on an airplane) affect output? How does the ritual of drinking tea compare to other writerly rituals? These are the sorts of mundane, yet potentially eye-opening questions that our field has yet to research. In the haste of resisting the more counterfeit-seeming or cliché-sounding parts of creative writing's powerful mythography, there's the very real possibility that we will discard time-tested strategies *that work for many students.*

Historiographical methods in creative writing studies

One method of "doing" history in creative writing studies is to take an etymological approach: identifying a particular unit of lore and then tracing its usage and derivation. To look specifically at one instance of "teaching lore" traveling through time, we might take the example of the writing advice, "kill your darlings." (In other words, delete your "best" sentences, since they are probably overwritten and mannered, and different in tone from the rest of the composition.) This advice is, without a doubt, repeated daily in English-speaking creative writing undergraduate and graduate workshops throughout the world. I had initially thought that this was either Gertrude Stein's or Ernest Hemingway's dictum, but web searches led me to believe my assumption was incorrect. I found reputable sites that attributed the bit of lore to Allen Ginsburg, William Faulkner, and Stephen King. I eventually found a piece by Forrest Wickman on Slate.com that considered the origins of the title of the 2013 film *Kill Your Darlings*. Wickman traced it back elsewhere, to Arthur Quiller-Couch, in fact, from a Cambridge lecture in 1914 entitled "On Style," in which Quiller-Couch criticized "extraneous ornament" and advised his audience, "Murder your darlings."[13] While this piece of lore, once Quiller-Couch delivered the statement, clearly took on its own life, I believe it is helpful and elucidating to trace it backward through time, to its origins. For instance, an apprentice writer encountering this piece of advice might—given its context—be better able to weigh whether or not to embrace this idiosyncratic method of editing. What was the stylistic paradigm Quiller-Couch had in mind, when he made this utterance? What does the context of 1914 and Cambridge tell us about the *type* of writing toward which this particular unit of lore aims to direct its practitioners? How and why have notions of "taste" and minimalism/maximalism shifted through time? It is always up to the individual writers to curate their own archive of practices and beliefs—which will propel them through the drafting and editing processes. But by understanding where lore comes from, and how it has been used through time, we can help students choose wisely.

To better understand how lore operates discursively and "to endanger the propagation of unexamined lore,"[14] I recommend turning to historiography and the philosophy of history. Histories need not be chronological or linear, and so while tracing "kill your darlings" might suggest one way creative writing lore moves through time, we should strongly consider how the fields of historiography and philosophy of history might suggest otherwise. In the context of composition studies, Geoffrey Sirc describes how the journey to become an innovative practitioner and scholar in one's field involves doing historical research with a critical historiographical bent. That means looking to the footnotes and also the seemingly mundane to invigorate our scholarly journeys. To get around the conventional wisdom of the field, and "find the stuff in the field that really glitters, you've got to root through the discard heap. Your history has to be alternative or, as Byron Hawk calls his, 'counter.'"[15]

One philosopher of history capable of re-invigorating our study of lore is Hayden White. In White's *Metahistory*, he explores how historians claim objectivity, but are in fact *making* history as much as—or more than—they are *uncovering* history. In creative writing, we have the choice to step back and not only examine our use of lore in our classrooms, but also to consider how each time we engage with lore, we are making a historical appeal to our students. In developing this idea, we might turn to White in philosophy of history and specifically his use of the Ricoeurian notion of "emplotment": the way historians combine smaller stories into larger stories using plot techniques strategically to give a purportedly complete account of a series of events. Lore has often been linked to romantic emplotment and its powerful mythos invoked by heroic narratives: the "genius (male) writer"[16] achieving eminence is one narrative that critics of lore seek to correct. Surely there are lore-based metanarratives that are in need of revising: and yet that does not mean we should go too far in the other direction, and encourage students to take on a fully satirical or ironic stance toward all writing advice.

Like any historical narrative, lore has both form and content, and the concert between the two will yield both useful and harmful results. A unit of lore, for instance, that epitomizes "the writer" as a white male in a corduroy jacket, leaning over a desk in an empty room with an open bottle of whiskey at his side, has its own historiographic story. In order to correct it, we need to understand how this myth-building took place and how and why and where it has been propagated. Less nefarious, though still outdated, bits of lore such as what a manuscript should look like, how long it should be to suit publishers' recommendations, etc. will likewise possess an undeniable historical valence. By working with students to train them to recognize how these clichés and truisms came about, we are, in effect, attempting to understand the value of lore within the complex cycle of writing activities and processes. Even when the tidbit of lore is untrue, it still recollects a history of the field, and is useful to our disciplinary histories and ripe for further study, remix, revision, and response.

The problems we continually run up against in lore-based pedagogy are the problems of any grand narrative: In the vast majority of cases, beginning creative writing instructors will hit against very little counterpoint and/or theoretical challenges to however they have decided to run their workshops. Though there are some exceptions, most MFA programs do not run pedagogy seminars specifically designed to teach undergraduate creative writing, with the result that there is little encouragement of critical perspectives within the field, even for beginning instructors. Mayers, who sees certain problems with an overly accepting attitude toward lore, describes lore operating within creative writing departments as such:

> [Institutional-conventional wisdom] denotes a system of belief that often appears to some creative writers to be a form of "natural" or "commonsense" knowledge. Thus, it is "conventional wisdom," believed by many to be beyond dispute. But it is also "institutional" in the sense that it has become embedded within institutional structures and therefore has helped to form the kind of academic enterprise creative writing is.[17]

Lore, in other words, has its reasons for being advanced and favored; much in the way that "official" historical records that aim for objective standards of truth are constructed, and possess a content inherent in their form as "official." This marks a sharp contrast to the way that composition has sought out published research that uses all available methods and methodologies to endorse and/or discourage certain teaching practices (among other topics). Mayers illustrates the cycle by which lore—within creative writing departments (i.e., this is how we workshop, this is how we ask students to distribute their work, this is how we ask students to engage with new media)—is institutionally re-inscribed without such checks and balances. As North describes, lore is not comprised of "isolated settlements"; instead, there's an aspect to lore that guarantees parts of it will be abandoned only to be picked up again later.[18]

Recovering and remixing historical relics

When looking at the formal definition of "recovery," in the larger context of historical recovery, the third of three basic meanings catches one's attention.

Recovery, in this particular sense, is "the act of obtaining usable substances from unusable sources."[19] In the context of lore, when students think critically about outdated maxims or cliché advice that they have encountered, they are performing an act of historical recovery—something akin to remix. And while I agree with historian David Lowenthal's observation that the preservation of the past has "dampened creative use of it,"[20] creative writing pedagogy is one site where practitioners still have the opportunity to use the past in novel ways, especially when the House of Lore has "many rooms that look very much alike."[21] The dustbin of history, to borrow Lowenthal's term, is often the most pragmatically useful, and just because the oft-repeated advice is institutionally re-inscribed at the MFA or undergraduate level, or just because it has attained mythic or iconic status, does not mean that it has not exerted influence over generations of writers, or been deployed in a variety of ways. Even if we were to deem "kill your darlings" as a cliché, now emptied out of original pizzazz, do we truly believe that students have moved beyond the *topos* of efficient editing? By looking at lore as a fundamentally historical entity comprised of writers discussing writing, and in turn making their own lore, we can better see the nature of lore existing in a chain of "powerful, complicated discourse" rather than existing as "small, uncomplicated utterances."[22]

More generally, I believe a misconception about creative writing lore exists, specifically because we can't view individual units of lore as entities that may be conventionally "true" or "false." Teachers of writing will often hold antithetical positions on various issues (the role of the unconscious, writing routines, the value of formal study/training, the use of symbols, or considerations of aesthetics), and this raises obvious questions: if these units are fragmented, contradictory, and conditional, then why does lore dominate the prevailing creative writing pedagogy? Is this not the pedagogical equivalent of throwing darts at a dartboard to tailor feedback and/or pedagogy? And yet, I believe we can easily circumvent this criticism by using a historiographical lens. Again, we are considering lore not as proscriptive maxims, but as local contested histories of the writing act. Texts in the archive of writers on writing (or as Wendy Bishop calls it, "collections of writers' wisdom") possess conditional accuracy and a truth-value dependent on their specific contextualization.[23]

Take the example of Author 1. Author 1 achieves literary fame and respected status from her novels and essays on the literary life. The essays—which often mix memoir and craft advice—occasionally come in the form of maxim or parable. These essays are assigned in graduate creative writing workshops, which MFA Student 1 thinks about privately and engages with, in the writing of his or her own work. Later MFA Student 1 begins teaching undergraduate creative writing, and shares Author 1's advice with a new class of students. The assumption—through this process of idea distribution—is that Author 1's approach to and reflection on creative writing processes worked. They were successful. But the propagation of Author 1's advice depends mostly on the fact that MFA Student 1 has tested them and deemed them useful. Perhaps a different Author and MFA Student would not have experienced this bond or connection—but *this* particular web of influence is formed, and will likely repeat for a handful of students in the next generation.

Or else, consider the possible reach of Anne Lamott's hugely popular *Bird by Bird*. While there are certainly pithy truisms put forward in this text, a prolonged engagement with Lamott's work might move beyond the advice to write "shitty first drafts" and her "bird by bird" refrain. Her writing may, over time, provoke a subterranean response from the reader. That reader-writer might consider his or her life as a first draft, or consider "bird by bird" as a kind of logic to deal with the more quotidian concerns in life. From these first-level significations, the book may take on a form of lore that carries a particular, not always languaged, second-level signification. This signification may exist as cultural mythologies exist—as shaping mechanisms that do not fully reveal themselves to their users. Whether or not Lamott's advice will provide this response in *everyone* is beside the point: it only matters that for *some* people, Lamott's advice produces this profound engagement.

Self-reflexivity and pedagogical metanarratives

Distrust is a healthy part of a creative writing education, and is particularly essential for students building their own educational narratives in relation to lore. Hayden White's work on metahistory calls for greater self-reflexivity and awareness of metanarratives, and I believe we can benefit from a similar intervention within creative writing studies. One response to the flow of endless lore is to locate almost scientifically what is useful and what is unhelpful to a majority of writers—all in the name of recovering a kind of fixed and reproducible view of the writing process. But an alternative mode might be to accept this flow of lore and information, and lore's ability to sometimes delightfully contradict itself and surprise us. One craft book that tries to chronicle every step of the process of writing a short story is *Ron Carlson Writes a Story*. Carlson, novelist, short story writer, and essayist who teaches in the MFA program at UC Irvine, places himself in the work, using a mode of self-reflexivity, as one would expect in many kinds of postmodern histories. It's a move that many postmodern scholars call for in the field of historiography, and also one which historiographers and philosophers of history have long argued brings about a heightened awareness of metanarrative. In different fields, we can think of the graphic novels *Maus* or *Persepolis* here and countless other works on creative nonfiction that are self-reflexive in their telling; that is, they grapple with the work of writing history.

In the pages of *Ron Carlson Writes a Story*, Carlson offers tidbits and advice about the writing life: Drink one cup of coffee. Twenty minutes after you want to stop writing for the first time, stay seated. He analyses the anatomy of a story he's published, describing, for instance, dialogue as a dance. But we get a lot more from this book than a typical offering of "lore," precisely because Carlson re-imagines "the mangle of practice"—to again borrow Pickering's notion of "a performative understanding" of making rather than a "representational understanding"[24]—that put his work together. Carlson discusses the small serendipities and elements of chance that were involved, as well as the deceptively mundane aspects of daily life that merge actual event with revision. In the end, we get something more than a creative nonfiction hybrid craft book: we get an attempt at a chronological play-by-play of how a work comes into existence.

Of course, as Carlson well knows, neither he nor any other writer-teacher, can write an adequate "how to write a story" on the blackboard with diagrams. Rather, the effective writer-teacher, in sharing his or her knowledge, must be content to *perform* a form of history in order to tell the story of craft more adequately. It's almost as if Carlson, in this text, is grappling with his own local, contested history in order to demonstrate or enact the process of historical recovery. We can view *Ron Carlson Writes a Story* as a narrative history, a self-reflexive series of reflections on the rhetorical choices that went into his creative production, as well as a document that involves all of the basic aspects of any historical writing: sociohistorical context; pedagogical and ideological background; serendipity; and new relational encounters.

Given this example among so many others, and though Ritter and Vanderslice have rightly encouraged us to collect lore in the hopes of "moving beyond personal anecdote and myth"[25] in our scholarship, I'm hesitant to jettison anything from the House of Lore no matter how bogus or counterfeit it seems. My fear is that by too hastily discarding myth and anecdote, we annihilate the histories of how works came into being. For if we are truly to follow Hesse's call in "The Place of Creative Writing in Composition Studies" to "examine writerly activities and processes,"[26] then our investigations should be as inclusive as possible, and should aim to understand where that advice comes from and how it continues to be deployed. We're at an odd moment in creative writing where many lore-based tidbits have been so overused in the classroom and in the archive of writers on writing (e.g., "Write what you know") that they have become cliché.[27] It would seem, at least on some level, that experimental pedagogies need to break free from the past and from unenlightened or unexamined traditions of teaching; but is it in fact the lore itself or only our understanding of lore that needs a fresh look? We seem to be on the verge of, or in the midst of, a paradigm shift within creative writing studies. While D.G. Myers's *The Elephants Speak* paved the way, the topic of history and historiography is only recently finding its way in journal articles and creative writing studies scholarship. Our field is beginning to do, in earnest, what many disciplines do—looking at our own disciplinary histories and place in the academy not only as foundational but as instrumental in shaping our future work. The imprimatur of history may come with added conceptual or practical questions, but no one can deny a fundamental importance in looking at the development of ideas over time.

Lore 2.0

Although I have defended lore as a fuel for writerly production, this is not to say that we should indiscriminately reinforce the status quo in creative writing pedagogy, which still relies heavily on "institutional-conventional wisdom." Rather I'm looking to put a new frame on lore, "Lore 2.0": a self-conscious, self-reflexive, skeptical curating of lore that emphasizes prosumer creative literacy, and reflects remix culture of today. The best way to treat lore, in other words, is to hand agency over to our students. We stand at a slightly different vantage point with respect to lore in 2017 than we did in the earliest inquiries into creative writing studies and the resistance of lore. This is particularly relevant to composing in the digital era, when there is an enormous body of information, communal, reasonably accessible, and not necessarily sourced. Apprentice writers are already seeking out this material on their own, so why don't we try to engage with it and connect with students at the level of lore? We certainly still need to be wary of accepting unexamined beliefs that give rise to counterfeit pedagogy and stereotyping. But these corrections can often be done *within* the House of Lore, not necessarily from *without*. Lan Samantha Chang, for instance, remembers when Frank Conroy, at the time the director of the Iowa Writers' Workshop, advised her: "If you don't want to be typecast, don't keep writing stories about Chinese-American characters."[28] Chang did not follow his advice. Today she holds the same position Conroy once did, as the director of Iowa's workshop, and has many acclaimed books to her name. This particular story about Conroy, which she has shared in interviews and likely with her own students, is now lore in its own right, and works as a corrective for the lore of a previous generation.

Of course, Lore 2.0 has resonances to Web 2.0, and the added frame of "2.0" might be a handy way to consider the networked way that students are interacting with lore. The degree to which digital tools, new media, and networked culture have affected writers and writing is one of the key compositional questions of our time.[29] Student writers are surrounded by narrative accounts of composing, whether in the form of Elizabeth Gilbert's TED Talk on "Your Elusive Creative Genius," Octavia Butler's inspirational letter to herself (featured on The Huntington Library's Instagram), the Foo Fighters' documentary project *Sonic Highways*, Jerry Seinfeld's *Comedians in Cars Getting Coffee*, various advice-related Twitter accounts like "Quotes for Writers" or *Writers Digest* that post writing aphorisms and how-to briefs, the Twitter accounts of publishing writers, countless podcasts devoted to discussions of art and artistry, or the ever-popular National Novel Writing Month (NaNoWriMo). New media outlets serve as conduits for collective wisdom and encourage input—and user-generated content—from professionals and non-specialists alike.

Given this context, it's almost impossible to dismiss lore as an unfortunate by-product of the institutional machine. In fact, lore has become instrumental in our field's sociality and its connection to popular culture. Harper, among others, has noted the "interconnection" and "reciprocal human connectedness" made possible through "synaptic technologies."[30] Additionally, Chris W. Gallagher asserts that "teaching and learning ... are acts and arts of engagement, and they succeed or fail on the strength of *relationships*."[31] If creative writing studies neglects to acknowledge the potency of process narratives in forming our field's social bonds, we might lose the most essential source of our pedagogical persuasiveness.

In *Ron Carlson Writes a Story*, Carlson writes: "I've also become convinced that a writer's confidence in his or her process is as important as any accumulated craft dexterity or writing 'skill.'"[32] This is a marked turn away from what has been drummed into creative writing students: "writing is a craft" and "only craft can be taught."[33] This notion of craft has been one of the hallmarks of creative writing pedagogy in the Program Era, and even "craft" discussions have become a kind of lore in and of themselves. But perhaps we should begin taking a wider view: and acknowledge that lore may help us identify how and why one student develops a process he or she believes in while another may not.

As creative writing studies continues to emerge and define itself as a socially-attuned field—both in scholarship and in pedagogical preoccupations—I predict we will need to keep actively addressing the alternate histories of people, languages, ideologies, and pedagogies. We should continue our mining of tidbits of lore, reminding ourselves that lore, when viewed via the philosophy of history, is a potential source of sociality for our field, as well as of writerly confidence, rather than mere confidence trick. I encourage teachers and scholars in creative writing studies to engage with—in the form of remixing/revising rather than discarding—the archive of writers on writing with this new framework in mind. Simultaneous acceptance and resistance of lore defines the condition contemporary students face; let's meet them there.

Notes

1   Ritter, Kelly and Stephanie Vanderslice. "Teaching Lore: Creative Writers and the University." *Profession* (2005), 105.

2   Ritter, Kelly and Stephanie Vanderslice. "Creative Writing and the Persistence of Lore" in Kelly Ritter and Stephanie Vanderslice (eds), *Can It Really Be Taught? Resisting Lore in Creative Writing Pedagogy* (Portsmouth, NH: Boynton/Cook Heinemann, 2007), xvi.

3   North, Stephen M. *The Making of Knowledge in Composition: Portrait of an Emerging Field* (Portsmouth, NH: Boynton, 1987), 29.

4   Prior, Paul. "Tracing Process: How Texts Come Into Being" in Charles Bazerman and Paul Prior (eds), *What Writing Does and How It Does It* (Mahwah, NJ: Routledge, 2004), 171.

5   Harper, Graeme. "Creative Writing in the Age of Synapses" in Michael Dean Clark, Trent Hergenrader, and Joseph Rein (eds), *Creative Writing in the Digital Age: Theory, Practice, and Pedagogy* (London: Bloomsbury Academic, 2015), 14.

6   Pickering, Andrew. *The Mangle of Practice* (Chicago: University of Chicago Press, 1995).

7   North, *The Making of Knowledge in Composition: Portrait of an Emerging Field*, 28.

8   North here refers to practitioners as "relatively free agents."

9   See Steve Healey's "Beyond the Literary: Why Creative Literacy Matters" in Donnelly and Harper's *Key Issues in Creative Writing*, as well as Healey's "Creative Literacy Pedagogy" in Hunley and Peary's *Creative Writing Pedagogies for the Twenty-first Century*.

10 Harkin, Patricia. "The Postdisciplinary Politics of Lore" in Patricia Harkin and John Schlib (eds), *Contending With Words* (New York: MLA, 1991), 125.

11 Rittter and Vanderslice, "Creative Writing and the Persistence of Lore," xvi (emphasis mine).

12 Hesse, Douglas. "The Place of Creative Writing in Composition Studies." *College Composition and Communication* 62.1 (2010), 33.

13 Wickman, Forrest. "Who Really Said You Should 'Kill Your Darlings?'" *Slate* (October 18, 2013). http://www.slate.com/blogs/browbeat/2013/10/18/_kill_your_darlings_writing_a dvice_what_writer_really_said_to_murder_your.html

14 Rittter and Vanderslice, "Creative Writing and the Persistence of Lore," xix.

15 Sirc, Geoffrey. "Resisting Entropy." *College Composition and Communication* 63.3 (2012), 511.

16 Katharine Haake quoted in Mayers, Tim. *(Re)Writing Craft: Composition, Creative Writing, and the Future of English Studies* (Pittsburgh: University of Pittsburgh Press, 2005), 59.

17 Mayers, *(Re)Writing Craft,* 13.

18 North, *The Making of Knowledge in Composition: Portrait of an Emerging Field*, 29.

19 The American-Heritage Dictionary, s.v. "recovery," https://ahdictionary.com/word/search.html?q=recovery [accessed July 18, 2016].

20 Lowenthal, David. *The Past Is a Foreign Country* (New York: Cambridge University Press, 1985), xvii.

21 North, *The Making of Knowledge in Composition: Portrait of an Emerging Field*, 27.

22 Rittter and Vanderslice, "Creative Writing and the Persistence of Lore," xvii.

23 Bizzaro, Patrick. "Writers Wanted: A Reconsideration of Wendy Bishop." *College English* 71.3 (2009): 263.

24 Spinuzzi, Clay. "Reading: The Mangle of Practice." Spinuzzi: A Blog About Rhetoric, Technology, Research, and Where We're Headed Next. (August 11, 2004). http://spinuzzi.blogspot.com/2007/01/reading-mangle-of-practice.html

25 Rittter and Vanderslice, "Creative Writing and the Persistence of Lore," xv.

26 Hesse, "The Place of Creative Writing in Composition Studies," 43.

27 This phenomenon has historical forbearers. For example, Erasmus, Montaigne, and others rejected the use of Ciceronian stock phrases, which were being used in increasingly formulaic ways, with the ideas themselves increasingly emptied out of meaning by imitation of Cicero's style.

28 Neary, Lynn. "In Elite MFA Programs, The Challenge of Writing While 'Other.'" (August 19, 2014). http://www.npr.org/sections/codeswitch/2014/08/19/341363580/in-elite-mfa-programs-the-challenge-of-writing-while-other

29 In addition to recent collections such as *Creative Writing in the Digital Age*, Adam Koehler provides an excellent overview of the disciplinary and craft-related pedagogical questions related to creative writing's digital turn ("Digitizing craft: Creative writing studies and new media: A proposal." *College English* 75.4 (2013): 379–97.)

30 Harper, "Creative Writing in the Age of Synapses," 8.

31 Gallagher, Chris W. "Being There: (Re)Making the Assessment Scene." *College Composition and Communication* 62.3 (2011): 463. http://www.jstor.org/stable/27917908

32 Carlson, Ron. *Ron Carlson Writes a Story* (Saint Paul: Graywolf, 2007), 4.

33 McFarland quoted in Hesse, "The Place of Creative Writing in Composition Studies," 36.

References

Bizzaro, Patrick. "Writers Wanted: A Reconsideration of Wendy Bishop." *College English* 71.3, 2009: 256–70.

Carlson, Ron. *Ron Carlson Writes a Story*. Saint Paul, MN: Graywolf, 2007.

Gallagher, Chris W. "Being There: (Re)Making the Assessment Scene." *College Composition and Communication* 62.3, 2011: 450–76.

Harkin, Patricia. "The Postdisciplinary Politics of Lore." In *Contending With Words*, edited by Patricia Harkin and John Schlib. New York: MLA, 1991, 124–38.

Harper, Graeme. "Creative Writing in the Age of Synapses." In *Creative Writing in the Digital Age: Theory, Practice, and Pedagogy*, edited by Michael Dean Clark, Trent Hergenrader, and Joseph Rein. London: Bloomsbury Academic, 2015, 7–16.

Hesse, Douglas. "The Place of Creative Writing in Composition Studies." *College Composition and Communication* 62.1, 2010: 31–52.

Lowenthal, David. *The Past Is a Foreign Country*. New York: Cambridge University Press, 1985.

Mayers, Tim. *(Re)Writing Craft: Composition, Creative Writing, and the Future of English Studies*. Pittsburgh: University of Pittsburgh Press, 2005.

Neary, Lynn. "In Elite MFA Programs, The Challenge of Writing While 'Other,'" *Code Switch: Race and Identity, Remixed* (blog), NPR.org, August 19, 2014, http://www.npr.org/sections/codeswitch/2014/08/19/341363580/in-elite-mfaprograms-the-challenge-of-writing-while-other.

North, Stephen M. *The Making of Knowledge in Composition: Portrait of an Emerging Field*. Upper Montclair, NJ: Boynton/Cook Publishers, 1987.

Pickering, Andrew. *The Mangle of Practice: Time, Agency, and Science*. Chicago: University of Chicago Press, 1995.

Prior, Paul. "Tracing Process: How Texts Come Into Being." In *What Writing Does and How It Does It*, edited by Charles Bazerman and Paul Prior. Mahwah, NJ: Routledge, 2004, 167–200.

Ritter, Kelly and Stephanie Vanderslice. "Teaching Lore: Creative Writers and the University." *Profession* (2005): 102–12.

Ritter, Kelly and Stephanie Vanderslice. "Creative Writing and the Persistence of Lore." In *Can It Really Be Taught? Resisting Lore in Creative Writing Pedagogy*, edited by Kelly Ritter and Stephanie Vanderslice, Portsmouth, NH: Boynton/Cook Heinemann, 2007, xi–xx.

Sirc, Geoffrey. "Resisting Entropy." *College Composition and Communication* 63.3 (2012): 507–19.

Spinuzzi, Clay. "Reading: The Mangle of Practice," *Spinuzzi: A Blog About Rhetoric, Technology, Research, and Where We're Headed Next*. August 11, 2004, http://spinuzzi.blogspot.com/2007/01/reading-mangle-of-practice.html.

White, Hayden V. *Metahistory: The Historical Imagination in Nineteenth-century Europe*. Baltimore: Johns Hopkins University Press, 1973.

Wickman, Forrest. "Who Really Said You Should 'Kill Your Darlings?'" *Slate*, October 18, 2013, http://www.slate.com/blogs/browbeat/2013/10/18/_kill_your_darlings_writing_a dvice_what_writer_really_said_to_murder_your.html

9

"We don't need no creative writing":

Black Cultural Capital, Social (In)Justice, and the Devaluing of Creativity in Higher Education

Tonya C. Hegamin

Hidden behind the statistical relationships between educational capital or social origin and this or that type of knowledge or way of applying, there are relationships between (and within) groups maintaining different, and even antagonistic, relations to culture, depending on the conditions in which they acquired their cultural capital and the markers in which they can derive most profit from it (my addition in italics).[1]

I want to talk about anger, about how important it is as a part of the process of coming to one's voice, about how it is inevitable in a diverse classroom. . . . If we don't recognize anger . . . if we don't, in fact, welcome it as a creative force, then I think we're going to end up blaming and dividing people even more.[2]

". . . the myth [is] that Creative Writing is a neutral space that is just about teaching craft, when in fact, it is not a neutral space."[3]

Imagine, if you will, a minor conference room at a small, predominantly black, urban institution of higher education. The walls are decorated with gilded Egyptian papyrus, beautifully framed. Hathor, bovine-headed goddess of the muse, gazes down at an oval table. High backed, maroon leather chairs cradle three women of various shades of brown and various levels of graduate degrees (MA, MFA and PhD), and each occupy different levels of academic hierarchy; one is an academic affairs administrator (AA), one is an untenured assistant professor (UAP) in the English department and coordinator of the Creative Writing Concentration, the other a full professor and chair of the Education department (DC). They are on a compulsory hiring committee, conducting interviews for an administrative position; it is and probably will be one of the only times these three would find themselves together. As they wait for the next applicant, the small talk topic meanders to problems with students and their lack of preparation, especially in writing.

> AA: I can't believe how poorly our student interns write. I spend so much time just revising their work I can hardly do my own!
>
> UAP: You should try teaching writing and grading papers! It's SO painful.
>
> AA (laughing):   Yeah, what *are* you all teaching in the English department?
>
> UAP (feeling slightly slighted):   Well, we *are* understaffed and not really equipped to teach standard academic English to students who are not even proficient in standard written English. Most of our students speak English as a second or third language. They have me teaching remedial writing but I'm not trained in that field! I mean, I can teach creative writing to remedial and mid-level students to help them to express themselves, to root themselves in revision, language, and craft, which is important . . . ."
>
> DC (sucking her teeth):   Our students don't need no creative writing! They need the basics!

A knock on the door announces the next candidate. The conversation ends, but the implication hangs above the untenured professor like a thick and rigid noose.

In his recent book, *Where Everybody Looks Like Me: At the Crossroads of America's Black Colleges and Culture*, Ron Stodghill interviews Johnny Taylor, president and CEO of the Thurgood Marshall College Fund, whose job it is to not only be a representative and resource for black students, but to also examine and hold Historically Black Colleges and Universities (HBCUs) and predominantly black colleges to task for their recent decline in enrollment and rise in corruption:

> 'That's the new black on black crime,' [Taylor] said. 'If you're going to take the unprepared or underprepared student, you have a moral

obligation to make good on somebody investing twenty-five thousand dollars a year. That means over four years these kids have given you a hundred thousand dollars. If that kid has given you a hundred thousand dollars, his parents and grandparents and everybody else have made huge sacrifices. If that kid leaves your university unable to really compete in the job market, shame on you, shame on you."[4]

What Taylor is saying is absolutely true; however, what isn't acknowledged is that most higher education institutions in America are run in exactly the same way. Many students, regardless of race or class take an average of four years to graduate from associate degrees, and often six years to complete a bachelor's degree because of financial or personal reasons. Although HBCUs and predominantly black colleges provide a microcosm to see these issues amplified, the specific problem or answer is not solely due to black students, teachers, or administrators. The "new black on black crime" is black educational institutions falling in line with the dominant paradigm for survival, adopting not only dominant culture as the highest valued currency, but also adopting the capitalist business models as their organizational system. Most black institutions also admit an increasing portion of international, Hispanic, Asian, and white students; they, too, have to practice inclusion to remain relevant in the global job market. We need to effectively reach students on creative levels in ways that might eventually innovate the system, to use their cultural currency for empowerment. Giving students, "just the basics" is not what college is for, nor should we try to fool ourselves that any one department, or even a whole school is responsible for any one set of students' failure or success—the problem is a Hydra that cannot be defeated with one sword.

Educational access is rooted in the promise of economic and cultural capital that U.S. higher education institutions blatantly and rampantly market today. "You can't get a job without a college degree" is parroted all over the country, yet a quality education is a dangling carrot for many who cannot or will not access the dominant economic or cultural systems. This essay examines the clash between black cultural capital and academic capital highlighted because of the racist, classist economic system many HBCUs and predominantly black colleges have been forced to adopt that then reduces the innate value of black creativity and skews interpretations of taste based on the dominant paradigm of U.S. educational system. In addition, the national epidemic of police and civilian violence toward young people of color and the Black Lives Matter movement heightens the need for creative writing skills and the valuing of black and cross-cultural capital, especially in urban and highly inclusive institutions.

Pierre Bourdieu's seminal work *Distinction* is a study on how "taste" is based not only on a personal aesthetic but a means of perpetuating dominant class structures, mainly via culture and education, in other words, ". . . art and cultural consumption are predisposed, consciously and deliberately or not, to fulfil a social function of legitimating social differences"[5] and that ultimately, "[t]astes (i.e., manifested preferences) are the practical affirmation of an inevitable difference . . . because each taste feels itself to be natural— and so it almost is, being a habitus—amounts to rejecting others as unnatural."[6] In a predominantly black college, the need for access to a higher class status is at a premium because of the realities of racism, classism, and heterosexism. How do black schools and students advance when their cultural capital is viewed as "unnatural" by the dominant class? Unlike in the past, black college administrators are not only competing with other HBCUs, but with predominantly white institutions that may have the similar limited resources and low enrollment/retention rates, but because they are simply not predominantly black, they carry a higher cultural currency in the workforce. Students become dollar signs and for those who have already been disenfranchised from the educational system as well as from the dominant social system, college life presents a crossroads for their personal and cultural expression and how one will fair in "the real world."

The previous conference room dramatic reenactment is indicative of the paranoid schizophrenia or "institutional low self-esteem" that many predominantly black colleges are suffering across the states. The question of what is valuable *for* our students is not necessarily answered by what is valuable *to* their current or aspired social or economic position. As an educator at a predominantly black four-year college, I know that creative writing is important and transformational for students in multiple ways and for multiple reasons. Students cite that my Creative Writing classes help them to better articulate themselves and "to see people and situations from a variety of alternate perspectives." They leave my classes understanding the importance of form and the craft of standard and vernacular language, but also with a respect for their own voices and experiences. They even get strategies for moving linguistically between their own "mother tongue" and the dominant culture. However, since I began coordinating the Creative Writing Concentration in our English department, I have had to fight to have my credentials and publications acknowledged and translated into a tenure track position, and I still receive no teaching credit for the administrative work that I do running the Creative Writing Concentration that graduates the most majors in the entire department. In this struggle, I realized that I wasn't only fighting to be acknowledged by white mainstream culture, but to be accepted by black academic "petite bourgeois" culture, which in turn, is struggling to be accepted by and to perpetuate/replicate white academic bourgeois culture. I began to absorb the "institutional low self-esteem" syndrome by questioning the value of the subjects I taught as well as the value of my own field of study. Bourdieu found that:

> Dominated life-styles . . . which have practically never received (*or been equally valued for*) systematic expression, are almost always perceived, even by their defenders, from the destructive or reductive viewpoint of

the dominant aesthetic, so that their only options are degradation, or self-destructive rehabilitation (my additions in italics).[7]

What, I wondered, could these "unprepared, underprepared" students really get from majoring in Creative Writing? I was brutally honest with my students about my own experiences being "the only one" in all-white classes, something they could barely fathom since many live in uber diverse Brooklyn. I stayed awake wondering: What was I really preparing my students for?

Very few black students apply to MFA programs; fewer are accepted. Against my advice, one of my students applied to several top-tier graduate programs. I tried to suggest low-residency programs or non-academic programs to start with because although her writing was passable in our school, it was still sub-par according to most graduate standards, and it was from a distinctively black cultural perspective. She refused my advice and was rejected from everywhere she applied. Another student, a queer identified Haitian-American woman whose work was strong from a mainstream perspective, was interested in applying to an MFA, but the internalized racism she felt at our predominantly black school against her country, culture, and sexuality was too debilitating for her emotionally to put herself "on the block" for an all-white audience. A Chinese-American student has been applying to the same two programs for almost two years—although her work is innovative, her insecurities about code-switching and anxiety of "getting the English right" has kept her from submitting any of her applications, even with my extensive editing and support. She also struggles with her family not supporting her creative endeavors, and describes her life as spent "alone in my room writing fan-fiction," yet she cannot envision herself living away from home, much less going to a graduate program where she would have to fully acculturate herself into a white-washed world. One African-American student described how she had taken a literature class at one of our "sister" schools within CUNY, and found herself to be "the only one." When the professor found out her home school, he spoke at length about what he felt was a "ridiculous" paper one of our faculty members wrote which speculated on the cultural blackness of Gatsby in *The Great Gatsby*, as though this student were somehow responsible, somehow to blame. "He talked as though he would have rather spit on our school than walk past it," she said. "I never felt embarrassed to go to this school until then. I always do well in literature but I failed that class." Many students feel the same:

At the college level, we may also find evidence of **stereotype threat**. According to psychologist Claude Steele, stereotype threat is 'the threat of being viewed through the lens of a negative stereotype, or the fear of doing something that would inadvertently confirm that stereotype.' This sense of social mistrust may cause some African-American writers . . . fear that their scores will confirm negative stereotypes . . . (bold in text).[8]

Creativity is a life force for many of us who have occupied the privileged spaces of undergraduate and/or graduate creative degree granting programs; we see creativity as the most basic expression of our humanity. Not all of us see the depth of that privilege, or acknowledge that it is a place of privilege. For those of us who went to good high schools, good colleges, and good graduate programs, the entitlement that a "good" education provides is an invisible extension of ourselves. I am admittedly one of those people, however my entitled stance is mired in otherness—I identify as African-American, bisexual, and am differently abled. However, since I appear multi-ethnic, straight, and the difference in my abilities isn't easily detected, I have spent large portions of my life explaining myself to white and black peers: defending my race, my color, my sexuality, and my learning/physical abilities. "Stereotype Threat" affected me deeply in my educational experience, I was often asked to represent my race in all-white spaces since I started school; I experienced physical and sexual violence as well as verbal bullying by black peers for "acting white" because I was into books, spoke standard English, was tracked into 'gifted' programs and lived in a predominantly white neighborhood. I was similarly harassed by white peers just for being in that same neighborhood. I was called nigger more than once before I was in second grade and some of my white peers were not allowed to have me in their homes, even though my parents both had white collar jobs. Our cultural ideals of "distinction" can create spaces where "[a] esthetic intolerance can be terribly violent. Aversion to different life-styles is perhaps one of the strongest barriers between (*and within*) the classes . . ." (my addition in italics).[9] One of the ways I healed myself was through exploring black literature and history.

In the Pitt library, during my sophomore year, I found the anthology *This Bridge Called My Back* edited by Cherrie Moraga and Gloria Anzaldua. In it was Kate Rushin's "The Bridge Poem":

> I will not be the bridge to your womanhood
> Your manhood
> Your human-ness
> I'm sick of reminding you not to
> Close off too tight for too long
> I'm sick of mediating with your worst self
> On behalf of your better selves[10]

Those words are still a balm for me, simply because they acknowledged that I was not "the only one" after all. Back when I was a kid, I would sit in the bookstore and lose myself in the shelves and stacks, opening books as though they were beautiful bottled messages and I had washed upon *their* shores. Because of the minimal cultural capital black literature held in 1980s rural Pennsylvania, few books sold there were written by people of color; I had to "borrow" those books from adult family members—it was a desperate search mission. Years later, Rushin's poem resonated with me like a beacon, a warning that I could not rest until I set sail on my own journey, untethered from the messages other people had left behind. I photocopied the poem and plastered it all over campus. I desperately needed to be heard, to be understood. It was at that time that I took my first poetry class with Toi Derricotte.

Toi embraced us all with her effervesce, her honesty, and her passion for the word. I finally felt at home in my writing self—I produced more work in her class than I ever had, and I had been filling notebooks since I was twelve. I had only had two black teachers throughout my entire education until then—both were math and science teachers. There were no limits to where I could stretch my imagination just because Toi Derricotte existed and wanted to read what I wrote, she allowed me to see my worth. That was probably one of the most powerful times I have ever felt in my life. She quoted Red Smith in class and in her book *The Black Notebooks*: "There is nothing to writing; all you have to do is sit down and open up a vein,"[11] which I still quote to my students today. In her class I learned how deep my need to write was in a space where my cultural capital was valued, that it wasn't a frivolous or "white" endeavor. I could share all of the parts of myself I had kept hidden and an understanding nod from Toi was immensely validating and motiving—she encouraged me to be myself. We read Cornelius Eady, Li Young Lee, and Marilyn Hacker. I experimented with forms like sestinas and produced an entire chapbook. At home, my family told me that majoring in Poetry was fruitless, that I couldn't make money writing full time, that I should "just" be a teacher and write during the summers "if I still wanted." I faced deep internalized fear of black creative cultural capital's ability to maintain middle-class status and using expression for means of obtaining economic capital. Although these fears of the value of a creative writing degree is common in most middle-class homes, it is amplified exponentially within the cultural subtext.

Despite this, Toi gave me license and freedom to say what I felt unabashedly—to heal the fear, isolation, and resulting rage, to take risks in my work, my life; to this day my gratitude makes me uncontrollably emotional whenever I see her. She and Cornelius have introduced and connected now nearly an army of poets to a new way of living (and making a living); they have created constellations of poetry rock stars. When she first told me that she and Cornelius were going to start a retreat for black poets, she might as well have said she had a flying rainbow unicorn in her back pocket—I didn't believe it could be possible. I didn't believe there could be enough black poets in the world to make it happen, a result of my own internalized racism but also because at the time I was the only black undergrad majoring in Creative Writing. I know that Toi and other writers of color have had to fight to get their credentials and publications recognized by white institutions because it is based on a racist dominant ideology of "taste" that consistently dismisses black cultural currency as inherently inferior, but I did not expect it to be so in a predominantly black institution. The symbol for the Cave Canem organization is a black dog with a broken chain, a metaphor for the one who has been kept now breaking free. The symbol is not specifically about physical freedom, but more about mental and emotional slavery—as much about how we enslave ourselves as we are enslaved by others.

Black cultural capital is complicated because what is produced and consumed by the masses is most often funded by white capital, therefore often skewing its presentation. There are currently more black millionaires and even billionaires who have turned this practice a few degrees, however most who create black culture are not able to be sustained solely by black audiences. Black cultural capital encompasses literature, fine arts, fashion, music/dance, and other creative expression. However, when I was growing up and for many in the African-American middle class, the assumption was that ". . . black cultural capital does not yield students high academic marks, get them into college, or even acquire them jobs."[12] But now more than ever, students of color are more interested in careers producing cultural capital that rejects (or seems to reject) the dominant paradigm. Black Lives Matter has created a class of activist entrepreneurs who invest back into their communities to create more cultural and economic capital. It has also brought awareness to those in privileged white spaces that there is an undeniable issue that must be addressed as an American problem. This same movement has created a critical need for autonomous and authentic creative expression to heal the fear and rage that inhabits many young people's lives.

Prudence L. Carter studied high school students in Yonkers, New York to discover the power of cultural capital in urban educational settings in her 2005 book, *Keepin' It Real: Why School Success Has No Color*. Based partially on Bourdieu's *Distinction*, she found that "[f]or many African-American students, non-dominant, or more specifically 'black,' cultural capital matters because it signifies in-group allegiance and preserves a sense of belonging"[13] and that "[a]nother function of black cultural capital is to create a coherent, positive self-image (or set of images) in the face of hardship or subjugation."[14] Students clung to black cultural capital because it gave them a sense of purpose, especially in educational systems that refused to acknowledge the powerful contributions of black cultural capital to American culture. However, students who refused to accept dominant culture traits in institutional settings (like wearing urban fashion or maintaining black vernacular in their speech at school) were often dismissed as being disinterested or somehow less capable in academic performance. Most of these students feel disempowered by their education because they no longer readily buy into the dominant paradigm. Because of the devaluing of education in today's world (there are more millionaires without degrees than with one), the increasing easily accessible and non-traditional/non-dominant knowledge and perspectives available on the Internet, they recognize the institution as stiflingly racist, classist, and heterosexist. Bourdieu also found that:

> The structural de-skilling of a whole generation, who are bound to get less out of their qualifications than the previous generation would have obtained, engenders a sort of collective disillusionment: a whole generation, finding it has been taken for a ride, is inclined to extend to all institutions the mixture of revolt and resentment it feels towards the educational system.[15]

Considering the display of violence that young people experience, students are in especially dire need of creative agency. Creativity and creative communication is a necessity in our educational system not only for generating innovative, divergent thinkers but also to promote cross-cultural access and communication.

Although many Creative Writing teachers embrace the range of emotions that students inhabit and encourage it to be expressed in their writing, many would like to only focus on craft to distance themselves from the sticky ectoplasm of feelings. I admit to feeling the same way at times, I wish it were simpler, more straightforward, that "the basics" were all that was necessary. I have developed strict rubrics that make sure students adhere to form and structure because that is a tool to be used within and sometimes even against the dominant paradigm. I focus on craft when I'm feeling the weight of the same paradigm, when I need to feel validated by a mainstream audience, but that is not what brings me to the page, it does not sustain my creative life force. I know many Creative Writing educators who would rather teach "tangible skills" than have to evaluate subjective expression. I don't blame them or myself for needing distance in this way, but I must remember that without these murky waters of expression the potentially transgressive workshop is essentially reduced to a glorified typing class.

Occasionally I use a craft prompt that requires students to write about a meaningful, painful experience from their lives in the second person. They are meant to detach themselves from the experience by writing in this way, to describe the emotions as if they were an instruction manual. After, the work is given to another classmate who then re-writes the piece in first person and finally reads the work aloud. One of my students, "O", a heavily tattooed young man with cornrows and a tough, streetwise demeanor, had his work read aloud by an openly gay and pagan male student, "P". O had written about his grandmother's death and how she had raised and protected him from succumbing to the streets. As P read the piece in first person, O kept his head down and began to visibly shake with emotion. P could see this and paused, looking at me for guidance. I didn't react because I wanted to see how things unfolded. P continued to read the emotional tribute, how O had sat by his grandmother's hospital bed for weeks, witnessing dismissive and sub-par care by the white hospital staff while watching his beloved grandmother die. When he equated his experience with the death of his innocence, the entire class, myself included, was unable to contain our sympathy. I could see tears dropping from O's face onto his notebook, and P's voice wavered. He looked at me again, wondering if he should stop but I encouraged him to keep going. To my surprise, P put his hand lightly on O's shoulder in support; I steadied myself for O's response. In our school, homophobia is rampant and the administration does not do much to change that. P was a student who waded through name calling and obvious disdain from not only students but also from teachers. O was a sincere student, but also a part of the dominant heterosexist culture and within that culture it was important to maintain a highly masculine persona. To my surprise, he lifted his head slightly and grasped P's hand quickly with obvious gratitude. After that, the class applauded loudly and there was not only congratulations for O's courage for writing, but also for P's sensitivity during the reading. After many tears were wiped from many eyes, I asked O to reflect in his journal on not only writing the piece in second person, but also about hearing it read by someone else in first person.

> O: When I wrote it I still thought about it from far away, you know. I haven't gotten emotional about my grandma in years. I had pushed it away, and writing in the "you" voice did the same thing. I kept my distance. When I heard someone else read it like he had experienced it too, I felt sympathy for him more than me. Then I remembered that it WAS me. He wasn't just him, he was me, too.

That type of experiential learning can really only happen in a Creative Writing classroom. Not only did it help this student access parts of himself, but it allowed him to see past the labels forced upon P, and to see him as a fellow human. Carter poses that:

> If we can figure out how to acknowledge and affirm the multiple capitals that exist while avoiding the structuring of achievement by race and ethnicity, then we could be one step closer [to] increasing these students' attachment and engagement in school.[16]

Creative Writing, when taught with compassion and sensitivity, has the ability to "acknowledge and affirm . . . multiple capitals" because it is dependent on a multiplicity of perspectives, even in homogeneous classrooms. Teaching students how to respond critically to all types of texts is paramount, but so is teaching them how to respond to the text in their own way, even if it rails against the dominant culture. However, it is up to the teacher to open the space for "difficult" emotions to exist as a part of the creative process, to commit to exploring craft's effect on emotion and vice versa. A transgressive creative classroom is key to the larger problem of institutionalized education. Inclusivity is deeper than a marginalized student sitting in a classroom as "the only one," that perspective must be included, no, embraced, in the dominant paradigm or else diversity is meaningless. The value of that student must be recognized and supported with examples of how they are not alone. The disenfranchisement of an entire generation depends on it; if black, brown, yellow, queer, and differently abled creative perspectives are dismissed as "unnatural" or of lesser value there will never be cross-cultural or intercultural communication that can lead to peace. At this critical point in history, it is not enough that MFA or undergrad Creative Writing programs hire a few teachers of color who have been accepted and valorized by the dominant culture, they have to examine how students experience the classroom, how their expression is valued or dismissed by reading lists, teaching styles, peer micro-aggressions and alternative expression that goes beyond "the basics." It is even more important for HBCUs and predominantly black colleges to embrace black cultural capital as a valuable modality for healing as well as imperative for black cultural and economic gain. As Teresa Redd eloquently explains in her essay, "Keepin It Real: Delivering College Composition at an HBCU": ... *true power lies not only in the mastery of the game but the ability to change the rules ...*[17]

Notes

1   Pierre Bourdieu, *Distinction: A Social Critique of the Judgement of Taste.* Translated by Richard Nice (Cambridge: Harvard University Press, 1984), 1.

2   Toi Derricotte, *The Black Notebooks: An interior Journey* (New York: Norton, 1997), 125.

3   Stephanie Vanderslice, Personal Correspondence with Author, July 13, 2016.

4   Ron Stodghill, *Where Everybody Looks Like Me: At the Crossroads of America's Black Colleges and Culture* (HarperCollins: New York, 2015), 121.

5   Bourdieu, *Distinction,* 7.

6   Bourdieu, 56.

7   Bourdieu, 48.

8   Teresa M. Redd and Karen Schuster Webb, editors, *A Teacher's Introduction to African American English: What a Writing Teacher Should Know.* NCTE Teacher's Introduction Series (Urbana, IL: NCTE, 2005), 68–9.

9   Bourdieu, *Distinction,* 56.

10   Kate Rushin, "The Bridge Poem," *This Bridge Called My Back.* Edited by Cherrie Moraga and Gloria Anzaldua (New York: State University of New York Press, 2015), xxxiii).

11   Derricotte, *The Black Notebooks,* 121.

12   Prudence L. Carter. *Keepin' It Real: Why School Success Has No Color* (Cary, US: Oxford University Press US, 2005), 66.

13   Carter, 51.

14 Carter, 57.

15 Bourdieu, *Distinction*, 144.

16 Carter, *Keepin' It Real*, 76.

17 Theresa Redd, "Keepin' It Real: Delivering College Composition at an HBCU."
    Delivering College Composition. Ed. Kathleen Blake Yancey. (Portsmouth:
    Boynton/Cook, 2006), 84.

References

Bourdieu, Pierre. *Distinction: A Social Critique of the Judgement of Taste*.
    Translated by Richard Nice. Cambridge: Harvard University Press, 1984.

Carter, Prudence L. *Keepin' It Real: Why School Success Has No Color*. Cary, US:
    Oxford University Press (US), 2005.

Derricotte, Toi. *The Black Notebooks: An interior Journey*. New York: Norton,
    1997.

Redd, Theresa. "Keepin' It Real: Delivering College Composition at an HBCU."
    Delivering College Composition. Edited by Kathleen Blake Yancey. Portsmouth:
    Boynton/Cook, 2006.

Redd, Teresa M. and Karen Schuster Webb, eds. *A Teacher's Introduction to
    African American English: What a Writing Teacher Should Know*. Urbana, IL:
    NCTE Teacher's Introduction Series, 2005.

Rushin, Kate. "The Bridge Poem." Edited by Cherrie Moraga and Gloria Anzaldua.
    This Bridge Called My Back: Writings by Radical Women of Color, 7th edition.
    New York: State University of New York Press, 2015.

Stodghill, Ron. *Where Everybody Looks Like Me: At the Crossroads of America's
    Black Colleges and Culture*. HarperCollins: New York, 2015.

10

Genre Fiction, and Games, and Fanfiction! Oh My!:

Competing Realities in Creative Writing Classrooms

Trent Hergenrader

Conceits of the fiction writing workshop

This course requires all new fiction to be scene-based in the realist tradition. Therefore, none of the following will be allowed: fairies, vampires, horror, children's fiction, flying saucers, zombies, hobbits, laser guns, vigilante cops, anything related or derived from Lord of the Rings, Star Wars, Star Trek, *etc. Also be careful of derivative fiction:* The Sopranos, Leaving Las Vegas, *Quentin Tarrentino-esque [sic] fiction,* Stephen King-esque *fiction, etc. It is hard to write anything new about drunks, drug addicts, hit men, mobsters, and evil cars.*

Joshua, a former student of mine at the undergraduate level, posted to Facebook this excerpt from a Fiction Workshop syllabus along with the comment, "See Katharnia [a friend he tagged], no zombies or anything else I'm interested in." She ironically replied (all caps hers), "NO LASER GUNS?! WHAT'S WRONG WITH YOUR PROFESSOR?"[1]

As an instructor who writes science fiction, fantasy, and horror, I found this genre fiction injunction, and the underlying assumption about its inferiority, entirely unsurprising. What did surprise me, however, was the sophisticated way in which the subsequent comments deconstructed the genre ban. Kent, another former student of mine, wrote:

> I don't think [the instructor] cares too much for those kinds of genres, however, the reasoning was that it's good to practice writing "ordinary" life, with characters and events based in our reality. With science fiction and fantasy, you add a whole spectrum of new things to keep track of, keep consistent, and research. i.e. It's supposed to be less complicated.
>
> That said, [the instructor] does allow magical realism. Just make sure you don't accidentally write a fantasy story. [tongue emoticon]

Others soon added their opinions:

> Kyle: Shit sucks.
>
> Dave: I'm not seeing any prohibition on humans with superpowers on the list. just a thought.
>
> Kyle: Probably falls under that "etc" or maybe, by a stretch, vigilante cops
>
> Kyle: Also, if you have no horror, does that mean you can't have scenes where, say, a normal person is in realistic scary scenarios? Like can you not write a story about someone's house burning down while they're inside?
>
> Kent: I'm sure they mean supernatural horror. You could write about a vigilante cop who has mad parkour skills and BAM! You've got a Batman.
>
> Kyle: If I were in that class, I'd write a story that purposely has a bunch of tropes and stereotypical stuff hinting at the stuff that's not allowed, but never actually goes to it
>
> Dave: nice, kyle! suggested title for your story: "In Your Face".

Then another former student of mine, Ashley, popped in with her two cents:

> I will say that in my [Fiction Workshop], in general the stories that proved to be most problematic in terms of creating a realistic and believable world while also balancing the other key elements of good short stories were those that involved speculative elements. That's not to say that they shouldn't be allowed, but I guess you should just be sure that you can effectively cover an entirely different universe of stuff within the page limits. Because many of my peers (myself included) struggled with that. Also, fellow workshoppers who are not well-versed in the genre get hung up on details inherent to the genre that are unfamiliar to them, which results in an entirely unhelpful critique.

This online conversation helped crystalize a number of thoughts I'd been having regarding how the fiction workshop commonly operates in the academy. First, that the default for fiction courses should be literary realism. Second, that the tropes of genre fiction are necessarily entangled with media—the syllabus invokes film (*Leaving Las Vegas*, films of Quentin Tarantino), television (*The Sopranos*), and works that have been adapted from print to film or vice versa (*Lord of the Rings*, *Star Wars*, *Star Trek*, and the many works of Stephen King). Third, that it's "hard to write anything new" in genre fiction because it has been rehashed a billion times and is thus creatively exhausted. Rather than merely being a genre itself,[2] literary realism serves as a stylistic description *and* a judgment of quality.

The syllabus dismisses an awful lot in three sentences. The one nugget of truth is that young writers should attempt to bring a fresh perspective to their fiction, regardless of the subject matter—and I would add a reminder that it's not just tropes from genre fiction that feel stale if handled poorly. A professor in my graduate program often categorized student stories by using phrases like "a domestic plate-thrower" to describe fiction that dealt with marital angst. Tellingly, he did not use such phrases as judgments, but rather as a way to group stories that bore certain hallmarks so he could then better refer the writer to other work of that kind. For example, he might recommend the writer of a domestic plate-thrower read John Cheever to compare how he dealt with themes of suburban crisis. This mimetic approach to teaching the craft of fiction is a well-established approach in fiction workshop,[3] and happily it can be just as easily applied to genre fiction. A student writing on themes of first contact with an alien species could be referred to the work of Isaac Asimov or Arthur C. Clarke. This requires, however, that the instructor actually be familiar with such themes and authors in order to make a relevant recommendation.

What I found compelling in the Facebook thread is how the students recognized genre slipperiness better than their instructor. What separates magical realism from fantasy? How does the genre of horror differ from the detailed accounting of a horrific event? Is genre fiction too difficult for beginning writers, or does it disrupt the workshop format and render peer advice useless? Not only do these students find these questions interesting enough to debate on social media in their spare time, but the entire conversation was borne from frustration: why are the things we're interested in banned from this class?

A syllabus should not establish an oppositional relationship between the instructor and students from day one. This fundamental mismatch between an instructor's literary sensibilities and the interests of the students proves a serious obstacle to teaching and learning, but where do we locate the problem? In inferior genre fiction? In the poor taste of students who enjoy it? In the instructor who preemptively bans it? In a workshop model that (allegedly) can't handle it? Or is the problem actually that these two groups—the literary-minded instructor and genre-inclined student—are less in opposition than they are working at cross-purposes? I argue that the problem does not reside in the workshop format itself, but rather on the default assumptions on which such workshops are built.

A semiotic what? Why the writing workshop works, except when it doesn't

The workshop is creative writing's signature pedagogy[4] that encompasses a wide set of practices that are "not a packaged pedagogical tool set,"[5] as evidenced by the range of approaches described in Donnelly's *Does the Writing Workshop Still Work?* To these excellent examples of what constitutes a successful workshop, I wish to add a perspective drawn from the field of linguistics and literacy studies that helps explain why the workshop's success can vary so greatly between programs and even from class to class. The success of a creative writing class relies heavily on student motivation, which in turn relies on students feeling comfortable and confident as they work toward a common goal. I will leave aside for now what we mean by "success" or what that "common goal" might be, and instead introduce the related concepts that elucidate this point: that of *semiotic domains* and *affinity groups*.

In his landmark work *What Video Games Have to Teach Us About Learning and Literacy*, linguist James Paul Gee describes a semiotic domain in lay terms as "an area or set of practices where people think, act, and value in certain ways" and is defined by "any set of practices that recruits one of more modalities (e.g., oral or written language, images, equations, symbols, sounds, gestures, graphs, artifacts, etc.) to communicate distinctive types of meaning."[6] Some examples of semiotic domains include bird watching, physics, anime, or any area where people draw from, and contribute to, a body of knowledge around a specific topic.

To use an example from my own life, I've followed world soccer for nearly thirty years. I, and millions of other fans of international soccer, instantly recognize the crest of Real Madrid C.F. For people who participate in the semiotic domain of world soccer, this symbol could prompt a casual conversation between strangers about the play of Cristiano Ronaldo, the results of Madrid's recent Champions League match, and whether we think the away goal rule will decide the tie. A more casual fan who doesn't follow soccer closely may grasp bits of information in that preceding sentence, but they wouldn't be able to engage in a meaningful discussion; for those who don't follow soccer at all, the sentence is impenetrable jargon. Those who could instantly slide into the conversation are part of what Gee calls an *affinity group* for world soccer; the affinity group consists of people who operate comfortably within a semiotic domain and can easily recognize other "insiders." In Gee's words, members of an affinity group "recognize certain ways of thinking, acting, interacting, valuing, and believing as more or less typical of people who are into the semiotic domain."[7] Membership to an affinity group is fluid; in this example, a casual fan could watch a few more games, read some websites describing tournament rules, ask questions on online discussion boards, and over time become more at ease in the semiotic domain.

The concept extends to professional pursuits and includes distinctive sub-types as well. For example, new English graduate students will learn the general language of academia (e.g., tenure clock), the language specific to their discipline (e.g., Russian Formalism as a school of literary criticism) and then a highly specialized area of study (e.g., Bakhtinian heteroglossias). Feelings of belonging increase with experience and achievements. A well-received conference paper boosts confidence and encourages further participation; a few peer-reviewed publications cements a sense of belonging in that community; and with that positive feedback, the one-time student develops into a recognized authority in the given area. By the time one lands a tenure-track job, the academic community expects the person to contribute regularly to their field of scholarship.

The concepts of semiotic domains and affinity groups explain people's participation in careers and hobbies because their motivations are clear. The goal is not to be a passive recipient of information but rather an active participant in the domain. Furthermore, an active, critical learner

> needs to learn not only how to understand and produce meanings in a particular semiotic domain but, in addition, needs to learn how to think about the domain at a "meta" level as a complex system of interrelated parts. The learner also needs to learn how to innovate in the domain— how to produce meanings that, while recognizable to experts in the domain, are seen as somehow novel or unpredictable.[8]

Truly successful students are able to *innovate*—to take old forms and received knowledge and transform them into something new. This should ring true for any dedicated educator, and it also describes what we hope to accomplish in our creative writing classrooms. Even when we use the mimetic approach, we don't want students to replicate literary heavyweights, but rather adapt them into something unique.

Semiotic domains, affinity groups, and mastery within a specific domain have particular significance for the creative writing workshop, whose invention is commonly traced back to the Iowa Writers Workshop in 1922. It was then that the school began accepting creative work for advanced degrees and offered courses in writing where "selected students were tutored by resident and visiting writers"; during the Second World War the program admitted only a dozen students, but a number that would grow into hundreds in the post-war era.[9] The Iowa-style workshop became the model for the dozens of creative writing programs emerging around the country in the latter half of the twentieth century, but interestingly the program claims little credit for the accomplishments of its graduates:

> The fact that the Workshop can claim as alumni nationally and internationally prominent poets, novelists, and short story writers is, we believe, more the result of what they brought here than of what they gained from us. We continue to look for the most promising talent in the country, in our conviction that writing cannot be taught but that writers can be encouraged.[10]

Thus, what the lauded Iowa Workshop offered was not a revolutionary approach to teaching creative writing, nor was it muse-inspired magic; rather it offered the time and space for a carefully selected group of motivated, talented, like-minded writers to discuss literary craft. To use Gee's language, the Iowa Workshop provided an ideal environment for an affinity group to operate within the semiotic domain of literary publishing. The fact that the Iowa Workshop can state that its graduates have won every literary award on record[11] suggests innovation certainly occurred and the workshop proved to be a springboard to publishing success.

In an era when both communication and travel over long distances was slow, unreliable, and expensive, it makes sense that a like-minded (and largely homogenous) group working toward a common goal would gather for an extended period of time in a specific location to do their work. Given those conditions, it makes sense that the workshop proved to be a success at Iowa and elsewhere. As Gee notes, affinity groups operating within a specific domain of knowledge can be sites of deep learning—even if they have very little to do with deliberate pedagogical design. In addition, there's no mystical connection between workshop efficacy and a specific *literary* style of writing. Prominent speculative fiction workshops such as Clarion or the Odyssey Writing Workshop operate in very similar ways to MFA programs in that participants generally wish to break into traditional publishing. These workshops also have competitive application procedures and use variations of the traditional workshop method, but their semiotic domain is that of science fiction, fantasy, and horror. Most participants enter the workshop feeling comfortable and knowledgeable about contemporary speculative fiction short story markets and publishers. Like the Iowa Workshop, these programs too boast lists of distinguished, award-winning graduates.[12] Again, motivated people with common interests and a desire to share knowledge can be powerful learning communities.

Yet, perhaps counterintuitively, the growth of creative writing programs has meant the ideal conditions for the successful literary-minded workshop are less common today than in years past. Where there used to be a handful of graduate programs nationwide, AWP reports there are more than 400 degree-conferring programs in the United States today.[13] This means that the once concentrated talent pool for students and instructors alike is dispersed the length and breadth of the country and in programs abroad. Today our culture is far more engaged with the narratives of film, television, and video games than literary fiction, and the publishing industry—no longer dominated by a few New York publishing houses—has yet to come to terms with a digital revolution that has forever altered how people produce and consume texts. Thus, inspirations and aspirations for students' writing can be quite diverse. The demographics of the student body have changed too, as they include a more diverse group of people of different genders, races, economic classes, and sexual identities, with different values and experiences than the affluent whites who populated university classrooms for the majority of the last century. Finally, people no longer need to be physically present to participate in a workshop as the Internet facilitates instantaneous communication with virtually every corner of the globe. Low residency programs mean participants no longer need to put jobs or families on hold to pursue their degree, and thus their attention might be understandably divided. Given all these reasons, there is no guarantee that an MFA cohort will naturally form an affinity group eager to work in the semiotic domain of literary publishing. Some students want to write genre fiction with literary sensibilities; others may want to experiment with digital narratives or write for film or games; still others might be doing an MFA to demystify publishing; whereas some students will still be trying to land a major book deal with a New York publisher. Their instructors almost certainly fall in that last category, and we see the evidence of the frictions between students and instructors with every interview with a literary superstar who decries the MFA as pointless or claims creative writing can't be taught.

If the traditional workshop yields uneven results in today's graduate programs, it can be downright dysfunctional at the undergraduate level. AWP reports that nearly 1,300 universities offer creative writing minors or majors at the undergraduate level—that's three times the number of graduate programs. What are the chances that these programs possess the ideal conditions for the traditional writing workshop to work at the undergraduate level? What are the chances that the semiotic domain of literary culture will naturally exist? In the institution where I've taught, the answer is never. However, a well-designed curriculum can *introduce* students to the semiotic domain of literary publishing by focusing on craft terminology and critique skills and using the workshop sparingly, if at all. With the proper approach, this can be a positive learning experience for students—provided they're motivated to learn about literary publishing in the first place.

However, more programs need to recognize that not all students taking creative writing classes are interested in literary publishing or literary realism, as evidenced by the student Facebook conversation that opens this chapter. An alternative to introducing students to the semiotic domain of literary publishing is for *us* to meet *them* in the affinity groups in which they're already comfortable—those of movies, games, and television programs that are often steeped in the genres of science fiction, fantasy, and horror. Starting in this familiar terrain can create a more cohesive writing community from the start and provides an ideal springboard, perhaps ironically, for engaged discussions about language and craft.

High tea with the barbarians at the gate: Common ground in creative writing classrooms

When I'm at conferences or participating on online conversations about creative writing, I often hear instructors describing students in oppositional terms: they don't read enough quality literature; they waste their time on their phones; they're self-absorbed and hide from adult topics behind trigger warnings; their choice in entertainment is trash, all zombies and superheroes and elves. In the minds of these critics, creative writing instructors are the self-appointed defenders of the last outpost of high culture. Their strategy, apparently, is to shame students into realizing how deficient their tastes are, and to supplant their media preferences with their instructor's culturally and aesthetically superior ones. Yet while creative writing at the university level has boomed in the last fifty years, the popularity of literary reading in that same time has not. Using creative writing classes as a venue to refine literary sensibilities and to revive literary readership has proven to be a failed strategy, at least in terms of increasing the numbers of books people buy. These critics seem to have not noticed that the barbarians aren't assaulting the outpost of culture; rather, they knocked down the walls long ago and wander to and fro as they please.

In a similar move to the genre fiction moratorium that opens this chapter, Adam Brooke Davis bans what he calls "alt-worlding" in his workshops because of the derivative and cliché riddled stories in his advanced workshop. He explains that:

> On their own, students were reading *The Hunger Games*, *Twilight*, and *World War Z*, and most of their experience of narrative came from time-constrained, market-determined, sponsor-vetted, focus-group-tested, and committee-created television and movies. I tried to provide some other models, including contemporary writers like Annie Proulx, Ha Jin, Margaret Atwood, Joyce Carol Oates, Louise Erdrich, Alice Walker, and Raymond Carver.[14]

Davis makes several errors with this equation. First off, he's comparing two works explicitly marketed as young adult novels (*The Hunger Games* and *Twilight*) with literary fiction intended for mature audiences. A fairer comparison would be between these genre fiction works and a popular novel in the realist tradition, perhaps Nicholas Sparks's *A Walk to Remember* or Jodi Picoult's *My Sister's Keeper*, both of which have been adapted into maudlin Hollywood films. Secondly, and more problematically, throughout the article he links the sub-par qualities of formulaic genre fiction with their *speculative* elements rather than their weak *craft* elements. It's not the presence of vampires or zombies that makes certain texts poor models for classroom use but rather the predictable plots and wooden characters.

Ironically, at least three authors in Davis's list—Joyce Carol Oates, Louise Erdrich, and Margaret Atwood—have deployed speculative elements prominently in their work, as have other literary darlings. George Saunders has a zombie story ("Sea Oak") and his collection *CivilWarLand in Bad Decline* presents a series of dystopian futures; Karen Russel includes lycanthropes ("St. Lucy's Home for Girls Raised by Wolves") and bloodsuckers ("Vampires in the Lemon Grove"). Aimee Bender, Michael Chabon, Kelly Link, and Jonathan Lethem have all enjoyed such "alt-worldbuilding" too, to great acclaim. Critics will argue that these authors aren't writing the boilerplate genre fiction they don't want in their workshops, but prohibitions specifically ban speculative elements—zombies, elves, vampires—from workshop. Actually, what these instructors really want is to ban *poorly written fiction*. For a course that's supposed to be teaching students the principles of fiction writing, this is problematic.

Christ Gavaler welcomes genre fiction in his classroom but insists that the stories have a literary sensibility and be character-driven, rather than plot-driven. When he got his first zombie workshop story, Gavaler says, "I didn't flinch. I also didn't chuckle and dismiss the story as a warm-up. I critiqued it the same way I would critique a piece of narrative realism."[15] He deserves credit for allowing students to explore their interests in fiction, and for holding their writing to a higher standard than some of their source material. Where he misses the mark, however, is that we shouldn't simply ignore the speculative elements as if they didn't exist. In fact, it's those genre elements that offer a readymade semiotic domain on which we can build our workshops. We all know zombies are mindless shambling horrors; we all know vampires can't see their reflections; we all know Batman is a humorless vigilante haunted by his tragic past. That genre awareness becomes a common point for a class to begin with. Rather than challenging—or outright rejecting—our students' preferences for genre fiction, we can ask them interrogate the use of the speculative element, to complicate it, to challenge students to take the familiar and do something unique with it in their own fiction. Zombie stories existed in human culture centuries before *The Walking Dead*, and the same can be said for vampires, superhuman characters, and the whole lot. One useful question is simply *why*? What is it about the human condition that sees us return to these elements across time and cultures? What makes them compelling? Survivor stories in zombie apocalypses often deal with tensions between the individual and the community; vampires have always been associated with fear of the foreign invasion and perhaps are a metaphor for racial anxiety. These seem like worthy issues for students to grapple with in their fiction, at least as much as domestic crisis.

To requote Gee, an active learner should be able to "innovate in the domain—how to produce meanings that, while recognizable to experts in the domain, are seen as somehow novel or unpredictable."[16] Rather than introducing them to a new domain of literary publishing, we can encourage them to innovate, to be novel, to do unexpected things in the semiotic domain in which they already feel at home. The crucial point: *they need help doing it*. While an affinity group's discussion might be a site of deep learning, the content may be trivial. It's the *instructor's* job to design an educational experience that can make use of an existing semiotic domain. Unfortunately, too many creative writing instructors are unwilling or unable to meet their students half way. And hardly any programs make this a priority when hiring new faculty, which is a shame.

When you play the game of thrones . . . everyone wins! Experiments in fanfiction and games in creative writing

The HBO show *Game of Thrones*, based on George R.R. Martin's fantasy series *Song of Ice and Fire*, has been a pop culture phenomenon since 2011. Martin's series now spans over four thousand pages and fifty hours of television—with several books yet to be written before the conclusion. One of the most iconic quotes from the novel comes from the queen uttering the ominous line, "When you play the game of thrones, you win or you die."[17] While this might be true in the cutthroat political world of Westeros, it turns out that when you play the *Game of Thrones* in the classroom, it can be a transformative learning experience.

In the Game-based Fiction course I designed, one of the rotating course topics is "Tales from King's Landing," taking its name from the capital city of *Game of Thrones*. The course is a large-scale, collaborative, student-led project set in Martin's pre-existing world and uses the series' authorized role-playing game as the course's central text. I based the course on work being done in literacy studies on fanfiction, specifically online "textual poaching" in fan communities,[18] motivation for writers in online affinity spaces[19] and the range of media literacies practiced in online fanfiction communities. These studies have shown that while students complete school writing assignments with little interest or energy, in their leisure time many students participate with vigor and engagement with fanfiction communities. They are eagerly sharing their work and providing thoughtful feedback on their peer's work that were set in pre-existing worlds including Harry Potter, *Twilight*, *Hunger Games*, the Avengers, Pokémon, and countless others. Participants in these online spaces have no trouble shifting between media—borrowing from films, games, and comics to use in their fiction writing—and accompany their writing with drawings, digital images, audio, video, and more. This type of unrestrained creativity is something educators want to encourage more of in their classrooms, yet we must recognize that the motivation stems from the comfort they feel from working in their affinity group. While this research focuses on young teens, I was curious to try it with an older student population.

The popularity of *Game of Thrones* made it an obvious choice. In a pre-semester survey, 60 percent of the class had read the first novel in the series and 93 percent had watched the show's first season. This meant that on the first day of the semester the class would already have its affinity group—students could recite granular details about the cultures and customs of the realm. We read from the encyclopedic *World of Ice and Fire* and the *Wiki of Ice and Fire* to round out their knowledge about the cultural specifics of each of the Seven Kingdoms, including their defining legends and mythologies. We connected this back to legends of mythologies of the United States, from Paul Bunyan and Babe the Blue Ox to George Washington chopping down the cherry tree, and connected those to our own sense of national, regional, and personal identities. We had vigorous debates about familiar characters from *Game of Thrones* and talked about how they upheld or challenged the social norms of their kingdom and what motivated them to do so.

Using Green Ronin's *Song of Ice and Fire Role-playing Game* leads players through a detailed creation process for forming a noble house and an individual character, as the make-up of each has a great deal to do with a person's social standing and social mobility. Some house's reputations are connected to their martial prowess, others for their bountiful crops, others for their great wealth. In small groups, students used dice to bring their houses into being, providing backstories and histories to transform the unpredictable rolls into a coherent narrative. Each student repeated this process to create their own perspective character (PC), or the pro-tagonist in the stories to come. The rulebook provides both structure and freedom to ensure all PCs have unique traits and skills, personalities, strengths, weaknesses, backstories, and motivations, as well as differing social stations. The student PCs were scholars, servants, noble heirs, and scheming advisors.

In the last third of the semester, we played modified role-playing sessions where I gave groups problems that they needed to solve in character. For example, one soldier had to decide whether to obey his lord's order to participate in what seemed like a suicidal mission; in another, a young lady-in-waiting had to decide how to handle an aggressive suitor who was very ugly but very rich. Based on the students' decisions, PC stories intersected in exciting and unpredictable ways. Before the students made any decisions, they had to consider about their characters' motivations and weigh potential positive and negative outcomes, understanding that their choices would have consequences for more than just themselves. The intertwining of stories meant that their character would often show up in a classmate's fiction. This made our critique sessions lively; because they all owned part of this constellation of stories, they were eager to provide detailed feedback on other's work.

None of the student writing focused on gratuitous sex or violence that the HBO series highlights. Instead, most vignettes dealt with literary themes as their characters grappled with difficult ethical questions, often needing to choose between competing political and familial loyalties versus their own personal gain. When asked to reflect on the benefits of this experimental approach to creative writing in an end of the semester survey, students did not mention the class being entertaining, easy, or fun; rather focused on the craft lessons they learned. Representative comments include:

> This methodology really helped to create an almost surrogate life experience that is easy enough to relate to and thus creates an understanding that traditional methods can barely reach.

> The concept of actually acting out a character's actions allows the writer to get a more in depth view into the person they are creating. Actually living their experiences helps to think of how their character would feel, what they would do, and how they would plan ahead for the future. No other creative writing class that I've taken has done something like this.

> The two aspects that did the most for me were the role-playing game base and the established fictional world. The random nature of the role-playing really helped to make the writing born from it feel life-like and real. The established setting really helped as both a challenge and as an aid. Challenging aspects arose from having to curve writing and language to fit within the setting. The established world really helped to expedite the story telling process because of the common background of information between me and the reader.

> While every aspect was useful, I found the role-playing the most helpful. It helps shoulder the load when developing some of the plot, allowing the writer to focus more on their character.

In this methodology, student writers experience a fictional world through the subjective perspective of their detailed character, and watch as the narrative unfolds over time as their decisions, and the decisions of their classmates, combine and collide in unpredictable ways. Is this fun? Nearly all students say yes, absolutely. From my perspective, fun is less a design goal than a happy by-product of engaged learning. The *only* thing I give up in this approach is having students produce work in the genre of literary realism. Based on all we gain in return—community, collaboration, engagement, and even greater attention to craft issues—it's no great sacrifice.

Creative writing: The once and future king?

Reading and writing—or considered more broadly from a media studies perspective, the consumption and production of texts—underwent radical change during the twentieth century. English as a discipline has been slow to adapt to these changes, though it is increasingly common to find film studies, visual studies, and even game studies cropping up in English departments. Creative writing has been even more tightly wedded to print literature and its signature pedagogy of the workshop. As I have argued, the workshop as a methodology can still be very successful in producing publishing writers, at least given the right conditions. However, I wish to challenge the notion that the goal of creative writing programs is producing writers who will go on to read and publish in the genre of literary realism, especially for programs at the undergraduate level. Though a well-structured curriculum can introduce students to literary culture and literary publishing, we have many other options that will better serve a great number of students.

Creative writing has a unique opportunity to execute an about face, redirecting the entire field to be oriented toward the future rather than dwelling on the past. This means exploring where writing is going and includes collaborative writing projects, narratives that incorporate media, and designing classes that speak to our students' interests and experiences rather than rejecting them. We can do this and still retain our expertise in the craft of language and the written word, which is what many students come to our classes for anyway. How do we do this? One way is to ask students what they're interested in and to listen when they speak. Over 10 percent of this chapter consists of direct quotes from students I've had the privilege of working with in these experimental courses over the years, and I've used their input and advice to fine tune my methodology. In a role-playing game, the game master sets up a scenario for the players and works with them to make it an engaging, rewarding, memorable experience. Should our teaching approach really be any different?

Notes

1   Special thanks to Joshua, Katharina, Kent, Kyle, Dave, and Ashley for their permission to reprint this online conversation with minimal alteration.

2   Elizabeth Edmondson, "The Genre Debate: 'Literary Fiction' Is Just Clever Marketing," *The Guardian*, April 21, 2014.

3   Dianne Donnelly, *Establishing Creative Writing Studies as an Academic Discipline* (Bristol, UK; Tonawanda, NY: Multilingual Matters, 2011).

4   Donnelly, 1.

5   Graeme Harper, "Foreword: On Experience." *Does the Writing Workshop Still Work?* (Kindle: Multilingual Matters, 2010).

6   James Paul Gee, *What Video Games Have to Teach Us About Learning and Literacy*, revised and updated edition (New York: Palgrave Macmillan, 2007), 19.

7   Gee, 27.

8   Gee, 25.

9   Iowa Workshop. "History."

10   Iowa Workshop. "Philosophy."

11   Iowa Workshop. "About the Workshop."

12   Clarion. "Alumni"; Odyssey. "Graduate Publications."

13   AWP. "Guide to Creative Writing Programs."

14   Adam Brooke Davis, "No More Zombies!" *The Chronicle of Higher Education*, October 14, 2013.

15   Christopher Gavaler, "How to Teach Zombies," The Chronicle of Higher Education Blogs: The Conversation, October 29, 2013, http://chronicle.com/blogs/conversation/2013/10/29/how-to-teach-zombies

16   James Paul Gee, *What Video Games Have to Teach Us about Learning and Literacy*, revised and updated edition (New York: Palgrave Macmillan, 2007), 25

17   George R.R. Martin, *A Game of Thrones* (New York: Bantam Books, 1996): 471.

18   Henry Jenkins, *Textual Poachers: Television Fans & Participatory Culture* (New York: Routledge, 1992); and *Convergence Culture: Where Old and New Media Collide* (New York: New York University Press, 2006).

19   Lammers, Jayne, Jen Scott Curwood, and Alecia Magnifico. "Toward an Affinity Space Methodology: Considerations for Literacy Research." (2012): n.p.; Curwood, Jen Scott, Alecia Marie Magnifico, and Jayne C Lammers. "Writing in the Wild: Writers' Motivation in Fan-Based Affinity Spaces." (*JAAL Journal of Adolescent & Adult Literacy* 56.8, 2013): 677–85.

References

AWP. "Guide to Creative Writing Programs." Accessed Aug 13, 2016. https://www.awpwriter.org/guide/guide_writing_programs

Black, Rebecca. *Adolescents and Online Fan Fiction*. 1st edition. New York: Peter Lang Publishing Inc., 2008.

Clarion. "Alumni." Accessed August 13, 2016. http://clarion.ucsd.edu/alumni.html

Curwood, Jen Scott. "'The Hunger Games': Literature, Literacy, and Online Affinity Spaces." *Language Arts* 90.6 (2013): 417–427.

Curwood, Jen Scott, Alecia Marie Magnifico, and Jayne C Lammers. "Writing in the Wild: Writers' Motivation in Fan-Based Affinity Spaces." *JAAL Journal of Adolescent & Adult Literacy* 56.8 (2013): 677–685.

Davis, Adam Brooke. "No More Zombies!" *The Chronicle of Higher Education* October 14, 2013.

Donnelly, Dianne. *Establishing Creative Writing Studies as an Academic Discipline.* Bristol, UK; Tonawanda, NY: Multilingual Matters, 2011.

Edmondson, Elizabeth. "The Genre Debate: 'Literary Fiction' Is Just Clever Marketing." *The Guardian* April 21, 2014.

Harper, Graeme. "Foreword: On Experience." *Does the Writing Workshop Still Work?* Kindle. Multilingual Matters, 2010.

Iowa Workshop. "About the Workshop." https://writersworkshop.uiowa.edu/about/about-workshop [accessed August 13, 2016].

Iowa Workshop. "History.". https://writersworkshop.uiowa.edu/about/about-workshop/history [accessed August 13, 2016].

Iowa Workshop. "Philosophy." https://writersworkshop.uiowa.edu/about/about-workshop/philosophy [accessed August 13, 2016].

Jenkins, Henry. *Convergence Culture: Where Old and New Media Collide.* New York: New York University Press, 2006.

Jenkins, Henry. *Textual Poachers: Television Fans & Participatory Culture.* New York: Routledge, 1992.

Lammers, Jayne, Jen Scott Curwood, and Alecia Magnifico. "Toward an Affinity Space Methodology: Considerations for Literacy Research." (2012): n.p. urresearch.rochester.edu [accessed February 13, 2016].

Martin, George R. R. *A Game of Thrones.* New York: Bantam Books, 1996.

Odyssey. "Graduate Publications." http://www.sff.net/odyssey/gradpubs.html

Snyder, Thomas D., and National Center for Education Statistics. *120 Years of American Education: A Statistical Portrait.* Washington, D.C.: U.S. Dept. of Education, Office of Educational Research and Improvement, National Center for Education Statistics, 1993.

11

Disability Culture and Creative Writing Pedagogies:

When having Fun Together is Radical Practice

Petra Kuppers

All of us, disabled and nondisabled alike, will never truly understand disability experiences and identities unless we examine what we think we know. We all have a lot of relearning to do.

PAUL LONGMORE

Creative writing and disability culture are two areas of practice that can come together very well, or can create major train wrecks. Much of the existing literature focuses on the train wrecks, usually when non-disabled folks try to use disability as a metaphor, sometimes with interesting, but more often with sad results. This essay will not engage this particular terrain very much—for pointers on how to do this well, see for instance creative writer Jillian Weise's fun polemic in *Drunken Boat* (2012). She skewers the assumption of the "neutral" body, the non-spoken about "general" body, and shows how it works both as an originator of discourse (in a conference, or in writing), and in reading practice:

> To speak at a conference, I should not use the word *you*. I may use the word *we* but only in matters of general agreement. For example: "We all agree not to talk about our bodies." This is the contract to speak. It is much like the contract to read, where also I have to take possession of

someone else's body, although in a private way, just between myself and myself, in order to get through poems that use disabled characters, so I can think, "Oh, that's not me." For example, when I read the title of Louise Glück's poem, "Cripple in the Subway," I take possession of someone else's body, put on the arms and legs, make sure the back is straight, zip everything up, and resume reading. Now I am safe. This new body has never been called a cripple, and so can read the word *cripple* without even flinching.[1]

Weise has to go into non-cripple mimicry to make her way through the cripple minefield. This is a position probably familiar to many of us who teach creative writing and have to think about when to give trigger warnings. Our students are asked to engage in the "oh, that's not me" two-step whenever they read about the girl with schizophrenia who has escaped the mental asylum, or the self-cutter who eviscerates herself, or the maybe-yes-maybe-no autistic boy who can't look anybody in the eye. Any "real" experiences of mental health difference, institutionalization, medication, or self-cutting have to curtsey and duck out of sight under the weight of disability stereotypes. No one like that living around here.

Being a wheelchair-using teacher helps me, and presumably my students: I get a lot less of the "evil dried-up wheelchair-using hag" stories than others do (I presume, finding this trope again and again in the literature). I can just see my students lifting their fingers off the keyboard, rethinking their strategy, as they are trying to work out how to defend this use of the wheelchair to me, their teacher with a sardonic eyebrow.

But what about other differences? What student will wish to identify their mental health differences as a motor for writing sensitivities when their classmates happily write about escapees and pill-popping loonies? Let us agree not to do the "this is the real face of disability" unmasking in our classroom. Nothing "real" can really happen while we live in stigmatizing societies. As education and disability specialist Linda Ware reminds us in the literature about how to reshape stereotypes of disability in writing classrooms:

> Lessons about democracy, social justice, and the essence of humanity are performed in public schooling not only by students but also by the adults in schools. The messages are clear about what is valued, who is valuable, and whose stories matter. In the example of disability, the script is often written well before the student arrives. Calls for a new cultural story of disability must begin in K–12 educational context before internalized social norms are brought to bear on issues of access.[2]

The internalized negative social norms around disability are deep and limit cripple stories. So, one of the potential violences of disability and creative writing is the endless and repetitious (as well as boring) recycling of existing

152

CAN CREATIVE WRITING REALLY BE TAUGHT?

stereotypes as narrative shorthand (something the disability studies field calls "narrative prosthesis," following David Mitchell and Sharon Snyder). This violence is done to the disabled student (and the teacher), and also to anybody who wants to see some more interesting readings on their desk.

Toward fun

So, what do we do with disability in the classroom? The composition field has yielded more writing on disability than the creative writing field, and there are useful collections that can point teachers to think creatively about access provisions and ways of introducing disability as a critical and interesting topic.[3]

How do we mark or stress human diversity in our spaces, and their effects on and engagement with the creative writing we do, with the narratives we develop, with our styles of writing? As long as disability is a spaceholder for abjection, or some "radical otherness," there can't really be a "good" way of engaging it and exploiting its juicy narrative and sensory potential, and it's highly unlikely that any of our disabled students will want to play openly with us, whether we identify as disabled or not. Once there are more disabled writers getting published, more disabled teachers, disabled readers who are critics, and more disabled people in the creative writing world in general, we can revisit this play with disability's abjection. For now, let's keep exoticism at bay, and agree not to use shorthand disability references to scaffold our stories or wrench poetic emotions. I could reference all the essays on how not to use blackface, but I think you get the point.

Of course, writers will write, and don't like prohibitions in the first place, and that's a good thing. So, a better avenue toward avoiding bad stuff is to present good stuff that is seductive and weird fun. Here, think about books like Samuel Delaney's *Through the Valley of the Nest of Spiders*, in which queer, disabled, black men (no women, sorry) care for each other in a hedonistic utopia of sex and abject play.[4] Of course, this means opening up our canon to be aware of writing "from the edges" (I realize that for some literary classrooms, Delaney or Octavia Butler might still be considered edge-spaces). When body play and mind play become interesting and not just sad negative moments of social ostracization, things get more interesting.

Fun and seduction are the avenues I wish to pursue in this essay. Meta-analyses of the use of expressive writing in inclusive learning classrooms have consistently shown that writing toward audiences and expression is helpful to disabled students.[5] I am a disabled teacher and writer who incorporates creative writing in her classes, with the aim of helping my students to see the richness of difference.[6] My classroom tends to focus on particular branches of creative writing that are more suited to disability representation (and other forms of difference) in unequal times: the condensory of poetry, the interdependent citational forms of speculative and horror writing, and the self-witnessing of creative non-fiction. No realist fiction, basically, not just because of the dried-up wheelchair hags, the spooky guy with the cast in his eye, or the saintly blind girl. Also, because I do not enjoy stories of fathers shooting their foot off on camping trips with their sons. Or mothers with Alzheimer's. Genre fiction, on the whole, tends to be more aware of the recycling and repurposing of literary mechanics, and, on the whole, seems to have a better sense of humor about it.

The student who sent me emails before class asking me for trigger warnings about sexual assault and mental health institutionalization in stories (easily done, part of my work in ensuring that workshopped stories can work for all) writes beautifully about trans werewolves, about changing shape, finding community and love, engaging in territorial wars, and drinking shimmering blood. Werewolves and vampires crop up a lot in my student portfolios. They seem to offer more potential than realism as interesting sites for engagement with gender play and sexuality.

In one of our in-class writing assignments, we prepare by reading two stories from *Accessing the Future: A Disability-Themed Anthology of Speculative Fiction*, edited by Kathryn Allan and Djibril al-Ayad. In two stories, disability's difference meets trans space in exciting configurations. In Jack Hollis Marr's piece, "into the water i rode down," a wheelchair-using deaf person interfaces with a catsnake living in a river on a planet that the corporation is trying to colonize. In Toby McNutt's contribution, "Morphic Resonance," a wheelchair-using protagonist finds themselves (the appropriate pronoun at this point) part of a hacked illegal body modification gang, with their sexuality/sensuality/senses rewired. The arc ends in one of the lovely recycled archetypes of sci-fi stories: the alien bar, familiar to anybody who has ever watched a Star Wars movie. In our in-class writing, we engage this fantastical space of the alien bar. In timed writing, we all work out how relaxation, sensory stimulation, thresholds, and social interplay can happen in this bar space, imagining ourselves in contact with other ways of being *without* having to construct narrative arcs around them.

How to make disability interesting and deep: that is one of the core issues my particular creative writing classroom faces. In the next section, I offer an exercise that starts from everybody's embodied/enminded difference, and finds richness in slowness and mindful attention.

Case study: Embodiment and the world

Here is a pedagogical exercise that allows us to relearn being in space, combining attention to embodiment with writerly expression. The exercise confounds conventional disability simulation exercises, imagining ourselves to be different than who we are, by substituting an experience of who we are already, perceived differently, with a more mindful attention. This kind of exercise, going out and being attentive to ourselves in the world, is the foundation for many of my creative writing classroom exercises, and the basis of much of my work on the difference disability makes. The session takes about twenty minutes of silent walking on our campus (on the Diag: the green space between our main university buildings), with a group of four, keeping each other in sight. Group members may wander away from one another, so long as all members of the group are visible to each other at all times (when we have people with visual impairments among us, we switch things up a bit, and might incorporate touch).

Student perspectives: What changes

In this section, I am sharing writings from the student blogs (with permission from the students), giving perspectives on the exercise.

> Jenny Wang: Walking around with a group I wasn't just taking in the scenery around me, but I was also taking in the sounds. When no one in the group is talking, when there wasn't any music blasting in my ears, I had to make up for the "sound gap" with sounds from all around me. Our group went around the Diag area, so we were really close to the actual streets. I eavesdropped on conversations, on music, on the cars that drove by.

> Niko Natsis: I have never simply just walked around and taken in the environment for the sake of enjoying it. I live in the mountains in Los Angeles by the beach and have never taken the time to stroll through either area. I noticed how quickly I normally walk. During this assignment, there was no end goal to reach or place to be. I have never walked at a pace that did not require any sort of extreme urgency to be somewhere.

> Amy Milewski: I really enjoyed feeling the differences beneath my feet, how different the concrete feels from the grass, how some areas of grass were softer than others, how some areas had fallen acorns that changed how your foot related to the ground, and how my preferences for a particular "ground-feel" led me to wander more in some areas than others. Also, I enjoyed not being confined by needing to walk in a straight line. I am sometimes wobbly on my feet and may "misstep" sometimes, with this wandering exercise those "missteps" were simply the first steps in a new direction.

> Alicia Wheeler: Walking around with my group was calming and energetic at the same time. In the almost 4 years that I have lived in Ann Arbor I have never taken the time to simply wander around the campus enjoying the nature, the artwork and the people walking by. I noticed so much more about this city than I think I ever have.
> It was so interesting and shocking to hear people speak especially when they spoke near us loudly or with aggressive words while we were

silent. It made that noise much more crass to hear than when I am speaking or on a mission to get somewhere.

Cari Carson: Perhaps the distinction is less between ability and disability than between appreciating and not appreciating. The characteristics of our bodies and minds could result in appreciation or not. Simulating a different ability-ness may heighten the appreciation; complacency with our own different abilities may lessen it.

But I wasn't thinking of any of this while wandering. When wandering, I just was. With ability and disability blurred, independence and dependence on other group members breathing life and accountability and creativity into my wandering, there was a playfulness and a joy and I-don't-have-more-nouns-that-mean-what-I-want-to-say-except worship.

This is not primarily a writing exercise, of course: this is an exercise in being, and in paying attention. It is also an exercise that can deeply impact how students write creative work afterward, with a lot more attention to space and description, stepping back from plotting into a different realm.

One of the follow-up exercises to this work brings this closer into creative writing practice.

Deepening space: Creating sense libraries

I begin most of my class sessions with a meditation: 5 minutes of sitting with each other, just paying attention to our breath, observing ourselves being in space. We listen to our minds' chatter, to the noises of the building, to the way we are bodily interwoven into the fabric of the university. Then we start our exercise.

As a prep for this exercise, I write down spaces on scraps of paper, twice as many as students in the class. Library, mansion, swimming pool, living room, alley, forest, ice-skating rink, etc. The students pull two of these.

We meditate again, sinking ourselves into our current space. Halfway through, I invite students to go to the first space, the one written on their first scrap. Sense it, listen to it, smell it, taste it, hear it, see it.

Freewrite.

Now the next exercise, again a short meditation, sinking into space. Halfway through, I invite students to be present as a persona in the space named on the second scrap paper: who are you, what do you experience, what do you feel as you hear, sense, taste, etc.?

Freewrite.

In a last go-around, students connect the sensory richness of space one with the experienced space in space two, and create a story that gets from A to B.

Freewrite again.

To honor the writing that took place throughout these hours, I invited students to share selected material from their freewrite, in couples.

We end the day by discussing the way writing emerges in these kinds of exercises: what happens, how does the writing and the results relate to how you normally write, how you set yourself up for entering a story? What works for you, and why? These reflections on writing process, in close proximity to the actual creation process, garners deep levels of engagement with the activity of writing, the way our juices can flow. We can have discussions that lead us to the kind of environments and structures that support our creativity.

This session allows us to step away from relentless plotting, and into experience, without losing sight of character and motivation. The students' own bodily specificity in sensing the world becomes central to their experience. They do not need to reach toward "being someone else" in order to enter altered states, heightened sensitivity. And if they want to change their bodily and minded being, they are welcome to do so—but from a place of richness and sensory overload, not from diminished narrative stereotypes.

The stories resulting from these kind of exercises can be remarkable in their depth. I used these experience-gathering exercises in my International Horror class, a half-critical, half-creative undergraduate class occupied with borders and their piercing, and with different perspectives on space and immigration (for instance, comparing Lovecraft's racist New York view with contemporary horror writer Victor DeValle's *Ballad of Black Tom*, a revisioning of Lovecraftian stories imagined from a Harlem center).[7] In addition to the exercise above (which took up one three-hour class session), we also explored creative writing while sitting next to dinosaur skulls in the Natural History Museum.

My undergraduate Space and Site class, another mixed critical/creative class, went to the Map Section in the University of Michigan Library, and the librarians pulled maps of Michigan for us—ancient ones, maps with battle lines, and indigenous maps of pathways and river crossings. My students were particularly taken with a huge map spanning multiple tables that showed old and new structures at the university: ruins of buildings, dreams of buildings, a foreshadowing of the current campus as imagined in the 1970s. In response, my students created their own mapping procedures. One mapped the Diag (the long green thoroughfare on campus) by leaf shapes, commenting on all the tree species that flourished in it. One team wrote a memory map, charting what had happened to them on the Diag and its surrounds over their time here as students.

The day at the Clark Library went so well, I visited the maps with my International Horror class, too. We scanned maps of Ann Arbor: we looked at the group affiliations of different areas of Ann Arbor over time, at toxic brown field sites, and for the outdoor sports activities available to students with and without access to cars. Then we wrote our own stories of space traversal, and a new and quite spooky Ann Arbor emerged.

One of the students in this class writes this about the use of bodily experience (cited with permission):

Phy Tran: I think that the idea of having the class have these visits and have some sort of physical experience, like the map room visit, the natural history museum visit, and the meditation, all enriches the experience of writing for this class. It also helps us sort of—build a library of experiences to draw on, as well.

A library of experiences: this is a rich way to explore difference, to enlarge one's vocabulary, to draw upon sensation.

This way of thinking about disability can also richly engage disabled writers in the classroom. Even if disability culture invites us to value difference, the social stigma of disability, including mental health difference, is severe, and, as noted earlier, usually well sedimented and established by the time a student is in our university creative writing classes. One of the most helpful things one can do as a teacher to shift disability stereotypes is to offer intriguing texts that provide evidence for disability's interest. These texts include realist novels like Susan Nussbaum's *Good Kings Bad Kings* (highly accessible and gripping, with Young Adult genre features), poetry/poetics collections like the *Beauty is a Verb* anthology, poetics essays like Jim Ferris's "Enjambed Body" (2004), short story collections like Anne Finger's *Call Me Ahab*, poetry collections like Leah Lakshmi Piepzna-Samarasinha's *Body Map* (2015) or Qwo-Li Driskill's *Walking with Ghosts* (2005). Classes can look at the emergence of a press run by neurodiverse authors, Autonomous Press, and its outputs, like the *Spoon Knife Anthology*.[8] They can read memoirs like Eli Clare's 1999 classic *Exile and Pride*, reissued in 2015; Corbett O'Toole's memoir *Fading Scars* (2015), or Terry Galloway's *Mean Little Deaf Queer* (2009), or, to bind us back to the experiential exercises I discussed above, the little flashes of jewel-like sense openings in Stephen Kuusisto's creative non-fiction collection on hearing and blindness (2006).

Slowing down

There is another violence associated with disability and creative writing, one much less common than narrative shorthands and boring storylines, but much more spectacular: the linking of real-life violence and violence in fiction. This particular connection came to the fore in the aftermath of the Virginia Tech school shooting, in 2007, when many who use creative modalities in the classroom were touched by what we read of the local creative writing instructors wrestling with themselves. The shooter, Cho, had written violent fantasies in his creative writing classes, and although his teachers had taken him aside and referred him to student services, the issue of creative writing teachers' supposed ability to diagnose real-life violence was part of the public discourse.

English composition specialist Margaret Price has studied the newspaper and media coverage surrounding this case, and she ends her account of the coverage with one of Virginia Tech's teachers, Edward Falco, who taught Cho in a playwriting class, and who addressed his students in this way:

> There was violence in Cho's writing—but there is a huge difference between writing about violence and behaving violently. We could not have known what he would do. We treated him like a fellow student, which is what he was. I believe the English department behaved responsibly in response to him. And please hear me when I say this: It was our responsibility, not yours. All you could have done was come to me, or some other administration or faculty member, with your concerns—and you would have been told that we were aware of Seung-Hui Cho, we were concerned about him, and we were doing what we believed was appropriate. Look, all our hearts are broken. There's no need to add to the pain with guilt.[9]

Price writes:

> I find this message extraordinarily hopeful, for several reasons. First it refers to all persons respectfully, and without resorting to derogatory remarks. Second, it does not attempt to pretend that the mystery of Cho's violent actions has an easy answer. Third, it names Falco's own emotion and indicates to his students that emotion is an appropriate response— "all our hearts are broken".[10]

With her writing, Price slows down any machine that wants to find answers to how to respond to violence in student writing. There is no answer. Most likely, genuine human concern and engagement will go a long way toward alleviating human distress. The vast majority of students who experience mental health distress, and even those who use writing as dark fantasy, will not become violent, and are in fact much more likely to become the subject of violence themselves. The school shooter exception, even if endlessly discussed in creative writing lore, is not the rule, and should not undermine the slowness, kindness and compassion with which we read each other's work.

As creative writing teachers, we are more likely than others to read of students' fears and desires, to get a glimpse into what is going on. But we also have tools to offer students ways out of their own (at times confining) universes, and into the wider realm of literature, language, and the imagination. The kinds of alternative and additions to workshopping methods that I discussed in this essay can offer genuine ways out of scenarios that see creative writing teachers struggling with students' misogynistic serial killer short stories or suicide fantasies. Students can ground themselves differently, can step away from stereotypical fantasies, when they are offered other tools toward becoming creative writers. Prompts that point outside of one's self can be useful. One of the most interesting poetry tools in undergraduate classes can be erasure work, using an existing text and working into and onto it, erasing, highlighting, creating a new work out of its bones. In exercises like these, dialogues can happen: the archive becomes material, and enacting procedures upon it can offer new perspectives toward future living and writing. Race, class, disability, gender: we can reimagine a world shaped by perspectives different from ours. We offer students distance between themselves and language's play, distances they can grow into.

Restriction is violence: let's point outward, offer new ways of telling old stories and finding new forms.

Conclusion: Finding creative community

To end, I move from disability's conventional relentlessly singular focus toward the notion of community. Kris Bigalk investigated the usefulness of "tribes" in creative writing classes, and takes the isolating experience of disability diagnosis as her starting point. A student who had a disability diagnosis flourished in creative writing once he received a writing award. She writes:

> The next day, he was waiting for me at my office. "Do you think I could be a writer?" he asked. "I think you already are a writer," I replied. After we sat down and talked awhile, he confided that as a student labeled as having a disability, he had always disliked school, and thought that his complex writing was a liability, not an asset. Winning the award had finally made him realize that he might actually be good at something— writing—and that other people might make a connection with him, and be interested in what he had to say.[11]

Convoluted, complex writing here became an asset, an interesting thing, something others might be drawn to. I am glad to include this quote here, as it is so rare to find something positive about disability experiences in education settings. This one is a bit hopeful, of course: not all our disabled students will win awards. But it's a good start: here is a tribe, the creative writing world, that is interested and thrives on difference, on new stories, on whole libraries of experience. Bring it on.

Notes

1   Jillian Weise, "Cloning Disabled Subjects," *Drunken Boat* 15 (2012): n.p., http://www.drunkenboat.com/db15/jillian-weise

2   Linda P. Ware, "A Moral Conversation on Disability: Risking the Personal in Educational Contexts," *Hypatia* 17:3 (2002): 160.

3   See, for instance, Cynthia Lewiecki-Wilson and Brenda J. Brueggemann, *Disability and the Teaching of Writing: A Critical Sourcebook* (Boston: Bedford/St. Martin's, 2008), and a rich web-text about multimodal teaching, Melanie Yergeau et al., "Multimodality in Motion: Disability and Kairotic Spaces," *Kairos* 18:1 (2013): n.p.

4   Samuel Delaney, *Through the Valley of the Nest of Spiders* (New York: Magnus Books, 2012).

5   See: Russell Gersten and Baker Scott "Teaching Expressive Writing to Students with Learning Disabilities: A Meta-Analysis," *The Elementary School Journal* 101:3 (2001): 251–72.

6   See: Petra Kuppers, *Studying Disability Arts and Culture: An Introduction* (Harmondsworth: Palgrave, 2014).

7   Victor DeValle, *Ballad of Black Tom* (New York: Tor Publishing, 2016).

8   Michael Scott Monje Jr. and N.I. Nicholson, eds, *Spoon Knife Anthology* (Fort Worth: NeuroQueer Books 2016).

9   Falco quoted on CNN, in Margaret Price, *Mad At School: Rhetorics of Mental Disability and Academic Life* (Ann Arbor: University of Michigan Press, 2011).

10   Margaret Price, *Mad At School: Rhetorics of Mental Disability and Academic Life*, 174.

11   Kris Bigalk. "Creative Writing at the Two-Year College: Creating Opportunity and Community," *Teaching English in the Two Year College* 42:2 (2014): 138.

References

Allan, Kathryn and Djibril al-Ayad, eds. *Accessing the Future: A Disability-Themed Anthology of Speculative Fiction*. New York: Futurefire.net, 2015.

Bigalk, Kris. "Creative Writing at the Two-Year College: Creating Opportunity and Community." *Teaching English in the Two Year College* 42:2 (2014): 136–41.

Clare, Eli. *Exile and Pride: Disability, Queerness, and Liberation*. Durham: Duke University Press, 2015, originally 1999.

Delaney, Samuel. *Through the Valley of the Nest of Spiders*. New York: Magnus Books, 2012.

DeValle, Victor. *Ballad of Black Tom*. New York: Tor Publishing, 2016.

Driskill, Qwo-Li. *Walking with Ghosts*. Cambridge: Salt Publishing, 2005.

Ferris, Jim. "The Enjambed Body: A Step Toward a Crippled Poetics." *Georgia Review* 58:2 (2004): 219–33.

Finger, Anne. *Call Me Ahab*. Lincoln: University of Nebraska Press, 2009.

Galloway, Terry. *Mean Little Deaf Queer*. Boston: Beacon Press, 2009.

Gersten, Russell and Baker Scott. "Teaching Expressive Writing to Students with Learning Disabilities: A Meta-Analysis." *The Elementary School Journal* 101: 3 (2001): 251–72.

Kuppers, Petra. *Studying Disability Arts and Culture: An Introduction*. Harmondsworth: Palgrave, 2014.

Kuusisto, Stephen. *Eavesdropping: A Memoir of Blindness and Listening*. New York: W.W. Norton, 2006.

Lewiecki-Wilson, Cynthia and Brenda J. Brueggemann. *Disability and the Teaching of Writing: A Critical Sourcebook*. Boston: Bedford/St. Martin's, 2008.

Longmore, Paul. *Why I Burned My Book and Other Essays on Disability*. Philadelphia: Temple University Press, 2003.

Mitchell, David T. and Sharon L. Snyder. *Narrative Prosthesis: Disability and the Dependencies of Discourse*. Ann Arbor: University of Michigan Press, 2000.

O'Toole, Corbett Joan. *Fading Scars: My Queer Disability History*. Fort Worth: Autonomous Press, 2015.

Piepzna-Samarasinha, Leah Lakshmi. *Body Map*. Toronto: Mawenzi House, 2015.

Price, Margaret. *Mad At School: Rhetorics of Mental Disability and Academic Life*. Ann Arbor: University of Michigan Press, 2011.

Ware, Linda P. "A Moral Conversation on Disability: Risking the Personal in Educational Contexts." *Hypatia* 17:3 (2002): 143–72.

Weise, Jillian. "Cloning Disabled Subjects." *Drunken Boat* 15 (2012). http://www.drunkenboat.com/db15/jillian-weise

Yergeau, Melanie, et al. "Multimodality in Motion: Disability and Kairotic Spaces." *Kairos* 18:1 (2013): n.p.

12

Polemics Against Polemics:

Reconsidering Didacticism in Creative Writing

Janelle Adsit

All art is quite useless.
OSCAR WILDE

The very uselessness of literature is its most profound and valuable attribute.
MARJORIE GARBER, *THE USE AND ABUSE OF LITERATURE*

This semester, a student in my fiction workshop, Jacquelyn Lowe, introduced her final portfolio with these words:

> Before this class I never considered my audience and wrote stories for my own therapeutic self-indulgence without ever considering the power and influence they could have over other people. I also never considered the technique of 'destabilizing' stereotypical conventions or that fiction could be used as a tool to influence people politically, socially, or otherwise. I never saw the storytelling world as a place for challenging authority and other institutions which I oppose. I almost changed my major to Journalism because I assumed that this was the most effective way to convey meaningful information to the public. Over the course of the semester, I have realized that I was wrong . . . I have learned that fictional writing is subtle and timeless.

Following this preface, Jacquelyn included a serial story inspired by Susan Minot's "Lust"—a story which Jacquelyn wrote with the express purpose of dismantling slut-shaming tendencies in contemporary culture.

The preconceptions about fiction writing that Jacquelyn describes in her portfolio introduction are reflected in creative writing's pedagogical discourses. Craft texts rarely provide an in-depth discussion of audience or the sociology of literature. Moreover, craft texts warn against didactic or polemical approaches to creative writing. They warn students like Jacquelyn against writing fiction with a clear rhetorical purpose, such as her Susan Minot-inspired story. How many students like Jacquelyn are discouraged by this orientation of creative writing? How many more would find power and potential in a critical understanding of the political role of literary writing?

Despite creative writing's pedagogical warnings against didacticism and polemics, there is a preponderance of activist work in our contemporary literary milieu that addresses specific audiences, that seeks to intervene in contemporary political situations, that advocates on behalf of communities. Take #BlackPoetsSpeakOut, for example. Or read the works of indigenous activism that are anthologized in *The Land We Are: Artists and Writers Unsettle the Politics of Reconciliation*, edited by Gabrielle L'Hirondelle Hill and Sophie McCall—a book that interrogates the relationship between "land, the role of the artist and the contested discourse of reconciliation in Indigenous cultural politics"[1] in the context of the Canadian Truth and Reconciliation Commission. Browse the cli-fi anthologies, such as the edited collection *I'm With the Bears: Short Stories from a Damaged Planet*, or the many anthologies of ecopoetics. Consider the articulations of a feminist aesthetics by such writers as Rachel Blau DuPlessis who observes that "when the phenomenological exploration of self-in-world turns up a world that devalues the female self, . . . [the feminist artist] cannot just 'let it be,' but must transform values, rewrite culture, subvert structures."[2] The feminist artist DuPlessis describes creates art as activism. Christina Davis's list of activist poetry collections, from her article "Is the Constitution: Some Notes on Poetry & Activism" includes, for example, M NourbeSe Philips' *Zong*, Juliana Spahr's *This Connection of Everyone With Lungs*, Claudia Rankine's *Citizen: An American Lyric*, Anne Waldman's *The Iovis Trilogy* and *Civil Disobediences*, Thomas Sayers Ellis' *Skin, Inc.: Identity Repair Poems*, Frank Smith's *Guantanamo*, C.D. Wright's *One with Others*, Fred Moten's "The University and the Undercommons," Gabriel Gudding's forthcoming *Rivers for Animals*, poet-journalist Eliza Griswold's *I Am the Beggar of the World: Landays from Contemporary Afghanistan*, Cecilia Vicuña's *A Menstrual Quipu: The Blood of the Glaciers Journal*." And, as Davis notes, there are countless other examples.[3]

The legacies of political art, critical art, awareness-raising art, guerilla art, progressive art, public art, activist art, interventionist art, socially engaged art are long and proliferating. Yet how often are these histories and movements left beyond the scope of the creative writing class? Looking over even the cursory list above, the need to interrogate creative writing's biases against political writing becomes clear—not only because the examples of activist art-making are many, but also because of the particular privilege that comes with a denial or marginalization of these examples. To ban political writing from the study of creative writing is to potentially silence or ignore the exigencies that give rise to these forms of art-making. The alternative should be that we invite these exigencies into the classroom and ask our students to grapple with the risks and possibilities of art that has a cause.

I argue that our students can learn to write art that makes sophisticated political interventions, art that avoids parroting party lines. The stated warnings against the didactic and polemical in the creative writing classroom are insufficient. As creative writers, we do well to historicize our positions— in our work on the page and in the classroom. Rather than putting a series of "dos and don'ts" before our students (e.g., don't write didactic/polemical work), we can identify how our aesthetic values and criteria came to be and how these values risk keeping some works of creative production on the margins. Rather than barring activist art, we can help students gain an artistic sensitivity to navigate the problems and potential of making an intentional intervention in art.

Historicizing anti-didacticism in creative writing craft texts

Given the preponderance of activist writers and activist texts, what can we make of the repeated admonishment we find in the craft texts: to avoid writing that makes an argument? Stephen Dobyns, in the highly circulated craft text *Best Words, Best Order*, explicitly devalues forms of political art. "We have seen antiwar poems . . ., radical feminist, black, gay, and Marxist poems," he writes. "Every belief has its partisan art, which either speaks to those already convinced of its truth or bullies those who aren't. The difficulty is that while extreme partisanship is easy to spot, its subtle forms can be insidious. Any kind of bias is a form of partisanship and if it enters the work, it then weakens it."[4] The optimism of this belief in a bias-less writing notwithstanding, Dobyns's view is representative of a tendency in creative writing. Warnings against didacticism and politicized or "moral" art pepper creative writing craft texts. Burroway and Weinberg's best-selling craft text *Writing Fiction,* for example, explicitly encourages writers to avoid the political: "The writer, of course, may be powerfully impelled to impose a limited version of the world as it ought to be, and even to tie that vision to a political stance, wishing not only to persuade and convince but also to propagandize. But because the emotional force of literary persuasion is in the realization of the particular," they argue, "the writer is doomed to fail."[5] In warning against this failure, Burroway and Weinberg are here preserving the literary community's values of complexity and the destabilization of institutionalized truths, yet they do little to chart a path toward writing the "political." The political becomes conflated with the propagandistic under Burroway and Weinberg's broad brush, foreclosing the possibility of a political literary art that offers complexity and non-programmatic critique. Surely these warnings against political art are borne of experience with reductive student texts that become "preachy" and flat in their fervor; at the same time, these warnings derive from a long history of aesthetic debate—a history that we should make known to our students and that should ground the craft recommendations we proffer in our courses.

In his 1934 craft text titled *Verse Writing*, William Herbert Carruth describes two opposing pulls in theories of literary art: "On the one hand it has been maintained that the artist must be ... impelled by love of beauty and the irresistible desire to express it; that he must either be wholly unconscious of any audience and the effect of his outpouring upon them [. . .] This is the doctrine of art for art's sake."[6] "On the other hand," Carruth continues, the artist is expected to "consider the effect of his product upon his fellows." In this second paradigm, which Carruth calls "the doctrine of art for man's [sic] sake," the artist becomes "responsible for the ethical influence of his output, and must accordingly calculate the moral value of his work."[7]

It is worth pausing to trace several centuries of Western aesthetic history to find how these two opposing pulls—art for art's sake and art for the good of humankind—has been inherited by contemporary creative writing. As early as the writings of Homer, historian of aesthetics Monroe Beardsley notes, "The functions of poet and seer, or prophet, were already distinguished." Yet these two figures were also at times conflated: "For both the poet and the seer, like the oracle, spoke in heightened language, in words that moved and dazzled, with an inexplicable magic power." The effect of this, Beardsley explains, "was to stamp Homer and Hesiod as wise men and teachers, and to link poetic greatness with epistemic value."[8] The poet becomes linked with wisdom— with the capacity to, as the Horatian dictum has it, "delight and instruct."

This dictum—to "delight and instruct"—is often repeated throughout the aesthetic tradition (along with the rhetorical tradition—Cicero says that rhetoric and oratory should likewise "delight and instruct"). It is reiterated in works such as Sidney's famous defense of poetry. Indeed, Horace's *Ars Poetica* is a touchstone for poets and aesthetic thinkers, especially in the Renaissance and Long Eighteenth. However, the "delight and instruct" pairing was to see a split that was hinted at even in the Renaissance. Renaissance writers like Castelvetro "denied explicitly that poetry has the aim to teach, and ... insisted that pleasure is its sole purpose."[9] Later, Romantic writers would take up this prioritization of pleasure and delight, rejecting didacticism in poetry.[10] P.B. Shelley, for instance, excoriates poets who have "affected a moral aim," claiming that "the effect of their poetry is diminished in exact proportion to the degree in which they compel us to advert to this [their moral] purpose."[11] Having a moral aim diminishes "the poetical faculty" in Shelley's formulation, yet—as he is famous for saying—"Poets are the unacknowledged legislators of the World."[12] Poetry strengthens "the moral nature of man [sic]," but it does so not through persuading an audience of assured moral directives. Shelley emphasizes that "A Poet . . . would do ill to embody his own conceptions of right and wrong, which are usually those of his place and time."[13] The poet should neither participate in, nor forward, these conceptions of right and wrong, which are short-sighted and fixed in time and place. Shelley, true to the transcendent subjectivity that characterizes the Romantic period, looks toward a morality that is beyond the here and now.

This sense of a transcendent and indirect moral benefit of art, a morality that cannot be delivered in doctrine, is reflected in several Romantic and pre-Romantic theorists of the poetic and aesthetic. These thinkers turned away from the given mandate that the artist reflect and reinforce established morals and decorum. Arguing against polemical and didactic poetry, Keats declared, "We hate poetry that has a palpable design upon us—and if we do no not agree, seems to put its hand into its breeches pocket."[14]

U.S. creative writing has inherited this legacy of skepticism toward the didactic, a legacy to which many theorists of the aesthetic have contributed. Kant, as we know, is careful to differentiate aesthetic judgment from ethical thinking.[15] Kant's work remains influential in the common rejection of the didactic conception of literature. Literary writing is, in this view, "a good" even as it refuses to teach "the good"—a claim that Schiller underscores as well.[16] Schiller claims in *On the Aesthetic Education of Man* (1795) that "if we are ever to solve that political problem in practice, follow the path of aesthetics, since it is through Beauty that we arrive at Freedom."[17] Yet, while the aesthetic is clearly beneficial to the political and moral life of society in Schiller's view, it does not directly state political or moral truths. Instead, the poet satisfies "the noble impulses of his heart" by elevating society's thoughts "to the Necessary and the Eternal" and, by his creations, transforms "the necessary and the eternal into the object of [the heart's] impulses."[18]

Inheriting this tradition of objection to the Horatian dictum "to delight *and instruct*," twentieth-century craft texts often warn against didacticism in literature. Indeed, even the common workshop mantra "show, don't tell" can be understood as a form of anti-didacticism.[19] Chekhov's often-repeated statement to his editor—that of "answering the questions and formulating them correctly. Only the latter is required of an author"[20]—is likewise a warning against the didactic or polemical, an admonition against literature with a cause.

The destabilizing capacities of literature

The refusal to instrumentalize art into moral or informative discourse is most famously celebrated by Oscar Wilde and proponents of the Aesthetic

Movement and "Art for art's sake"—a phrase dating from the nineteenth century. Beardsley explicates the "code of professional ethics" that is embedded in this concept of "art for art's sake": "the demand for freedom from external pressures was a demand for the chance to live up to the artist's own highest obligation, to his art itself."[21] In this view, the obligation is to the form of the text being created—a conception of the art-making process that, as Mary Ann Cain argues in "Problematizing Formalism," continues to hold sway in creative writing.[22]

This formalist approach to art-making may at first appear to be depoliticizing or even apolitical. Yet even in formalism, art has the capacity to destabilize hegemonic moral claims—to make us think in new ways and see the world, in all its complexity, with penetrating eyes. This destabilizing capacity is routed through the affective and the sensory, circumventing the logics of morality. Creative writing's rejection of didactic and polemical writing is tied to a larger skepticism regarding formal reasoning, argumentation, and rhetoric. Evoking emotions in readers or causing them to experience something through the text are worthwhile intentions for the artist, but to deliberately argue something is another matter. To teach or influence readers through rhetoric runs too close to the feared possibility that art will become subsumed by established norms. Demonstrating this perspective, which transcends multiple decades of craft-text writing, Charles Glicksberg's 1953 *Writing the Short Story* argues that the writer must have a "creative truthfulness," an "unswerving integrity," and a "resistance to all forms of political coercion, to catchwords and gospels and creeds, since no commissar can presume to tell him what to write or how to write."[23] The writer, in other words, must have a vision of his or her own—a vision that transcends institutionalized discourse. Yet that vision is not meant to be translated into polemical or didactic discourse.

The complexities of this craft concept called "vision" are readily apparent, as this is a notoriously difficult concept to explicate for students in creative writing. Examining Charles Baxter's use of the term in his popular work of craft-criticism *Burning Down the House* points to some of the term's knots: Baxter writes, "Technique must follow a vision, a view of experience. No technique can ever take precedence over vision."[24] "Vision," for Baxter, is a "view of experience," but it should not be managed so calculatingly as to render a work that is overly controlled by it. "[A]rt that is overcontrolled by its meaning," Baxter writes, "may start to go a bit dead,"[25] so the artist cannot doggedly follow a vision, cannot launch a concerted argument. To Baxter, a text overly controlled by meaning would become a mere vehicle of the writer's opinions or views, something nearing propaganda. Arguing against overly manipulative writing that insists on designated conceptual or emotional responses from its readers, Baxter claims that each literary text must be true to the writer's vision, but should not be controlled by the writer's opinions, beliefs, intended meanings or effects. Baxter's theory of artistic vision is backed by the aesthetic thought that precedes him: In the conception of "vision" offered by this craft text, Baxter echoes warnings against the potential harms of the didactic in art, while preserving the writer's artistic freedom—a value that governed the art-for-art's-sake movement—to play out his/her own vision of the world.

Behind these statements in *Burning Down the House* is a rejection of approaches to art that treat literature as useful, or as determined to deliver a particular effect. But what is at stake in these common conceptions? What forms of literature are pushed to the margins in the value system this aesthetic legacy has erected?

Sharon Crowley has tied such anti-didacticism to a high/low distinction that stigmatizes certain form of art.[26] Crowley writes of the stratifying distinctions made between those "who possess the ability to discuss art . . . as objects of *taste* from those who treat encounters with them as *useful or moving* experiences" (emphasis mine).[27] Along similar lines, D.G. Myers notes in his history of creative writing instruction that the field "has acted with hostility toward two different conceptions of literature and writing, which for convenience might be labeled the scholarly and the socially practical"[28]—in other words, the useful. Creative writing, as a field emerging in the twentieth century, has a governing ethos that rejects literature as a body of knowledge or means to an end. While exceptions exist in craft-criticism—for example, Chris Green argues that "there are no such things as well-written poems, only contingently useful poems and less useful poems"[29]—creative writing craft instruction has tended to maintain an aesthetic perspective that divides high "literary" work from the socially practical—the "socially practical" here being inclusive of works intended to be entertaining and/or informative.[30] This high/low distinction is paralleled by an aesthetic/rhetoric distinction that holds the "appeal to an audience" as what separates rhetoric from the aesthetic. Myers notes that "[c]reative writing was formed by amputating 'expression' from a concern with the communication of ideas."[31] The anti-didacticism we have traced in craft texts, and their legacy in the aesthetic tradition, has been key to creative writing's self-forming identity as a field.

The way we handle political texts in the creative writing classroom is shaped by this history, and we do well to make this history—and all its contingencies—known to our students. Rather than banishing political art or "didactic art" from the classroom in sweeping claims, we owe our students a nuancing of the perspectives they find in craft textbooks. Our evaluations will be more legible to students if they can understand the theories and assumptions that have shaped the literary field. We can reconceive the creative writing class as an opportunity to decode the literary community for our students—to help emerging writers know how to navigate the cultures and conversations that constitute and promote contemporary literature.

Creating dangerously: Teaching political literature in the creative writing classroom

As we've seen, the aesthetic tradition has defended art as serving society while debating the means of achieving this outcome. To what extent can art be in the service of some larger purpose? What is at stake when the literary writer explicitly has an aim or intention for the work? Can we assume that every aesthetic object needs no other end than its own coming into being?

Rather than simply banning polemical art from the classroom (the irony of course being that in mandating against polemical literature, creative writing pedagogy erects a polemic of its own—a polemic against polemics, as it were), we can invite questioning and exploration of the intersections between art and activism. Rather than deploying "rules" about art, we can put a diverse range of texts into conversation and ask what is possible. How can the diversity of the textual landscape continue to grow? What is at stake in the choices we make as writers?

We can put our message in the means by taking a nuanced and probing approach to the subject matter that arises in the classroom—refusing to arrest writing into a set of rules, a list of dos and don'ts. Our goal should be to help students gain an artistic, rhetorical, and cultural sensitivity so that they can examine the risks and possibilities of each craft choice or writerly move, including those techniques that might construct a politically effective art—art that produces politicized effects.

The writer provides something important to society—as art gives people access to new modes of thinking and seeing. Art-as-critique can disrupt prevailing norms, can subvert knowledges of the status quo, and can produce new ways of thinking. Art gives us something to think with, as it also shapes our structures of feeling, when we approach political questions. And art indeed can intervene. The creative writing class has an imperative to take into account the effects of the cultural productions that we teach and the possibilities of art-making as a form of resistance. For example, we can prompt our students to ask the following about their own texts and the published and peer-written texts they encounter:

- What common ideas does this text reinforce or destabilize?
- Whom or what is the text meant to speak for or about?
- What is centered and what is left to the margins of this text?
- How does the text represent its subjects? Are the representations potentially damaging, alienating, silencing, or oppressive?
- What are the potential ramifications of the text's claims?
- Who or what stands to gain from the text? And who or what stands to lose or be lost? Whom or what does the text serve?

- What might this text do in the world? How might it change societal understandings, representations, or beliefs?
- What exigencies does the text call upon?
- Has the text avoided oversimplification? Has the text done justice to the multivalent, complex, and diverse nature of human experience with regard to the issues it invokes?
- What artistic responses might this text provoke? How can this text be generative of further artistic production and conversation?

In asking these questions, I want students to probe what it means to "create dangerously"—a phrase that Edwidge Danticat uses to name a "revolt against silence, creating when both the creation and the reception, the writing and the reading, are dangerous undertakings, disobedience to a directive."[32] Creative writing can promote such artistic disobedience to systems that perpetuate inequity and discrimination, the systems that shut down thought, the systems that materially affect lives. To "create dangerously" is not to trot out a party line; it is instead a way of honoring the fact that literature, in its creation, knows more than we do. We learn to critique, to create dangerously, in the process of art's coming into being. Our task as teachers of creative writing is to foster students' access to this power.

Our students can learn to write art that makes sophisticated political interventions. And, indeed, it may be imperative that they learn to do this—since there is no such thing as apolitical art. Depending on how the term is defined, activist literature may not be a small sub-genre, but may be the larger term—characterizing the majority of literary cultural production. Steve Westbrook has gone so far as to claim that it is much more difficult to list the names of writers who did not intend to change something with their words. It is, as Westbrook notes, "extremely difficult to think of writers who have not acted to change culture or alter discourse in some meaningful way, however minor or major, especially when we recall that even the New Critics, who tried to isolate writing from its social function, set out to change—and successfully changed—the culture of writing instruction and the discourse of writing pedagogy."[33] Aesthetic discourse has regularly been harnessed for its power to disrupt normative practices. To mandate against didactic writing without acknowledging this is to mislead our students. Instead, our work in creative writing should be to interrogate what Westbrook has termed "the illusion of the purposeless text."[34] What are the purposes that interest our students? How can their purposes become problematized, reimagined, and interrogated through the artistic work of the creative writing class? What does it mean to participate in world-making as a creative writer?

Accepting that one may have a purpose for writing does not require that we surrender the value we place on uncertainty. Writing from a place of uncertainty allows us to go deeper into our purposes, to offer stories and poems that have more layers to excavate. We can invite our students into this work of delving into the political spheres that matter most to them—not to the exclusion of other forms and approaches to creative writing, but to no longer dismiss the significance of politicized literary production.

Notes

1   Gabrille L'Hirondelle Hill, and Sophie McCall, *The Land We Are: Artists & Writers Unsettle the Politics of Reconciliation* (Winnipeg: ARP, 2015), 1.

2   Rachel Blau DuPlessis, *The Pink Guitar* (New York: Routledge, 1990), 17.

3   See Christina Davis, "Is the Constitution: Some Notes on Poetry & Activism," *Teachers & Writers Magazine* (November 12, 2014).

4   Stephen Dobyns, *Best Words, Best Order: Essays on Poetry,* 2nd edn (New York: Palgram Macmillan, 2003), 183.

5   Janet Burroway and Susan Weinberg, *Writing Fiction,* 6th edn (New York: Longman, 2003), 359. However, Burroway, in *Imaginative Writing,* seems to condone Imamu Amiri Baraka's belief that "the first thing you look for is the stance." Burroway responds to the quote, "Interestingly, Baraka is here arguing that all poetry is *political*—that poets reveal their way of looking at the world the moment they open their mouths." See Janet Burroway, *Imaginative Writing* (New York: Penguin, 2003), 314.

   Burroway does not take a clear position on this debate across these two texts and, instead, immediately leaves this topic after introducing it. It would seem that, for Burroway, this issue of the political in writing is a genre marker, separating fiction (which cannot be political) and poetry. Alternatively, perhaps Burroway accepts that all utterances are inevitably political, yet a writer should avoid taking an overt or conscious political stance. I am not confident of Burroway's viewpoint given how little she writes of this topic—the scarcity of discussion about ethics and politics in these two best-selling craft texts is perhaps most telling; it is naturalized as a relatively unimportant issue for the student writer.

6   William Herbert Carruth, *Verse Writing: A Practical Handbook for College Classes and Private Guidance* (New York: Macmillan, 1934), 48.

7   Carruth, *Verse Writing,* 49.

8   Monroe C. Beardsley, *Aesthetics: From Classical Greece to the Present* (Tuscaloosa: University of Alabama Press, 1966), 25.

9   Beardsley, *Aesthetics,* 136.

10 Another version of this split, "delight and instruct" is associated with another parallel dichotomy in discussions of art: form and content. The "delight" side of the two-pronged dictum would at times be associated with the prioritization of form, while "instruct" would be associated with content.

11 Percy Bysshe Shelley, "From a Defense of Poetry. Or Remarks Suggested by an Essay Entitled 'the Four Ages of Poetry,'" in *The Norton Anthology of Theory and Criticism,* ed. Vincent B. Leitch, 2nd edn (New York: Norton, 1959), 597.

12 Shelley, "From a Defense of Poetry," 613.

13 Shelley, "From a Defense of Poetry," 596–7.

14 Quoted in Marjorie Garber, *The Use and Abuse of Literature* (New York: Pantheon, 2011), 11.

15 As Kant delineates these two realms, he emphasizes that the ethical good is *interested*—invested in bringing about certain actions and dissuading other actions—and, in contrast, aesthetics are *disinterested*. Aesthetics bring about a certain type of pleasure, enlivening the mind. This type of pleasure in valued by Kant, but differentiated from the values connected to ethics. See Immanuel Kant, *Critique of Judgment,* trans. James Creed Meredith, ed. Nicholas Walker (Oxford: Oxford University Press, 1978).

16 In her 1908 handbook on the writing of the short-story, Evelyn May Albright warns: "The short-story has no call to preach. It does not need to teach a moral truth." At the same time, a story "must never be immoral; and it rarely is quite unmoral, if it is a story worth remembering." See Evelyn May Albright, *Short-Story: Its Principles and Structure* (New York: Macmillan, 1908), 227.

   Like Albright, Dobyns scorns writing that preaches. In his 2003 craft textbook, he cautions against the "partisan poem" which might try "to gain sympathy from the reader" (Dobyns, *Best Words,* 181). He defines the partisan poem as one that tells us how to think and feel. Yet, although Dobyns disparages the moralizing poem, he also preserves a moral role for poetry: He writes, "It is easy to say that art has no moral role—that, basically, it is a piece of instruction for the maker. Once the poem is made and has a public life, then it is impossible to deny that social and moral aspect. The poet is not attempting to teach, but, nonetheless, the poem teaches" (Dobyns, *Best Words,* 339). In Albright and Dobyns—writers who are separated by nearly a century—we find the formulation, common to Romantic theorists, that good literature is inherently also a moral benefit to society, even as it makes no effort to preach a moral good. It is the nature of good literature to be good for society, even as the literary writer makes no explicit moral claims.

17 Friedrich Schiller, *On the Aesthetic Education of Man,* trans. Reginald Snell (Mineola, NY: Dover, 2004), 27.

18 Schiller, *On the Aesthetic Education of Man,* 53.

19 Paul Dawson, *Creative Writing and the New Humanities* (New York: Routledge, 2005), 104.

20 Quoted in Dobyns, *Best Words,* 354.

21 Beardsley, *Aesthetics,* 289.

22 See Mary Ann Cain, "Problematizing Formalism: A Double-Cross of Genre Boundaries," *College Composition and Communication* 51 no. 1 (September 1999), 89–95.

23 Charles I. Glicksberg, *Writing the Short Story* (New York: Hendricks House, 1953), 200.

24 Charles Baxter, *Burning Down the House: Essays on Fiction* (St. Paul, MN: Graywolf, 2008), 116.

25 Baxter, *Burning Down the House,* 33.

26 Postmodernism has challenged these high/low distinctions—as Jim Collins
    notes, with postmodernity came "the notion that refined taste, or the
    information needed to enjoy sophisticated cultural pleasures, is now easily
    accessible outside a formal education." See Jim Collins, *Bring on the Books for
    Everybody: How Literary Culture Became Popular Culture* (Durham, NC:
    Duke University Press, 2010), 8. Creative writing's institutional discourses have
    yet to fully destabilize this binary.

27 Sharon Crowley, *Composition in the University: Historical and Polemical
    Essays* (Pittsburgh: University of Pittsburgh Press, 1998), 44.

28 D.G. Myers, *The Elephants Teach: Creative Writing since 1880*, 1st edn
    (Englewood Cliffs: Prentice Hall, 1996), 8.

29 Chris Green, "Materializing the Sublime Reader: Cultural Studies, Reader
    Response, and Community Service in the Creative Writing Workshop," *College
    English* 64 no. 2 (November 2001), 162.

30 There is a long-standing, entrenched norm in creative writing: Creative writing
    syllabi often include statements of the unacceptability of romance, science
    fiction, fantasy, horror, supernatural, mystery, crime, fairy tale, thriller, war,
    western, or ghost stories, favoring instead "literary" fiction; a similar statement
    is made for the poetry workshop, rejecting "Hallmark" and *Chicken Soup*
    poetry.

31 Myers, *Elephants Teach*, 61.

32 Edwidge Danticat, *Create Dangerously: The Immigrant Artist at Work*
    (Princeton: Princeton University Press, 2010), 11.

33 Steve Westbrook, "Just Do It™: Creative Writing Exercises and the Ideology of
    American Handbooks," *New Writing: International Journal for the Practice
    and Theory of Creative Writing* 1 no. 2 (2004), 142.

34 Westbrook, "Just Do It™," 143.

References

Albright, Evelyn May. *Short-Story: Its Principles and Structure*. New York:
    Macmillan, 1908.
Baxter, Charles. *Burning Down the House: Essays on Fiction*. St. Paul, MN:
    Graywolf, 2008.
Beardsley, Monroe C. *Aesthetics: From Classical Greece to the Present*. Tuscaloosa:
    University of Alabama Press, 1966.
Burroway, Janet. *Imaginative Writing*. New York: Penguin, 2003.
Burroway, Janet, and Susan Weinberg. *Writing Fiction*, 6th edn. New York:
    Longman, 2003.
Cain, Mary Ann. "Problematizing Formalism: A Double-Cross of Genre Boundaries."
    College Composition and Communication 51 no. 1 (Sep. 1999): 89–95.
Carruth, William Herbert. *Verse Writing: A Practical Handbook for College
    Classes and Private Guidance*. New York: Macmillan, 1934.
Collins, Jim. *Bring on the Books for Everybody: How Literary Culture Became
    Popular Culture*. Durham, NC: Duke University Press, 2010.

Crowley, Sharon. *Composition in the University: Historical and Polemical Essays*. Pittsburgh: University of Pittsburgh Press, 1998.

Danticat, Edwidge. *Create Dangerously: The Immigrant Artist at Work*. Princeton: Princeton University Press, 2010.

Davis, Christina. "Is the Constitution: Some Notes on Poetry & Activism." *Teachers & Writers Magazine*. November 12, 2014.

Dawson, Paul. *Creative Writing and the New Humanities*. New York: Routledge, 2005.

Dobyns, Stephen. *Best Words, Best Order: Essays on Poetry*, 2nd edn. New York: Palgrave Macmillan, 2003.

DuPlessis, Rachel Blau. *The Pink Guitar*. New York: Routledge, 1990.

Garber, Marjorie. *The Use and Abuse of Literature*. New York: Pantheon, 2011.

Glicksberg, Charles I. *Writing the Short Story*. New York: Hendricks House, 1953.

Green, Chris. "Materializing the Sublime Reader: Cultural Studies, Reader Response, and Community Service in the Creative Writing Workshop." *College English* 64 no. 2 (Nov. 2001): 153–74.

Kant, Immanuel. *Critique of Judgment*. Translated by James Creed Meredith. Edited by Nicholas Walker. Oxford: Oxford University Press, 1978.

L'Hirondelle Hill, Gabrille, and Sophie McCall. *The Land We Are: Artists & Writers Unsettle the Politics of Reconciliation*. Winnipeg: ARP, 2015.

Myers, D.G. *The Elephants Teach: Creative Writing since 1880*, 1st edn. Englewood Cliffs: Prentice Hall, 1996.

Schiller, Friedrich. *On the Aesthetic Education of Man*. Translated by Reginald Snell. Mineola, NY: Dover, 2004.

Shelley, Percy Bysshe. "From a Defense of Poetry. Or Remarks Suggested by an Essay Entitled 'the Four Ages of Poetry.'" In *The Norton Anthology of Theory and Criticism*. Edited by Vincent B. Leitch. 2nd edn. New York: Norton, 1959.

Westbrook, Steve. "Just Do It™: Creative Writing Exercises and the Ideology of American Handbooks." *New Writing: International Journal for the Practice and Theory of Creative Writing* 1 no. 2 (2004): 141–8.

13

"It's my story and I'll revise if I want to":

Rethinking Authorship Through Collaborative Workshop Practices

Joseph Rein

In recent years, I have come to the unsavory conclusion that my workshop undergraduates develop far less than I expect. For the most part—with key exceptions of course—my average student hands in a final portfolio only perfunctorily altered from its initial submission. They enter, they workshop, and after fifteen weeks, they exit relatively unchanged. As with any course, these students vary in their skill level; the chief similarity seems to be the odd phenomenon that they feel less inclined—and sometimes incredibly obstinate—toward revising their works. But wasn't revision, I asked myself, the exact skill for which workshop was meant?

I initially read this obstinacy as naiveté. My students were too close to their work, too early in their writing lives, to see revision as necessary. As such, each semester I varied my workshop style—more pointed critique, fewer global comments and more marginalia, multiple assigned revisions—to combat this naiveté. But no matter my efforts, the outcome remained the same.

Then, one conference with a particularly opinionated student changed my outlook. She came to me and, as kindly as she could, questioned why revision should be such a large part of her grade when her pieces were already substantially better than the norm. Putting aside that her assertion was likely true, I suddenly saw the problem not as naiveté but as stubbornness. This student was essentially telling me, *It's my story and I'll revise if I want to.*

But then a third, more complex idea arose. Perhaps my students—this opinionated one included—failed to revise because they hadn't yet developed the skills to do so. Workshop, at its heart, relies on both positive and constructive criticism: in workshop-speak, what "works" and what "needs work." Setting aside the problematic nature of this—chiefly, that these observations are often personal predilections masked as objective fact—we rarely acknowledge that these comments deal primarily in observation, not resolution. We most often point out instead of suggest, and when we do, we just assume the writer will have the skill necessary to implement such suggestions. Writers thus leave workshop knowing *what* their work needs, but not necessarily *how* to exercise it. In other words, if the amateur poet knew how to imbue his pastoral poem with rich sensory detail, wouldn't it be there already?

This is not to say the workshop doesn't help: identifying key areas of improvement proves vital to an amateur writer, because oftentimes they only see the piece itself and not its latent potential. However, identification and suggestion are only the first steps, and unfortunately, many workshops fail to move beyond them, or if they do, not far enough. As Ashley Cowger states, "the majority of class time is spent giving feedback that will amount to nothing if the writer doesn't use it."[1] It's one thing to note that a character needs development; it's another to actually engage the writer in developing her skills relating to character.

My assumptions led me to shift my own focus. Instead of wondering why my students did not revise sufficiently, I realized I needed to look more closely at their writing habits before entering my classroom, at their desires and self-perception in an artistic sense. What did they hope to gain from workshop in the first place? And what was their sense of authorship, of this murky business of "being a writer"?

The lore of authorship

One of the greatest obstacles to substantial revision comes from the popular perception of a successful writer's craft and lifestyle. Most of my students enter creative writing classrooms or majors with only a vague sense of their future goals. For many the idea of being an "author"—as a job title, as a person, as a way of life—looms in the distance as the final destination on a journey that began sometime in childhood, and on which their college education is a mere stop. Their investment in workshop courses becomes an extension of this end goal: their pieces exist as sounding boards for this progression, as road markers to see where—or how far along—on this path they land.

This self-serving impulse—to use workshop as a measuring stick for one's development—feeds into the popular notion that writers are solitary, singular, self-made. In this mindset, another's critiques may taint the originality, the purity, of a work. Alex Pheby refers to this as the "myth of isolation."[2] Jenn Webb and Andrew Melrose elaborate on this phenomenon as "the desire of so many writers to be *sui generis*; to be dependent on, and to collaborate with, no one; to see works emerge independent of other people"; they state that authors are often viewed, or view themselves, as "social isolates, or solipsists, or egoists."[3] These titles, generally seen as derogatory, become laudatory in the mind of amateur writers. To the amateur student, authors wear their solitariness not as a stigma but as a badge of honor. This isolation, this self-centered egotism, exists as a perceived form of cultural capital: the more alone we can be, the more time we can spend apart from other people, the better writers we will become.

We can hardly blame our students for harboring such perceptions, since popular culture and even published authors themselves misrepresent the real work of writing. In their article "Box Office Poison," Wendy Bishop and Stephen Armstrong highlight this lure of writers-as-characters and its impact on students who enter our classrooms.[4] They describe how writing as an exercise—the daily, dogmatic aspects of composition for professional writers—does not entice as does the perception of writers as tortured souls or truth-seeking vigilantes or even action heroes. Thus, students "learn the images and to live the image ... they are living the life they have seen depicted in countless films, held up to them as mirrors for manners."[5] Entering our classrooms, students often attempt to "be a writer" based more on these misconceptions than on the act of writing itself. Film and television rarely depict the act of composition itself, and when they do, the act is often dramatized as fevered, frantic, and most often fleeting. And if writing rarely takes the stage, revision never even enters the theater.

Our students' perceptions of professional writers as public figures, unfortunately, rarely differ. Our students see writers at readings, at book signings, at social events; in other words, students see the podium but not the countless hours of writing that earned those writers such a place. And very often these writers' re-creations of their own writing processes are obscure, indistinct: many act as though asking about a work's genesis is akin to asking a chef where he gets his ingredients. This leads to what I often call the fallacy of *abstruse inspiration*: the notion that a writer's inspirations and aspirations are unknown even to herself. When my students enter the classroom, their prevalent notion is that authors only write (successfully anyway) when they are under the throes of some strange passion that is neither creatable nor quantifiable. We isolate ourselves from each other, not to work but to await the muse.

As a realist, I understand that the myths of isolation and abstruse inspiration will in some senses always remain. As such, I never question my students' initial impressions of authorship, nor do I intentionally grate against them. However, these myths seem too often to stand in the way of a greater appreciation for revision, and for the work of workshop itself. So for me, the question became, what could I do to open their minds to revision while not attempting to shatter something that had been built from their childhood, that had perhaps lured them to writing in the first place? Something that, in a semester's worth of time, I may not undo if I tried? Most importantly, how could I teach my writers to revise, and revise well?

Revision revisited

Toward the end of a recent workshop, one student asked me how many versions of her story she needed to hand in with her final portfolio, because in the past, she had to submit four or more revisions of a single piece. Cowger details this "multiple revisions" method as a way to highlight the importance of revision in workshops; others include requiring at least one "significant revision" in a portfolio—although Cowger herself admits that "significant" is nearly impossible to define—and workshopping a single piece more than once.[6] Each of these has its benefits and drawbacks; however, most of them, like many graded measures of revision, tend to value quantity over quality. They assume that altering, and then perhaps printing out, a text a certain number of times will produce a requisite amount of revision. They also do not seem to fully engage the heart of true revision: the moments when a writer recognizes for herself what a work *can be*, and reworking it to approach—if not reach—that potential.

So, for reasons seemingly obvious to me, I didn't have a set number of revisions for my student. But her inquiry raised a good pedagogical question: how much weight should a professor attach to revision? In an ideal world, I would place their entire grade on it, because no piece of writing approaches its potential in one draft. But that would be unfair to those who struggle, strain, and sacrifice for their initial submissions, as I know many do. It also privileges those who submit work earlier in the semester, as they simply have more time. And anyway, when I have altered the weight of the grade in the past, it has done little to alter my students' investment in their revision processes.

Another avenue taken by many scholars is to assign revision narratives that require students to contextualize their writing processes from beginning to end. If anything, these narratives give me insight into the writer's initial motivations, and allow her a moment to speak directly about her work. But these rarely go deep enough. Like workshop critiques themselves, these documents often explicate what *what* the writer has changed, and often *why*, but rarely does it delve into *how*.

Toward a collaborative workshop

Though rarely considered in this light, workshop itself is an interesting exercise in authorship. When our students offer up work for communal critique, they in essence surrender their claim over it. They must admit, if unconsciously, that their work would benefit from collaboration. But this comes with caveats. Workshop is meant to aid, not control: to suggest, not direct. Though critiques are often subjective and stylized, the critics rarely invest themselves beyond recommendation. This caveat, often unspoken, will at times rear its head when a student stops to say, "But it's your poem, so you can do whatever you want." I am guilty of this myself; I will often say, "I don't want to write your essay for you," before offering a potential alternative. But afterward, I often feel the weight of a missed opportunity, as though the writer might have benefited more from these tangential possibilities than another comment on how she could use more setting detail. These moments feel closer to collaboration, to genuine communal meaning-making, and thus closer to moments where writers can truly see their work's potential.

Mary Ann Cain offers one of the practices closest to a collaborative workshop. Her method, which she titles the "OIE Method," exists in these fruitful moments by making observation only the first step: the second and third are investigation and experimentation.[7] This "thirdspace" created by observing, investigating, and experimenting allows for "the group to collectively explore the multiple possibilities for how [a] draft might be reconstituted."[8] It assumes not an "ideal text," but rather "a plethora of possibilities for what a draft *might* mean."[9] Here students are allowed, encouraged even, to explore revision not as a singular avenue toward a writer's initial intention, but rather as avenues pointing in many divergent, sometimes contradictory, directions.

But I wanted to go even further. In two of my non-workshop courses, I discovered that collaborative writing created spaces where experimentation and revision became not only augmented, but necessary. These courses spent less time on the genesis of ideas—less wallowing in the abstruse inspiration of a piece—but rather focused on identifying a piece's potential and exploring avenues to pursue it. These courses forced many of my otherwise obstinate writers into newer, and more complex, writing challenges, perhaps because co-writing as an exercise pushes against the notions of isolation and abstruse inspiration. These collaborative-based courses offered students a fresher insight into their revision processes, which seemed to me the aim of workshop itself. But since my workshop failed where these courses succeeded, I wanted to bridge the gap. It arrived at a simple, yet likely contentious, idea: in this experimental workshop, my students would rewrite *each other's* work.

This form of collaboration, as outlined by Donna Lee Brien and Tess Brady, fits under the "secondary collaboration" model, wherein one person begins a project and another finishes it.[10] This differs from models such as the contribution model, in which each person simultaneously contributes part to the whole; or the cooperative model, where one person begins a project and then circulates it through the group; or the synchronous model, where all members work collectively on every aspect.[11] In recent years, I have utilized parts of each of these collaborative models, and each has its positives and challenges. For my workshop, I ultimately chose a secondary collaboration model for two reasons. First, it would be the simplest to explain to my students. But second, and more importantly, my vision for this exercise highlighted revision above composition, re-envisioning above envisioning, development above conception. It would, I hoped, distance students from their own work initially; but then, through struggle with another's work, ultimately bring them back with renewed insight.

I did not come to this decision without hesitation. Collaboration and creativity, like warring siblings, often flock to opposite sides of a given room. And although creative writing scholars have begun to champion collaboration, doubts still exist: Webb and Melrose state that collaboration "aims at developing students' capacity, imbuing them with graduate attributes, and ensuring that they are better positioned to practice effectively after they leave the university" but then also add that "most of the benefits of collaboration seem directed to professional, rather than creative, practice."[12] Admittedly, the attributes commonly attached to collaboration seem more corporate than artistic. And for the most part, scholars paint students as at best hesitant, at worst outright hostile, toward the prospect of co-writing.

Once we began, however, I found much less resistance than I anticipated. Helpful was the fact that enrollment was small, and even: ten to be exact. Helpful too was my decision to withhold this assignment until the final weeks of the class. As Webb and Melrose state, "the secondary collaboration relationship relies on a great deal of trust and empathy between the collaborators," and though a professor can't necessarily create such attributes, she can help foster and develop them as a semester progresses.[13]

The class paired up, and I assigned each student two roles. As Writer One, the student would offer up his submissions, one of which would be revised by his partner. As Writer Two, the other student would take this submission and make substantial revisions, based not on Writer One's preferences or tendencies, but on her own. To start, each group collaboratively chose which submissions would work best for the project. Allowing this initial collaboration proved crucial; this way, no Writer One felt as though his favorite work, his "baby" so to speak, was being appropriated by his classmate. It also gave Writer Two the opportunity to explain which of Writer One's works appealed to her most, and to describe her thoughts on revision strategies. In many cases, the decision became a negotiation of sorts, which heightened both students' investment in the outcome.

Writer Two then had a week to substantially revise Writer One's initial submission. Returning after that week, I allowed the groups time to read each other's revisions, and then to discuss initial impressions. After this, we held a full-class discussion about the successes and struggles of tackling another's work. The discussion was lively, enlightening: along with some necessary venting of frustration, the class also—for the first time in any of my workshop experiences, student or professor—explored not just the *outcome* of their revisions but the *processes* that produced them. These students began to recognize that such collaborative work brought "the possibility of variation to a project," and that such variations, implicitly or explicitly, must happen in order for a piece to approach its potential.[14] It seemed as though, separated from their own initial intentions, my students finally focused on and found a deeper meaning for the work of revision.

Of course, not all students arrived at such epiphanies. In order to encourage engagement with the project, I allowed students to choose their own partners, but in retrospect I may have missed an opportunity. Those who worked well together—and in some ways wrote similarly—emerged the most positive about the project, but also likely learned the least. In at least one case, the parallels in the students' writing styles led only to minor, surface-level revisions. Those with different writing styles, or those paired together out of necessity, made more radical revisions and thus came closer to my learning objective. In the future, I plan to assign pairs based on my perceptions of the strengths and weaknesses in their writing. Pairing the plot-heavy adventure writer with the character study aficionado would likely allow each a better chance at seeing their work anew.

Another obstacle, inevitably, became the question of authorship, of ownership over the final products. Whose poems were these? At what point did Writer One's story end and Writer Two's begin? And most specifically: if Writer One wanted to aim for publication, would Writer Two's name need to be attached? I used these questions as the basis for a discussion on authorship itself. I showed collaborative creative works, in writing and visual art, in digital and print mediums. I pulled up two author's dedication pages from recent successful novels, both of which listed over twenty names of readers and editors (who, after all, are collaborators). I then encouraged my students to pursue their works in whatever capacity they saw fit, from continuing to work collaboratively all the way to accepting none of their peer's revisions, because for me, the end product meant less than the process. The exercise in collaborative revision aimed to disrupt my students' sense of isolation and abstruse inspiration by releasing their work from its usual confines. It required them to see not *what was* on the page after draft one, but *what could be*.

Collaboration in genre

In the next phase of this collaborative work, I plan to assign cross-genre revisionary work. For this assignment, Writer Two would use Writer One's work as a basis for a new work in a different genre. So, if Writer One submitted a short story, Writer Two could then compose a poem, nonfiction essay, one-act play, or short screenplay based on some aspect of Writer One's original work. The craft elements that Writer Two would utilize—be it character, setting, down to even specific lines or language—and the amount of homogenization would be entirely up to her. The class would then share the works similar to my exercise above, or even submit them for a more traditional workshop.

As is likely apparent, a truly collaborative workshop has only begun to form in my mind, and like collaborative work itself, it continues to coalesce and evolve. I do not intend, however, to suggest that such work should or will replace the traditional workshop. The pull of history, of traditional university structures, of the publishing world, still weigh heavily on our daily classroom practices. However, those who live in the world of creative writing long enough come to realize that nothing we do—not writing, not studying, not publishing—is solitary work. As an institution, creative writing, and the workshop on which it has been founded, would do well to acknowledge and utilize the immense potential in collaborative work. Doing so will help students see authors not as what they seem to be, as isolated, abstrusely inspired entities, but as they truly are: as workers, as lifetime learners, and as collaborators in every work they produce.

Notes

1   Cowger, Ashley. "Eradicating Reviser's Block: Bringing Revision to the Foreground." *Dispatches from the Classroom: Graduate Students on Creative Writing Pedagogy.* Eds Chris Drew, Joseph Rein, and David Yost (New York: Continuum, 2012), 16.

2   Pheby, Alex. "The Myth of Isolation: Its Effect on Literary Culture and Creative Writing as a Discipline." *Creative Writing: Teaching Theory and Practice* 2.1 (Feb. 2010), 51–8.

3   Web, Jenn, and Andrew Melrose. "Writers Inc.: Writing and Collaborative Practice." *Creative Writing Pedagogies for the Twenty-First Century.* Eds Alexandria Peary and Tom C. Hunley (Carbondale, IL: Southern Illinois University Press, 2015), 103.

4   Bishop, Wendy, and Stephen Armstrong. "Box Office Poison: The Influence of Writers in Films on Writers (in Graduate Programs)." *Can It Really Be Taught? Resisting Lore in Creative Writing Pedagogy.* Eds Kelly Ritter and Stephanie Vanderslice (Portsmouth, NH: Boynton/Cook, 2007), 91–104.

5   Bishop and Armstrong, "Box Office Poison," 100.

6   Cowger, "Eradicating Reviser's Block," 17.

7   Cain, Mary Ann. "'A Space of Radical Openness': Re-Visioning the Creative Writing Workshop." *Does the Writing Workshop Still Work?* Ed. Dianne Donnelly (Bristol, UK: Multilingual Matters, 2010), 224.

8   Cain, "A Space of Radical Openness," 227.

9   Cain, "A Space of Radical Openness," 226.

10 Brien, Donna Lee, and Tess Brady. "Collaborative Practice: Categorizing Forms of Collaboration for Practitioners." *TEXT* 7.2 (October 2003). http://www.textjournal.com.au/oct03/brienbrady.htm [accessed February 8, 2016].

11 Brien and Brady, "Collaborative Practice."

12 Webb and Melrose, "Writers Inc.," 113.

13 Webb and Melrose, "Writers Inc.," 118.

14 Webb and Melrose, "Writers Inc.," 114.

References

Bishop, Wendy, and Stephen Armstrong. "Box Office Poison: The Influence of Writers in Films on Writers (in Graduate Programs)." *Can It Really Be Taught? Resisting Lore in Creative Writing Pedagogy.* Edited by Kelly Ritter and Stephanie Vanderslice. Portsmouth, NH: Boynton/Cook, 2007.

Cowger, Ashley. "Eradicating Reviser's Block: Bringing Revision to the Foreground." *Dispatches from the Classroom: Graduate Students on Creative Writing Pedagogy.* Edited by Chris Drew, Joseph Rein, and David Yost. New York: Continuum, 2012.

Pheby, Alex. "The Myth of Isolation: Its Effect on Literary Culture and Creative Writing as a Discipline." *Creative Writing: Teaching Theory and Practice* 2.1 (Feb. 2010).

Web, Jenn, and Andrew Melrose. "Writers Inc.: Writing and Collaborative Practice." *Creative Writing Pedagogies for the Twenty-First Century.* Edited by Alexandria Peary and Tom C. Hunley. Carbondale, IL: Southern Illinois University Press, 2015.

14

Toward a Digital Historiography of Creative Writing Programs in Our Millennium

Ben Ristow

The historical development of creative writing programs has been well-documented and researched through Stephen Wilbers, D.G. Myers, Mark McGurl, and more recently, in Eric Bennett's book *Workshops of Empire* (2015).[1] In these historical accounts, the role of creative writing programs has focused on how broader socio-cultural, political, and educational movements came to determine what we now consider to be the culture and institution of "creative writing," one of the most anomalous and cavalier educational enterprises of the twentieth century. The institution of creative writing has come to be studied and historicized by the assumption that important cultural factors—within Progressive education or the Cold War, for example—created the foundation for the establishment and proliferation of creative writing in America. True to the cause of democratic ideals, progressive educational philosophies, and practitioner knowledge, creative writing has been historicized with ample and broad brush strokes for the educational and political movements in mid-century America.

These histories position creative writing as an "experiential commodity" (McGurl) or "elephant machine" (Myers) more than a teaching or artistic endeavor born of writer-teachers in contexts across America.[2] The focus on the Iowa Writer's Workshop (and its authors) in our histories serves to entrench and celebrate the most important creative writing program, but it also tends to obfuscate the variegated and complex development of individual creative writing programs at large. Our historical studies feeds the common lore of Iowa as the beginning and end of creative writing and feels a bit like we are writing a contemporary history of American agricultural development through a singular lens: *think corn*. A large segment of creative writing programs did originally develop through and as a result of the Writers' Workshop; however, I would argue that the development of creative writing programs since 1980 might be more fairly assessed as an attempt to distinguish themselves from Iowa rather than as an attempt to simply align with its originating philosophies. Part and parcel to this distinguishing of character, in authors, in aesthetics, and in geography, the contemporary creative writing program is distinguished as much by external cultural factors as by the textual, visual, and digital artifacts that arise from within each individual creative writing program. What happens to creative writing history when we work inductively and ascribe to each program its own history and legacy of writers? Also, what happens when future historians return to digital archives to understand the value and mission of creative writing culture? In a June 2016 article for *New York Times Magazine*, Jenna Wortham suggests: "this plethora of new media and materials may function as a totally new type of archive: a multidimensional ledger of events that academics, scholars, researchers and the general public can parse to generate a more prismatic recollection of history."[3] New histories of creative writing, then, necessitate a multi-faceted approach that accounts for new media now more than ever.

I argue in this essay that creative writing historians must now account for the ways that the digital and visual artifacts, in the form of traditional print media and new media especially, determine the ways we characterize and historicize creative writing culture. By referring to creative writing as a *culture*, I am necessarily choosing to see and analyse creative writing as a culture rather than as an *institution*. Institutions contain and harness human activity certainly, but the reference to creative writing as a culture provides us the connotations of human relationships and artistic practices. The culture appears to be headlined by canonized authors, or schisms, as Chad Harbach points out between NYC and the MFA; nonetheless, the analysis of individual creative writing program artifacts in print advertisements in the *Writer's Chronicle*, program website materials, along with promotional videos about and for individual programs, will determine the history of creative writing in the future.[4] Future historians will have to contend with the conditions of lore that position the names and faces of published authors teaching *in* programs with those students who are whisked *through* programs.

Curiously, the void in our histories of creative writing also highlights the omission of the individual student writer, and far from aligning ourselves with the promoters or detractors of MFA and PhD programs in creative writing, we must at least observe in the ways Howard Zinn might—how do students *experience* creative writing and how are their stories best told?

In looking at a small sample of digital artifacts for this essay, I am far from achieving a thorough treatment of creative writing history, but I hope to initiate a contextual and methodological shift consistent with Adam Koehler's call for more digital creative writing studies scholarship in his

College English article "Digitizing Craft: Creative Writing Studies and New Media: A Proposal."[5] Furthermore, the gesture toward more digital studies of creative writing has been made by the collection edited by Michael Dean Clark, Trent Hergenrader, and Joseph Rein *Creative Writing in the Digital Age: Theory, Practice, and Pedagogy.*[6] These studies of creative writing do more than cast the field in the light of the digital, they argue, more foundationally, that *creative writing is a digital and visual culture* that includes new facets, interfaces, and artifacts within its purview and therefore its study.

This essay sets out on a short journey into the world of YouTube promotional videos in order to determine the facets of creative writing culture. As a relatively new academic discipline, and one in which the printed word holds transcendent sway, writer-scholars are in danger of overlooking the digital and visual artifacts that creative writing programs disseminate. My argument is that creative writing programs have created a digital culture that calls potential applicants, their viewers, many of whom are attempting to mark the end of their adolescence, to claim an identity as writers and to authenticate that identity through the experience of workshop with established authors. By associating their identity with that of a "writer" and "reader" and sometimes "author," the program videos that I will analyse demonstrate how creative writing culture situates itself as a context—be it writing workshops or social gatherings—where apprentice writers can take rhetorical action and make claim to the identity of "The Author" and their place in the familial structure of their program. As Bennett points out in *Workshops of Empire*, the demographics of today's workshop differs greatly from the "mature and experienced" veterans that first entered Iowa, and it seems our methodologies should transform to account for a new historical moment.[7]

Before moving forward into the promotional video analysis, it seems productive to present a quick addendum to my claim: *creative writing is a digital culture.* One of these additions is supported by this essay collection and the premise that lore, in its historical myopia and stagnant workshop models, is counterproductive to pedagogical reform in creative writing. Lore is a paradoxical term though, as Stephen North reminds us, and it is possible to define lore as a concept with valuable import for historiographical and pedagogical reform.[8] Rather than wholly discounting "lore," creative writing studies scholars may choose to analyse creative writing as an oral or auditory culture in which practitioner knowledge is valued above theoretical knowledge. The separation of creative writing as a field apart from literary and composition studies hinges on its reliance the ideas of "lore," "craft," and "workshop." The redefinition of these terms may do more to change traditional practices than an outright dismissal of them. In the case of the oral tradition within creative writing and its status in the teaching context of workshops, we need testimonies of student workshop experiences, examinations of author interviews on teaching along with research on audio podcasts, traditional and new media discussions, and craft seminar interactions that demonstrate the ways that lore is defined in the culture of creative writing. Lore will continue to problematize reform to workshops where marginalized voice are suppressed or silenced, but it may provide the impetus for writing new histories and pedagogies within a predominately digital culture.

In our transition to secondary orality, as referenced in Kathleen Welch's foundational book *Electric Rhetoric: Classical Rhetoric, Oralism, and New Literacy* (1999) creative writing studies scholars will benefit from a robust examination of the visual, oral, and other *interactive media* that will come to dominate the ways we conceive of the pedagogical dimensions of craft and workshop.[9] Creative writing culture may appear to resist or discard, in some capacities, the progression away from a literate, text-based culture to one of an image and interaction-based culture. I argue though that precisely because of this perceived resistance and because creative writing's expansion (beginning in the 1960s) coincides with the evolution of new media and Web 2.0 and 3.0, we must now work to recognize the participation of creative writing in new media. For this essay, I am working with video artifacts in order to determine their rhetorical function and to propose a way of historicizing creative writing that adds to the examinations of Myers, McGurl, and Bennett. In this enterprise I touch upon Erik Erikson's sociological concept of identity formation and Murray Bowen's theory of family systems in looking at two creative program promotional videos (from Syracuse University and the Iowa Writer's Workshop).[10] In my analysis, I will suggest that that viewers of creative writing promo videos can authenticate and solidify their identities through joining an MFA program and securing their position in an existing family by differentiating themselves within a program.

Are MFA students in an *identity crisis* as they enter creative writing programs? The question feels moot depending upon who we imagine to be the audience and applicant for MFA/PhD programs in creative writing or which literary studies scholar we ask. Erikson's concept of identity formation and the crisis of late adolescences seems feasibly remedied by enrolling in an MFA program; however, Erikson's theory of psychosocial development has its limits and does not answer the question for all populations of writers entering MFA programs. Nonetheless, promotional videos invite applicants to situate their identities as writers within a context and to move from a sense of isolation to one of intimacy in a quasi-family unit. Watching videos for creative writing programs highlights how identity is *determined* and *differentiated* by the MFA program you choose (or that chooses you). Think of Uncle Sam or Smokey the Bear enlisting "you" and viewers will understand the ways that MFA promo videos offer a deterministic view on their support for writers within a differentiating community. Only you can choose to enroll (if selected) into a community that will determine your identity.

The root of creative writing culture is bound by the paradox inherent in what Erikson would call "individuation" and Murray Bowen characterizes as "differentiation."[11] Bowen claims that differentiation creates the self and distinguishes the self from those that support him/her. MFA programs, in promoting their community, culture, and family, have the interesting challenge of providing a social group—workshop mates and mentoring faculty—that allow the apprentice writer to develop their authentic voice and artistic vision in the Romantic tradition. Ironically, but perhaps not surprisingly, MFA promo videos must be necessarily deterministic and claim that mentorship in a particular environment by one cohort of peers and group of faculty authors will provide the best opportunity to differentiate oneself from other writers. This deterministic ethos, which has proliferated through the culture of AWP and the increased competition by a larger and larger group of programs, has given traction to the common *deterministic fallacy* that MFA programs produce aesthetically homogenous writing, namely literary realism or narrative poetry. The fallacy can have the sheen of truth, but upon closer examination of the videos, the discerning program can determine its history while showing how it is differentiated from others.

In the fiftieth anniversary video created for Syracuse University in 2012, interviewees argue that Syracuse University is distinctive from other creative writing programs. For Syracuse University's Creative Writing Program, this distinctiveness is manifested in the writers who have taught or graduated from the program, and these names materialize as images floating across the screen. The narrative initial centers around the concept of studenthood, and especially Brooks Haxton recalling of his mentor Hayden Carruth and other prominent Syracuse faculty, namely Ray Carver and Toby Wolff. Mary Karr continues by identifying the way social class characterizes and differentiates the Syracuse MFA program:

> It's a very scrappy program, I think we figured out at one point that Toby didn't finish high school, I didn't finish high school, I don't think Ray finished high school, Chris Kennedy didn't finish high school, actually it's kind of a blue collar program. We really just look at the work, we don't study academic records, so that might mean you have a student from Harvard and a student from Brown and some guy that has been working in the train yards and has been writing short stories at home in his spare time.[12]

George Saunders follows Carr in the video and identifies the ways that the program traverses class distinctions and is outside the framework of writing training. Of special interest here is how Saunders, Carr, and prominent grads recount their humble beginnings before entering the program as students. It would seem that identification as a writer serves (in part) as the resolution to the challenges that comes in the form of job dissatisfaction, poor academic performance, or financial hardship; however, I would argue that embedded in the commentary by Karr and Saunders is the challenge of differentiating their program. The Syracuse video artfully characterizes their program as one for the working class, and they successfully negotiate the question of an applicant—am I a writer?—by discussing their program's selectivity. By accepting, as they cite, six students out of 520 applicants, Saunders does a masterful job in articulating the enterprise as community building rather than as training in writing or as a stop on the way to a career. The rigor of the program is matched quite masterfully with the characterization of it as a home. Saunders teases out distinctions between the identity of student, writer, and author by articulating it as an "opportunity." He says:

> By the time you get to the top six [applicants], they are not only so talented, they're talented in six unique flavors, that you can see all the lives they have lived on the page, and it's just an amazing thing. So at that point, what are you teaching them really?
> Are you teaching them to write? NO. They figured that out years ago. What you really are doing, you're kind of bringing them along. Trying to get some sense of who they are. Then trying to get them to have the talent for having their particular talent. So that's something entirely different than teaching someone to write. And we make that particularly clear, we are not really there to get them a career, we may or may not, we are there to give them the opportunity to do this almost impossible thing. And then they go and do it, which is pretty cool.[13]

Saunders comments are significant in that they demonstrate that he and other program faculty are interested in the identity of the students, but that identity is not a question of whether they are writers or not or whether they can write or not; instead, he assumes that admitted students are already writers who need to develop their talent. The crisis seems then to shift toward publication, and the students and faculty emphasize that process is the focus rather than publication. No agents will be buzzing around the Syracuse campus they say, and it seems that the differentiation that informs those in the video is *the difference between being a writer and being a published author*. The latter is aspirational, but as emphasized in the video, not the objective of the program. So perhaps the resolution that Saunders presents is less stable. Sure, the students can write, "they learned that long ago," however, their identity as published author is not yet secure and this instability is assumed by Saunders commentary.

Given the stability of the identity of writer, but the instability of a claim to authorhood, the student commentators speak to the aspects of nurturing they received while in the program. Highlighted here are the pseudo-familial aspects of the program and the former students take up where Karr and Saunders left off. Elizabeth Koch says, "I had a family there. I mean. And it was not hierarchical like writing programs can be".[14] Another student says, "I remember Arthur Flowers taking me out for crappy Mexican food on Erie Boulevard [. . .] and I wondered what world I had just stepped into that my professor sat across from me feeding me tortilla chips. Not really feed me but [...]".[15] Sarah Harwell, another former student who is now a faculty member, discusses her relationship with Mary Karr. "It all changed my life. I became a writer. I also got a whole new wardrobe. I got a new boyfriend. And Mary Karr actually got me the boyfriend. Mary Karr said you can't wear any more hats."[16] The humor and intimacy that is communicated is significant and establishes a writer as they move from isolation into intimacy within their program relationships. The nurturing and intimate elements of the Syracuse's video speak to the ways that the program has characterized its distinctive qualities and set itself apart by alluding to the familial qualities at the core of its program. The familial themes that run through the video offer an effective counterargument against the common student perception that distinguished faculty will be aloof or highly differentiated to the concerns of writers in the program. *Differentiation* as a psychological concept is key in understanding the identity cast by the Syracuse University MFA program and other promo videos. On one hand the program could be characterized as poorly-differentiated, whereby writers are dependent upon the faculty to mentor and coddle apprentice writers. Students' commentaries are tongue-and-cheek at moments, but they cast the program in the light of dependency and intimacy, dangerous values for a program to taut if they would like also to demand rigor. Saunders commentary alongside the interviews with Karr, Haxton, and Arthur Flowers, however, are positioned with candid and heartfelt student commentary that give us a sense of student autonomy and a mentor's responsibility. The differentiation, between student and faculty authors, then seems well-differentiated, healthy, and the backdrop of a happy hour gathering gives the program the feel of a family reunion rather than a performed sell.

Bowen's theory of differentiation within family units and social groups has particular value when looking at The University of Iowa's "A License to Write" 2010 video.[17] By focusing on highly-differentiated individuals, those Iowa graduates who have become established authors, the program interviews focus on the ways that the Workshop cultivates rigor and competitiveness. Iowa's eighteen-minute video juxtaposes still and video images from the 1940s and 1950s with images of faculty authors at Iowa, and unlike the Syracuse video, faculty and former students are given a more formal distance and faculty are shown in still images while former students are interviewed. The interviews emphasize the ways that the highly-differentiated tact and philosophy of the workshop might produce better writers who are trained by fire and ice. As Nathan Englander puts it at one point, "we wrote as if there was a shelf that held only one book."[18] In contrast to the Syracuse program video, the Iowa video makes acceptance (an important highlight for interviewees) only the first step in a highly elaborate initiation into the Darwinian affair of workshopping.

The Iowa promo video jettisons the familial sentiments for an argument, which is both political and artistic, that authorship arrives in the face of a contest of ego whereby gladiators battle for authentication and differentiation. Englander's comments are echoed by other unnamed commentators who offer a range of experiences including: receiving their acceptance letter; living in Iowa City; sharing feelings of intimidation among peers; and describing the personality and approaches to teaching by current and past workshop authors. The effect of the video offers the same candid qualities of the Syracuse video while foregrounding the workshop experience as a painfully transformative experience. In this transformation, one that is easily associated with psychosocial crises of Erikson's theory, students present rigor, competition, and seriousness as a method of authenticating the identity of author.

One need only look at the violent imagery that interviewees conjure up to confirm this analysis of the video. One student writes that: "workshop was a shock, it was like having your head banged into a wall." Another student calls it "a medieval conquistador sea-faring queer ghost story" and more brutally, another says "in workshop, participants provide raw meat to the other beasts."[19] These reflections are echoed in the feelings of inauthenticity, what one interviewee calls the "imposter complex" that follows some students through their experience in the Iowa Writers' Workshop. This imposter complex is a way of naming the identity crisis that faces writers entering the program and it is also way of determining outsiders within the social unit of the Iowa Writers' Workshop. Here admittance, as Saunders suggested in the Syracuse video, does not guarantee acceptance or support in social group, in fact, the teeth of the program are bared toward the student in a way that should challenge and frightened them to produce quality workshop submissions.

Fear is meant to communicate and persuade the student that this art training is authentic; authentication here comes from differentiating oneself from one's peers. The workshop method as a human sport is meant to be brutal and implicitly offers the rationale that writers are best trained through hostile, impersonal, and images of animalistic brutality. The hyperbole of interviewees can be easily dismissed as braggadocio but it illustrates the commitment of the program to a level of differentiation that allows for the author to come into being. Is the rigor of the Iowa Writers' Workshop that distinguishes the program from others? In the video, the answer is clear, but the footage also conjures up the disaffected and castoffs who are made invisible by the workshop process—those who could not differentiate themselves and make their names as published authors after or during their time at Iowa.

Without aligning with detractors or apologists for MFA programs, the comparison between the Syracuse and Iowa promotional videos should give historians pause. Both programs would seem to share a lineage to Iowa, however, the videos separate their missions in profound ways. In the Iowa video, the *par excellence* is rigor and competition is not only valued it is promoted through the culture of the program. From this side of the spectrum, and in term of psychological differentiation, the Writers' Workshop is highly differentiated and calls its writers to make serious and meaningful strides toward contributing to contemporary literature. The suggestion here is that a highly-differentiated program will recruit and train a highly-differentiated group of writers to impact literary movements outside of The Workshop. There is not a whiff of dependency in the "License to Write" video and it is clear that the University of Iowa wants writers to differentiate themselves from within the program and as they succeed or fail as authors outside of the program. The Syracuse University program maintains what we would consider lower sense of differentiation and suggests that faculty and peers in the program will nurture students. As a highly competitive program with a strong history, Syracuse University creates a sense in the viewer that they are people (peers and faculty) who are willing to build upon apprentice writers' uniqueness and strengths.

Neither promotional video profiles any current or past students that have not published a book or more than one book in many cases. Graduates of creative writing programs that do not publish are invisible entities and therefore the nameless bodies that are backgrounded or erased in these videos. Does creative writing culture recognize and give identity to those former students who identify as academics, editors, publishers, or teachers? This question is a question of the digital omission and one that creative writing historians must address in their future work with programmatic artifacts. Looking at the promo videos for less prestigious programs, there is less emphasis on admittance or competition, and the videos highlight the emergence of students into the identity of writers rather than as authors.

In the AWP Campus Visit Series (2016), videos appear from undergraduate BFA programs at SUNY Oswego, low residency programs in Oregon, three-year MFA programs at San Jose State alongside programs at Austin Community College.[20] In many respects, the purpose is to find students an environment in which to move from studenthood to roles as writers—not authors. Unlike Iowa's video, the ethos of place (both in the sense of the geographical and artistic) is juxtaposed with the nurturing ethos of Syracuse's video. Backdrops of mountains and bodies of water emphasize the ways that attending a program can unify students' physical environment with their psychological environment. For Oregon State Cascades, this means featuring a background of trees and Florida Atlantic pans the dappling waters of the beachside while in San Jose State—it means that place is a "literary incubator" that sounds fitting for its proximity to Silicon Valley. The New School and New York Arts Program talk about being "in the middle of it, you feel the buzz of it."[21] The student testimonials sometimes—as is the case with The New School and Chapman University—serve more as welcome videos for those already admitted to the program, but they also highlight the ways that collaboration among the students is more important than connecting with faculty.

Syracuse University's video is notable for the ways that bridges the competitiveness of Iowa with the mentorship and collaborative focus of less competitive programs. The video synthesizes the rhetorical principles identified in the other videos by focusing on identity formation as an author, workshop experience with faculty mentors, and the sense of place that moves beyond upstate New York. The ingredients of geography, mentorship, and identity represent the major touchstones of MFA program promotion and it's these ingredients that measure whether a program promise a lower or highly-differentiated experience for their admitted students. Dependency does not cultivate rigor and rigor would seem to compromise the trust needed to train promising writers in a cohort akin to a family.

In using the term differentiation to characterize the rhetorical choices that programs make in promoting their ethos and values, the purpose is to distinguish oneself without suggesting that the program is overly deterministic. Many MFA/PhD programs in creative writing say quite candidly that writing cannot be taught and yet exist wholly on the principle that it can. The principle is paradoxical and critical to buttressing MFA program against the suggestion from detractors of MFAs that their students produce a homogenized product and brand of writing. To assume that student writing coming from MFA programs is undifferentiated would suggest that we couldn't differentiate one MFA program from the next. My examination of digital artifacts suggests that MFA programs, in their expansion or ballooning or proliferation, have attempted to differentiate themselves as units and as geographies and as aesthetically diverse educational programs and writers' workshops.

For creative writing historians, these digital artifacts allow us, first and foremost, to gage the educational values situated within individual programs and to see those values emphasized through various forms of new media. The imagery in video promos also highlights the ways that faculty authors are mythologized for the purposes of promotion. Beyond their function in story or lore-building, these videos give us a way to analyse creative writing culture in a way that works from within programs and complements those who would work deductively from the pervading social and cultural conditions of literary production. Adopting a historical archivist approach to the digital artifacts or conducting oral histories of individual creative writing programs will render an entirely new history than the ones we currently use in our work as creative writing scholars. These histories will emerge from lore as much as they may resist those traditions that function to silence or isolate students; in this work it will be our responsibilities as historians to utilize artifacts that emerge from new media and beyond.

Notes

1   Wilbers, Stephen. *The Iowa Writers' Workshop* (Iowa City: University of Iowa Press, 1980); Bennett, Eric. *Workshops of Empire: Stegner, Engle, and American Creative Writing During the Cold War* (Iowa City: University of

Iowa Press, 2015); Myers, D.G. *Elephants Teach: Creative Writing Since 1880* (Chicago: University of Chicago Press, 1996); McGurl, Mark. *The Program Era: Postwar Fiction and the Rise of Creative Writing* (Cambridge, MA: Harvard University Press, 2009).

2   McGurl characterizes creative writing in economic terms as an "experiential commodity"; Myers characterizes creative writing in terms of an oversized industry: "elephant machine."

3   Wortham, Jenna. "Section: On Technology." *New York Times Magazine* (June 26, 2016).

4   Harbach, Chad. *MFA VS. NYC: The Two Cultures of American Fiction* (New York: n+1 Publishing, 2014).

5   Koehler, Adam. "Digitizing Craft: Creative Writing Studies and New Media: A Proposal" *College English*, 75(4): 2013.

6   Clark, Michael Dean, Trent Hergenrader, and Joseph Rein. *Creative Writing in the Digital Age: Theory, Practice, and Pedagogy* (London: Bloomsbury, 2015).

7   Bennett, *Workshops of Empire*, 6.

8   North, Stephen. *The Making of Knowledge in Composition: Portrait of an Emerging Field* (Boynton/Cook Publishers, 1987).

9   Welch, Kathleen. *Electric Rhetoric: Classical Rhetoric, Oralism, and New Literacy* (Cambridge: MIT Press, 1999).

10 Erikson, Erik H. *Identity: Youth and Crisis* (New York: Norton, 1994); Bowen, Murray. *The Bowen Center for the Study of Family* [formerly Georgetown University Family Center], (2015). http://www.thebowencenter.org/theory/eight-concepts/differentiation-of-self/

11 Bowen, *The Bowen Center for the Study of Family*; Erikson, *Identity: Youth and Crisis*.

12 "Syracuse University Creative Writing MFA—50th Anniversary." Dir. Devereux Milburn. (Published November 26, 2012). https://www.youtube.com/watch?v=Zh6ykndMPKg

13 "Syracuse University Creative Writing MFA—50th Anniversary."

14 "Syracuse University Creative Writing MFA—50th Anniversary."

15 "Syracuse University Creative Writing MFA—50th Anniversary."

16 "Syracuse University Creative Writing MFA—50th Anniversary."

17 "A License to Write: The Iowa Writer's Workshop." Prod. Jennifer Proctor and Jennifer New. (2008, uploaded February 8, 2010.) https://www.youtube.com/watch?v=prSIokFqBdU

18 "A License to Write: The Iowa Writer's Workshop."

19 "A License to Write: The Iowa Writer's Workshop."

20 "AWP Campus Visit Video Series." (Last Modified 2016.) [Rotating Campus "Featured Video"]. https://www.awpwriter.org/guide/campus_videos

21 "AWP Campus Visit Video Series."

References

"AWP Campus Visit Video Series." [Rotating Campus "Featured Video"]. https://
www.awpwriter.org/guide/campus_videos [last modified 2016].

Bennett, Eric. *Workshops of Empire: Stegner, Engle, and American Creative
Writing During the Cold War*. Iowa City: University of Iowa Press, 2015.

Bowen, Murray. *The Bowen Center for the Study of Family* [formerly Georgetown
University Family Center]. 2015. http://www.thebowencenter.org/theory/
eight-concepts/differentiation-of-self/

Clark, Michael Dean, Trent Hergenrader, and Joseph Rein. *Creative Writing in the
Digital Age: Theory, Practice, and Pedagogy*. London: Bloomsbury, 2015.

Erikson, Erik H. *Identity: Youth and Crisis*. New York: Norton, 1994.

Harbach, Chad. *MFA VS. NYC: The Two Cultures of American Fiction*. New
York: n+1 Publishing, 2014.

Koehler, Adam. "Digitizing Craft: Creative Writing Studies and New Media: A
Proposal." *College English* 75, no. 4 (2013).

"A License to Write: The Iowa Writer's Workshop" Prod. Jennifer Proctor and
Jennifer New. https://www.youtube.com/watch?v=prSIokFqBdU [2008,
uploaded February 8, 2010].

McGurl, Mark. *The Program Era: Postwar Fiction and the Rise of Creative
Writing*. Cambridge, MA: Harvard University Press, 2009.

Myers, D.G. *Elephants Teach: Creative Writing Since 1880*. Chicago: University of
Chicago Press, 1996.

North, Stephen. *The Making of Knowledge in Composition: Portrait of an
Emerging Field*. Portsmouth, NH: Boynton/Cook Publishers, 1987.

"Syracuse University Creative Writing MFA—50th Anniversary." Dir. Devereux
Milburn. https://www.youtube.com/watch?v=Zh6ykndMPKg [published
November 26, 2012].

Welch, Kathleen. *Electric Rhetoric: Classical Rhetoric, Oralism, and New Literacy*.
Cambridge: MIT Press, 1999.

Wilbers, Stephen. *The Iowa Writers' Workshop*. Iowa City: University of Iowa
Press, 1980.

Wortham, Jenna. "Section: On Technology." *New York Times Magazine*. June 26,
2016.

15

Investigating Creative Writing:

Challenging Obstacles to Empirical Research

Greg Light

Introduction

Much of the field of theoretical scholarship and empirical research on the practice of creative writing in higher education has generally focused on four broad categories of study: the writer, the creative writing process, the creative texts and, of course, the reader. Debates about the usefulness or uselessness of these theories (and the research they encourage) for the practice of creative writing in higher education seem to abound. The latter, for example, frequently emerges in the shape of literary theory, critical theory and countless other academic formalisms where it is sometimes lumped under "consumption theory" as their focus is on the reader's reading of the text with somewhat negligible concern for the writer (Harris, 2011). The others rarely fare much better, stuck in the marshland of concepts such as voice, creativity, literature, and the like. Nevertheless, these four categories, broadly described, have come to constitute the curriculum of creative writing courses in higher education and their multiple theories and research projects claim the field—albeit often cantankerously.

There has, however, been scant research on learning within the curriculum categories mentioned above. This is a glaring omission in the research record, somewhat curious given the educational environment in which the creative writing practice is located. It is, perhaps, doubly curious given the recent expansion in research on learning and teaching in higher education, and subsequent calls for new approaches and methods of teaching in higher education (Barr and Tagg, 1995); methods which go beyond traditional teaching-centered, or even student-centered, approaches to encompass learning-centered approaches to teaching (Light et al., 2009).

In this paper I argue that dominant and pervasive underlying theoretical assumptions about the practice of creative writing result in substantive resistance to meaningful empirical study of the student-writer's learning experience. Drawing on my own research experience in this field, I argue for a learning-direct research approach which illustrates a challenge to the above resistance from three viewpoints: theoretical, empirical, and practical. But first I will briefly describe what I mean by learning-direct research of the practice of creative writing in terms of where exactly its challenge emerges in the broader research traditions of the field.

Researching learning vs researching creative writing

Empirical research on creative writing in higher education, such as it is, has tended to follow the lead of its theoretical companions and focused on the same categories and debates about readers, texts, processes, and writers. Alongside this focus there has also been a tendency to see the practice of the creative writing process—characterized by these four curriculum features— as inhabiting a fundamentally different kind of cultural category than similar descriptions of other socio-cultural practices, even other forms of writing or textual construction. Partly this draws upon the idea that the production of artistic and "creative" writing connect to more authentic, subjective experiences than the production of other kinds of cultural writing. The underlying assumption is that creative writing differs fundamentally from other forms of writing, more fully embedded, for example, in the personal and aesthetic experiences of the writer. The formalization of this distinction goes back at least as far as James Britton and Janet Emig's influential work in the 1970s. The distinction of reflexive versus extensive modes of writing which Emig (1971) identifies is mirrored in the contrast Britton (1970) makes between the personal nature of the writing self and its process in poetic writing with the more public writing self and process at work in transactional writing (Britton, 1970).

More recently these subjectivist assumptions have popped up in work in the flourishing field of creativity studies. In their work on creativity and creative writing, Kaufman and Kaufman (2009), for example, contrast "writers and artists who seek to express their feelings" with "scientists who seek to understand a complex phenomenon" (p. 154). This distinction has also been pointed out by writers contrasting traditional assumptions about the autonomous, individual self in creative writing programs with the idea of a socially constructed self which is more prevalent in composition theory

(Royster, 2010). Moreover, closely related to the idea of an individual, private self are normative descriptions of the writing process as authentic (versus inauthentic or "bad") writing where "authentic writing involves tapping the stream of inner speech and focusing it" (Moffett, 1981, p. 23). It is an idea reflected in a range of research approaches on the writing process, grounded in the idea of the writer's individual (and presumably authentic) unconscious, concerned first with "how one accesses the unconscious and second how one 'consciously' manipulates it" (Hecq, 2013). It is a short leap from "authentic" writing processes to the idea of "authentic" texts (Light, 1996) and all the attendant "literary" issues associated with the quality of both their production and consumption. It is no wonder that literary theory has emerged as a theoretical prism for investigating creative writing.

Ritter and Vanderslice (2005) have described the manifestations of these assumptions in practice and how they have been handed down from teacher to teacher and generation to generation in the spread of creative writing programs throughout the academy over the last number of decades as the:

> ... influential mythology or lore that perpetuates the public and academic perceptions of what writing classrooms can do and how this lore dictates what part teaching and teacher training can, and should, play in the education and development of writers to be in both undergraduate and graduate classrooms. (p. 105)

The lore which powers the pedagogy of these programs undermines the idea that creative writing can be formally taught in the same way as other academic subjects, thus situating creative writing in a unique (and isolated) position in the academy. More importantly it contorts the very nature of what learning creative writing might mean. If, as its lore suggests, creative writing cannot be taught, it also suggests that it cannot be learned, at least not in any formal sense. The idea of learning creative writing—other than perhaps acquiring a set of craft based techniques (McFarland, 1993)—is excluded from meaningful research and consideration.

It is not my objective here to rehash the theoretical debates about the creative process, their texts, and reading which dominate the focus of research. Other than to suggest that their assumptions run deep within the student understanding and experience of the practice of creative writing (Light, 1995, 2002), and can be deeply troublesome and misleading. They carry with them, for instance, the danger of promoting a type of pedagogical lore and mystique which questions whether "real" creative writing, characterized by personal inspiration, subjective expression, innovative ideas, and a touch of artistic genius, can even be taught. (Light, 1996). More importantly, they run the risk of undermining other important empirical research approaches which stand outside the lore-laden, curriculum-framed research approaches which currently dominate. It is my aim, here, to argue for a research approach unencumbered by the lore dominating the field.

This paper does not dismiss other research perspectives; however, it argues that creative writing is not simply characterized by the "creative" and "writing" nature of the experience (be it the text, the process, or the processor) but also by the "learning" nature of the experience. It is a perspective that shifts the focus explicitly towards the student as a learner and the process as learning. It maintains that the direct object of research is learning. And the indirect object is creative writing.

The theoretical and empirical research questions of this learning-direct approach are also not strictly about creative writing but rather about learning. How do students understand their learning with respect to the practice of creative writing, not what is the practice(s) of creative writing which students are learning, or what are the challenges of learning the practice, or even what are the critical and creative cognitive skills required in learning the practice. There is a fundamental difference here, often missed in the literature on creative writing, which has tended to privilege the subject matter of the learning over the learning. Indeed, prevailing theoretical assumptions about creative writing as a practice—the subject matter for students to learn—tends to undermine meaningful critique and empirical study of the student experience of learning the practice.

To illustrate this learning-direct research approach to creative writing, and the resistance of creative writing studies to research evidence derived from such a learning-direct approach this paper will consider the influence of such an approach to creative writing in terms of the impact of a study which I undertook twenty years ago looking at student learning of creative writing. I will situate the following discussion in terms of three perspectives of learning: 1) Theoretical: learning theory (variation theory) and a related research methodology (phenomenography); 2) Empirical: a brief description of empirical research results; and 3) Practical, the impact or lack of impact of these results on creative writing practice.

Theoretical: Creative writing, variation theory, and phenomenography

Variation theory is a theory of learning which has been widely applied to student learning in higher education. It was developed by Ference Marton and his colleagues in the latter decades of the twentieth century (Marton and Booth, 1997; Åkerlind, 2003). Briefly, the theory assumes there are a finite number of hierarchically related ways in which a learner understands or experiences a particular phenomenon such as a practice or a concept—in this case creative writing. Learning in terms of these different understandings or conceptions is not about being "correct" or "incorrect" but is described in terms of changes in the learner's conceptions of the particular phenomenon. Different conceptions are explained in terms of the learner's awareness of, and ability to, discern variation in the critical aspects of the phenomenon. Cumulative awareness of variation in the critical aspects of the given phenomenon results in a richer or more complex understanding. Empirical research informed by variation theory generally leads to a set of increasingly complex categories of understanding or conception (Marton and Pong, 2005).

The research methodology most associated with variation theory is phenomenography. Also developed by Marton and his colleagues, phenomenography is widely used to empirically investigate student learning in higher education environments. Phenomenography studies the different ways in which a phenomenon and the key aspects of that phenomenon are experienced within specific educational and learning contexts. Marton and Booth (1997) describe it as seeking "the totality of ways in which people experience . . . the object of interest and interpret it in terms of distinctly different categories that capture the essence of the variation . . ." (p. 121). This complete log is often referred to as the "outcome space" of the research results. It is not a record of individual experiences, but rather a set of finite categories of experience.

In so far as phenomenography focuses on the individual's personal perspective, rather than an external researcher-centered perspective, or a broader community perspective, it resembles phenomenological methodologies. They frequently use similar data collection methods, such as semi-structured interviews, and related textual and visual materials which can make them seem very similar. They differ in two fundamental respects. First, whereas phenomenology investigates common experiences of a phenomenon, (Van Manen, 1990), phenomenography looks at the ways in which learner experiences differ (Marton, 1988). Sampling procedures in a phenomenographic study focus on broadening the scope for variation of experience in the sample of students enlisted in a study. While keeping the educational phenomena under investigation steady, phenomenographic studies aim at diversity of student with respect to other variables: including the kind of course, program, level, gender, educational and socio-economic background. Secondly, phenomenography focuses on the experience of the phenomenon as opposed to phenomenology's focus on the phenomenon (Van Manen, 1990). These differences are precisely what distinguishes the learning-direct research approach from most of the research conducted on the practice of creative writing: i.e., the latter focuses on subject matter (phenomenon) rather than learning (experience of the phenomenon).

Empirical: Student learning and creative writing

The empirical research was based on in-depth interviews conducted with forty students selected from three creative writing courses in three different institutions in the United Kingdom (Light, 2002, 1995). The courses included both undergraduate and post-graduate courses. A precis of the results are presented to illustrate a learning-direct research approach to investigating creative writing practice in higher education. The student descriptions of their experience of creative writing are not simply based on their accounts of what they did or what they wrote or what they read but more deeply look at how they understood the experience, how they described their learning, and broadly how they conceived the practice of creative writing in the educational setting in which they were learning. The distinct categories of descriptions of the student's experience are referred to as student conceptions of creative writing.

The student conception revealed in this study were all framed within a broader perception of the nature of creative writing; a perception shared by all of the students involved in the study. Student reports all took a view of creative writing as distinctive and unique, particularly in contrast to their other educational writing such as the writing of essays or of journalistic kinds of writing. This perception reflects the kind of subjectivist or expressionist presumption that three decades ago Berlin (1987) described as one where "that which the writer is trying to express . . . is the product of a private and personal vision." Irrespective of the course level creative writing was consistently described by the students as *"more personal"*; *"your own writing"* with related feelings of freedom: *"much freer sort of writing . . . from your own experience"*; *"less restricted"*; *"less restrained"*; *"an escape."* This was not necessarily a comment about creativity—many students felt that they could be creative in other forms of writing—but rather about the subjectivist epistemology at the heart of their perceptions of creative writing and ultimately underlying their conceptions. It suggests that the influence of creative writing lore extends much further than college classroom.

Within this context, the study revealed a typology of four distinct student conceptions of creative writing in two general categories. Table 15.1 sets out an abridged version[1] of the types by category and by the main aspects of variation by which they are distinguished from one another. They are divided into contrasting categories each with two types of conception. The transcribing category is comprised of what are referred to as *releasing* and *documenting* conceptions, and the composing category of *narrating* and *critiquing* conceptions.

The critical aspect of variation which distinguishes the two main categories of conception is called *reader awareness*. It has two dimensions: the first reflects what Bakhtin (1986) calls the "addressivity" of writing: that aspect of being "directed to someone," an "addressee," who may vary from "an immediate participant-locutor in an everyday dialogue (to) . . . an indefinite, unconcretized *other*" (p. 95). It separates student-writers who in the act of writing do not see their writing as directed to a reader (detached from the reader), and those who do see their writing as directed to a reader

TABLE 15.1 *Student conceptions of creative writing*

Conceptions	Critical Aspects	
	Reader Awareness	
Category Types	Addressivity	Readership
Transcribing		
I Releasing	Detached	Dissenting
II Documenting	Detached	Assenting
Composing		
III Narrating	Integrated	Dissenting
IV Critiquing	Integrated	Assenting

Source: Light, 2002, p. 267

(integrated with the reader). The second dimension of *reader awareness* concerns readership, readers in socio-cultural situations in which they are reading, using specific cultural norms and forms: Williams (1977) describes such forms as "the common property ... of writers and audiences or readers, before any communicative composition can occur" (p. 187–8). The distinction here is whether the student "assents to" or "dissents from" the prevailing readership forms. Based on these two aspects of variation, the four conceptions—*releasing, documenting, narrating,* and *critiquing*—emerged from the analysis.

Releasing: In this conception creative writing is frequently understood as being therapeutic. The writing is seen as "working" for the writer if it is released onto the page so to speak and provides a kind of personal "therapy" and/or self-knowledge: *"It's an exorcism ... trying to express a sense of yourself, you in relation to everything else, trying to create your own history."* It is detached from the concerns of the reader. Indeed, seeing ones writing with respect to a reader is a kind of betrayal of self and of artistic integrity. *"I'm sure that most people who write ... cannot handle the idea of sharing, sharing their ideas. If they do it's very superficial."* The writer "dissents from" the prevailing forms of readership and "releases" his/her inner narrative in a personal form (sometimes linked to stream of consciousness).

Documenting: The student-writer recognizes that they are writing for a reader, but mainly at the level of the material they are writing about. They want to capture an experience, a scene, an idea, and transcribe or document it the way they see or feel it *"just putting it down and just keeping it for myself, hopefully as well I'm making a poem which would say, perhaps, something to somebody else."* While it would be nice if a reader liked their writing, the reader's reading of it is not something they feel they control. It is incidental, detached from the activity of writing. The writing "works" if the material is interesting and/or meets course requirements. They do accept readership forms, although the range is limited to reproducing very general genre forms (fiction, poetry, drama), those taken from course exercises, and/or market forms: *"you really have to structure your work depending on where you're going to send it."*

Narrating: Students with this conception describe an understanding of writing in which they integrate their material and the reader through the practice of writing. There is a recognition that *"writing isn't just something that hits you like a thunder bolt and you suddenly get this inspiration and scribble something down"* but rather something that means *"incorporating techniques whereby you impose a structure on yourself."* Along with this new sense of control is also a new sense of objectivity—*"I sort of see my work more objectively, without being biased about it."* Through this new awareness of writing that requires control, structure, and objectivity in the practice of writing, these students understand they can "narrate" their meanings vis-a-vis meanings shared with the reader. This new sense of control is related to the student's awareness on integrating the reader and readership forms. *"I guess I'm aware of trying to make sense to other people, yet at the same time, I don't—I think I make the reader work."* And alongside this recognition is a new sense of confidence about having the control which is associated with a more internalized awareness of the reader: *"I kind of can sense now what it is that would make somebody smile, what it is that would make somebody think that's a bit over the top, or what it is that would make somebody cringe."*

Critiquing: The students with this conception are aware of integrating the reader in their writing, but at the same time their understanding encompasses a critique, a new kind of dissent from important elements of the readership forms. *"Sometimes you can catch yourself lying I think . . . Um, because something's easy to say. Because you've got it pegged. And then you get a little niggle, niggling feeling in the back of your mind: but is that what I mean, is that really, is that really it, or is that really true?"* There is an element of questioning, of challenging oneself, of pushing the envelope so to speak, at the core of this conception. This critical dissent may be of themselves in practice of creative writing itself (integrated in the writing) and/or might consist of a dissenting critique of a wide variety of discourse issues, forms, conventions, and techniques of that practice. The concern is not simply to narrate one's personal material to readers through structure, technique, and craft to control the reader's reading of that material, but also an obligation to critique oneself and the reader during the writing: *"am I saying anything that they haven't already heard a million times before? . . . Or am I, you know, am I saying it in such a way that they are going to see something different about it even if they have heard it."* In this conception the student-writer conceives their writing as also challenging the readership norms in which they perceive the reader is situated.

Practical: Learning, creative writing, and pedagogy

The obstacles facing this learning-direct research approach to the practice of creative writing were predictable. It was naive to expect that this field— still a nascent in the UK at the time—might take more than a passing interest in the results above. It was busy trying to look and be academic, worthy of inclusion in the university. And student learning had never been a primary focus of higher education. On the other hand, these results offered the first, certainly a new and substantive framework for understanding and describing the student-writer in terms of their learning. And the hierarchical structure of this framework, provided a considerable tool for learning-based educational design. As a phenomenographic framework it lent itself particularly well to the design of learning objectives, pedagogical strategies, assessments, and evaluations (Micari, Light, Calkins, and Streitwieser, 2007).

But redirecting the educational focus on student learning and away from teaching, learning-direct research also posed a substantive challenge to existing practices of creative writing in higher education. It challenged the authority of the teacher. It is not by chance that there has been substantial discussion in the creative writing literature by teachers about types of pedagogy and curriculum design of creative writing courses at all levels from undergraduate to PhD, however, very few have been informed by rigorous studies of student learning of creative writing. Even fewer have been informed by published research.

While I published a number of early papers about this research in practitioner magazines such as *Writers in Education* (the magazine of the National Association of Writers in Education in the UK), practitioners did not readily take an interest in ways in which research data on learning could inform their practice. In part, this may be due to the fact that outside a comment or two in practitioner magazines, creative writing academics do not tend to publish educational research papers: their field is fiction, poetry, creative, drama, and nonfiction. This is primarily what they are rewarded for. In this, of course, they are no different than almost every other academic discipline. It does not in itself justify the continued use of pedagogy and curriculum uninformed by research evidence on learning. But it does go a long way to explain why serious research in the educational aspect of the discipline is fledgling at best, and why serious research steers clear. While my own papers on this research have been cited in many academic publications, the vast majority of those citations are in papers and books that are concerned with student learning and education, only rarely creative writing. And even in educational journals there was suspicion that learning in creative writing was not really a subject of study. Indeed, when I first proposed the idea for PhD study, it was rejected. Not a proper subject.

No appropriate supervisors. I was lucky to find a first champion in the learning field and only later advisors with creative writing interests. Needless to say, the dearth of interest by creative writing practitioners in what learning theory and research could provide, combined with the demands of academia to publish in peer reviewed journals, quickly diverted the direction of my work.

In hindsight, resistance by the creative writing field to evidence-based, learning-centered approaches to teaching and curriculum design is not that surprising. It is not just the lore of the creative writing classroom that presents an obstacle to learning research, it is also the lore of the university.[2] There is resistance in almost all academic fields to research on student learning and its perceived threat to the authority of the teacher. Despite evidence to the contrary (Marsh and Hattie, 2002), faculty tend to believe that if the teacher is an excellent practitioner, researcher, or scholar in their field, they will undoubtedly be a better teacher. And, as in other disciplines, the dominant pedagogical approaches and categories in creative writing eschew a focus on learning-centered classrooms in favor of a widely shared, handed down pedagogical lore embracing traditional teaching-centered or student-centered academic understandings of education (Light et al., 2009). In creative writing it includes the question as to whether or not it can be formally taught or learned which makes the obstacle to reform that much more difficult.

Conclusions: Promoting learning in creative writing

Drawing upon this initial research on learning creative writing, and later with similar types of research on student learning in fields as diverse as nanotechnology, study abroad, medicine, and history, I have worked with thousands of faculty across the world in looking at how the results of learning research might be used to help them design educational environments focused on learning as well as to assist them in considering their own transitions to learning-centered understandings of their encounters with students.

The most productive and interesting approach was informed by a broader aspect of the above research on creative writing. Conceptions it was found emerge from encounters between the personal histories and identities of students and the particular course environments (and readerships) in which they are learning and writing. The broader research revealed, for example, that gender, class, age, ethnicity/nationality, and educational background shape student interactions with the educational environment differently, and in the process enhance or hinder the development of their experiences and conceptions. These encounters are impacted (often quite negatively) by the students' relationship to the dominant "literary authority" characterizing the prevailing course readerships determined by the teachers, the interpersonal peer and teacher/student relationships, and the course and program curriculum (Light 1995, 1996). For example, one graduate student, who described himself as coming from a "working-class, non-literary background," reported feeling very bitter about the underlying literary assumptions in his program: "I think there are codes of what literary fiction is, and it seems clear to me that that I just don't get it, I just don't, can't crack the code." (p. 259).

In this respect, conceptions of creative writing, are—as Mihaly Csikszentmihalyi the guru of creativity studies has reluctantly come to describe creativity—not in the individual but in the individual's relationship with society. Creativity is constituted by the interaction of the individual with a symbolic domain within a field characterized by the authority of the field experts (Csikszentmihalyi, 2015). The difference here is that conceptions are not simply defined by the domain (readership) and the field experts (literary authority) but rather can be severely undermined by them in course encounters. This is particularly the case if the prevailing assumptions and lore (Ritter and Vanderslice, 2007) about the domain and the field are awash with the kind of subjectivist, personal, artistic, authentic, inspiration type notions which perpetually stalk creative writing, and which are by their very nature not assumed to be capable of change: you have it or you don't.

In a more recent study of how faculty (including creative writing faculty) understand learning in their field—both their own in their research or scholarship and that of their students in their courses—we discovered faculty understandings of the nature of their own ongoing learning was fundamentally different from the understanding of learning they expected of their students (Light and Calkins, 2015). The discovery revealed a learning gap at the heart of academic practice. This gap, moreover, was at the heart of teacher understandings of their teaching practice, often silently and insidiously compromising their students' learning. The key to faculty development of teaching was, therefore, less about providing a set of handed down teaching strategies and techniques and more about helping faculty to redirect their pedagogical thinking towards a deeper reflection on their own, ongoing learning as professionals and to apply this understanding to designing environments which promote richer and more complex forms of student understanding and learning (see for example Vanderslice, 2012). It raises new avenues for research on creative writing focused around the promotion of learning. And therein lies the key to whether it can be taught. It can.

Notes

1 A full description of the conceptions including two further aspects of variation and two additional conceptions can be found in Light, 1995.

2 Creative writing lore, however, is in many ways more insidious because it claims new pedagogies and unique educational perspectives which mask its resistance.

References

Åkerlind, Gerlese S. "Growing and developing as a university teacher: variation in meaning." *Studies in higher education* 28, no. 4 (2003): 375–90.

Bakhtin, Mikhail Mikhaïlovich. *Speech genres and other late essays*. Austin Texas: University of Texas Press, 2010.

Barr, Robert B. and John Tagg. "From teaching to learning—A new paradigm for undergraduate education." *Change: The magazine of higher learning* 27, no. 6 (1995): 12–26.

Berlin, James. *Rhetoric and Reality: Writing Instruction in American Colleges, 1900–1985*. Carbondale: Southern Illinois University Press, 1987.

Britton, James. *Language and Learning*. London: Penguin Books, 1970.

Csikszentmihalyi, Mihaly. "Society, culture, and person: A systems view of creativity." *The Systems Model of Creativity: The Collected Works of Mihaly Csikszentmihalyi*. Netherlands: Springer, 2015.

Emig, Janet. *The composing processes of twelfth graders*. Urbana, IL: National Council of Teachers of English, 1971.

Harris, Mike. "'Shakespeare Was More Creative When He Was Dead': Is Creativity Theory a Better Fit On Creative Writing Than Literary Theory?" *New Writing* 8, no. 2 (2011): 171–82.

Hecq, Dominique. "Creative Writing and Theory: Theory without Credentials." In *Research Methods in Creative Writing*, Kroll, Jeri and Harper, Graeme eds. New York, NY: Palgrave MacMillan, 2013.

Kaufman, Scott Barry and Kaufman, James C., eds. *The psychology of creative writing*. Cambridge: Cambridge University Press, 2009.

Light, Gregory. *The literature of the unpublished: student conceptions of creative writing in higher education*. PhD thesis. London: The Institute of Education, University of London, 1995.

Light, Gregory. The Literature of the Unpublished: Towards a Theory of Creative Writing in Higher Education. Paper presented at the Conference on Creative Writing, Middlesex University, London, UK, 1996.

Light, Gregory. From the personal to the public: Conceptions of creative writing in higher education. *Higher Education* 43, no. 2 (2002): 257–276.

Light, Greg, Calkins, Susanna and Cox, Roy. *Learning and teaching in higher education: The reflective professional*. London: Sage, 2009.

Light, Greg and Calkins, Susanna. "The experience of academic learning: uneven conceptions of learning across research and teaching." *Higher Education* Volume 69, Issue 3 (2015): 345–59.

Marsh, Herbert W. and Hattie, John. "The relation between research productivity and teaching effectiveness." *The Journal of Higher Education*, 73 (2002): 603–41.

Marton, Ference. "Phenomenography: A research approach to investigating different understandings of reality." In *Qualitative research in education: Focus and methods*, Sherman, Robert and Webb, Rodman eds, New York, NY: Falmer Press, 1988.

Marton, Ference and Booth, Shirley A. *Learning and awareness*. New York, NY: Routledge Press, Psychology Press Series, 1997.

Marton, Ference and Pong, Wing Yan. "On the unit of description in phenomenography." *Higher education research & development* 24, no. 4 (2005): 335–48.

McFarland, Ron. "An Apologia for Creative Writing." *College English* 55 (1993): 28–45.

Micari, Marina, Light, Gregory, Calkins, Susanna and Streitwieser, Bernhard. "Assessment beyond Performance Phenomenography in Educational Evaluation." *American Journal of Evaluation* 28, no. 4 (2007): 458–76.

Moffett, James. *Active Voice: A Writing Program across the Curriculum*. Montclair, New Jersey: Boynton/Cook Publishers, 1981.

Ritter, Kelly and Vanderslice, Stephanie. *Teaching Lore: Creative Writers and the University* New York, NY: Profession, Modern Language Association, Vol. (1), 2005: 102–12.

Royster, Brent. "Engaging the Individual/Social Conflict within Creative Writing Pedagogy." *Does the Writing Workshop Still Work?* Donnelly, Dianne ed. Toronto: Multilingual Matters Vol. 5 (2010): 105–16.

Vanderslice, Stephanie. "The Lynchpin in the Workshop: Student Critique and Reflection." *Teaching creative writing*. London: Palgrave Macmillan, 2012.

Van Manen, Max. *Researching lived experience: Human science for an action sensitive pedagogy*. New York, NY: State University of New York Press, 1990.

Williams, Raymond. *Marxism and literature*. Oxford: Oxford Paperbacks, Oxford University Press, 1977.

16

Creative Writing with Godzilla:

Welcoming the Monster to your Creative Writing Classroom

Graeme Harper

Godzilla is a state of mind.
WILLIAM TSUTSUI, *GODZILLA ON MY MIND* (2004)

Childhood and *Monsters Inc.*

"Good morning, Roz, my succulent little garden snail," chimes Mike Wazowski, the short green one-eyed monster of the Disney film, *Monsters Inc.*[1] "And who will we be scaring today?"

"Wazowski!" growls Roz, the overseer of operations on Scare Floor F, who is indeed monstrous, but sweetly so, as this Disney animation requires. "You didn't file your paperwork last night."

"Oh, that darn paperwork!" replies Mike. "Wouldn't it be easier if it all just blew away?"

Roz is seemingly only slightly moved. "Don't let it happen again," she barks.

"Yes, well, I'll try to be more careful next time," says Mike, and his dismissiveness is as obviously connected to his fictional stardom at Monsters Inc. as it is to his real stardom in the movie.

"I'm watching you, Wazowski," Roz responds, ineffectually, though there is a sense these two share a deep regard, a more than grudgingly monstrous acceptance. "Always watching."

So ends this innocent if bizarre exchange, giant garden snail and short green cyclops abandoning their brief tête-à-tête about the existence and submission of paperwork. The dichotomy in the scene is clearly that between the actions undertaken and the text that has resulted because of them, the "paperwork"—paperwork that purportedly reports on the actions, that is influenced by them, that stands as a form of evidence that those actions have occurred. What an interesting message such an opposition is sending, and largely one it is sending to children.

That perceived combative dichotomy is very simple: it is *Individual vs Text*. This dichotomization produces an anxious relationship, in this case one literally delivered from the *Monsters Inc.* Scare Floor, an animated binary filled with disquietude. *Monsters Inc.* is indeed a children's film. To explore this fact in meta context, the noted schema of the pioneer of child development, Jean Piaget, suggests that from birth each of us progresses developmentally through stages of limited knowledge and simple physical motor activities, onward to the use of language, memory, and the imagination, to discovering the external world and recognizing systems of symbols that represent and define; finally, to a point where we can assess life's variables, formulate hypotheses, and think about abstractions.

How intriguing to present such an oppositional picture as that depicted in the scene from *Monsters Inc.* to those of us beginning to develop concrete human reasoning and logic; that is to children who have not formed but form*ing* minds. Even more so perhaps, for those in the Piagetian earlier stages, "the preoperational stage" and the "sensorimotor stage" where language, memory, imagination, and symbolic abilities are developing. More broadly speaking, it is also a good example of the tension that exists between the philosophical position of idealism and that of physicalism; with the former suggesting everything is mental or mentally constructed and the latter suggesting everything is physical and that there is nothing over and above the physical.

To follow a Kristevan line of thought here: in a time in our lives before we each individually ordered the world, symbolically, such separations did not exist. Philosopher, psychoanalyst, feminist and, indeed, creative writer Julia Kristeva speaks of this time as a "pre-linguistic"[2] condition, of a point therein were identities barely exist,[3] referring in a somewhat different way to what Piaget is considering in a stage of childhood defined by him as being prior to the development of language abilities.

Kristeva's suggestion is that it is here in this primal condition where the "abject" exists—the abject referring to part of the self that has since been rejected in the dichotomous, linguistic, symbolic world in which we adults live. A world in which there is said to be "subject" as opposed to "object," a "self" versus an "other." Situated prior to the dichotomized representational order of this adult world—that is, in what Kristeva suggests is a primal condition, a primal site—the abject relates to those elements that are in some way taboo in our ordered adult existence, an existence that is based on a social constructs and socially structured identities. Abjection maintains boundaries, keeping otherness at bay. We see this abjection in depictions of the foreign, the uncanny and, indeed, in our representation, understanding, and rejection of the monstrous.

Adversarial lore

Both the Kristevan and the Piagetian critical outlooks offer something for considering how creative writing is actually situated, rather than how it is sometimes depicted as being situated. Creative writing, which employs the imagination as well as the intellect, language as well as creative interpretations of what language might actually entail beyond the linguistic, actions that produce no text, and texts that are produced and sometimes worked on extensively, the immaterial and the material so that the world as viewed through mental processes or the world as physical entity can equally exist. In that sense, creative writing is equally recognizable within the tenets of idealism or those of physicalism.

Even though that is the case, and creative writing is fundamentally cooperative rather than adversarial, much creative writing teaching and learning has been and continues to be a site of adversarial lore, traditions of apprehensive embattlement borne regularly in such oppositional questions as "Can it really be taught?" and "Is it literary?" This is not only because the true condition of creative writing has often *not* been the defining aspect of creating and delivering creative writing teaching—replaced by a dichotomy and promoting numerous binaries such as "literary/not literary," "draft writing/completed writing," "being a writer/not being a writer"—but also because surrounding conditions in the adult world in relation to abjection have fed such a fretful, oppositional approach.

Because of these things, many current approaches to creative writing teaching and learning do not recognize an uninterrupted primal site of exchange that Kristeva depicts, that is cooperative rather than adversarial, a place or activity that prioritizes neither subject nor object, that recognizes a human ontology of completeness, a becoming and a being all at once. Such teaching cannot thus easily embrace the unbroken "monstrous," where creativity and critical understanding are not symbolically cleft one from the other, as they have been (as though somehow it is not possible for us to both think and create at the same time!), where the self and the text are able to occupy the same human space.

Rather than the productive exploration of a natural internal exchange these pedagogic approaches promote a strongly symbolic as well as a literal epistemological separation, a cleaving of creative writing understanding and knowledge from the action of creative writing, of actually *doing it*. Figuratively, what these pedagogic approaches are doing in their cleaving is producing a combative monster movie rather than recognizing the natural primality of the monster. Such a cleaving lamentably falsifies the reality of creative writing, the way it might be learnt, the scope, style, and potential of the learning, and thus of course the way many of those who would teach it therefore approach teaching it.

In these ways a disingenuous "versus" consistently undermines the truth about creative writing, and threatens to undermine the positive nature of the creative writing experience shared between students and between students and teachers. The battle is further entrenched, and reasoning attaches itself to the blows that are dealt to greatest effect, the blood that is drawn by the victory of *The Self* in a dichotomy such as *The Self vs Others*, or of *Edited-Out* in the dichotomy *Edited-In vs Edited-Out*, or of the *Imagination* in the dichotomy *Imagination vs Intellect*, while the supposed opposite of each lies beaten, in the name of what we allegedly value most about our craft and its end results.

Over time this dichotomization has become paradigmatic in creative writing teaching. It is now skittishly present in many beliefs about it. It informs creative writing course structure and content and even gives credence to conditions of employment, advancement, and notions of academic leadership in the field. It is a source of tension reminiscent of a childhood apprehension of the dark, lore that is founded on abjection, specifically on a failure to recognize the boundlessness inherent in the practice we so often passionately enjoy, and that we attempt to describe, discuss, provide as experience, and portray as a way of being in the world to our creative writing students. These students surely deserve better from us than such adversarial falsehoods!

We find, because of this adversarial lore, a resistant fear of change in how we view the construction of creative writing courses (witness, in that vein, a concern about maintaining or advancing "the workshop," as if somehow other forms of teaching and learning creative writing can't even be imagined). We find this also in the ways in which questions are often framed regarding how and whether to research and potentially discover new things about how creative writing works, and about the modes for doing this. There is, in this case, a suggested separation between creative writing and the studying of creative writing—so, in practical terms, "creative writing" and "creative writing studies" portrayed as if they are devolved from each other rather than shared elements of the same enterprise. Considerable organizational, institutional, and individual investment, the latter defensibly found in forms of indoctrination not varieties of education, has been generated in retaining and validating that current dichotomy.

This socially constructed uneasiness around the abject, the monstrousness of completeness, manifests itself in a love of embattlement, a love of bloodletting between portrayed opposing forces, combatants in our particular movie, and is often contextualized and even promoted on occasions with an element of moral indignation—such as in the name of promoting

"Literature" or the beauty of "creativity" or the importance "good writing." All this is part of a continued attempt to keep in place a separation that undermines the reality of creative writing's responsiveness rather than supporting it, that makes the lore of communal consensus in our field a tool for enforcing an established social and ultimately pedagogic order not for best supporting the practice and understanding of creative writing we often actively wish to embrace and equally encourage our students to embrace.

With this in mind, and with such a lore of binarization so heavily embedded, many of our creative writing classrooms became some time ago, and continue to be today, sites of social and cultural control, often more than they are sites of real learning. For example, try answering this question, even if merely anecdotally: How many students become anxious at the thought of submitting a piece of creative writing for assessment? Is this anxiety connected to how they expect the piece to assessed, what elements they expect to be considered, or some insecurity about what those elements might be? Why would this be so? How many say that "grading in creative writing is often subjective"? How many "believe in" (and I use the expression to suggest a learned belief) the foundation of creative writing being "reading like a writer" combined with writing "practice" (as if somehow these are different things)? On how many occasions have you known of a course, or even an entire program, that seeks to include the study of finished texts with the workshopping of new work, but made these aspects "tracks," or separately defined "components" or "requirements." Why? That is to say, based on what empirical evidence of the success of such a split approach has this construction been undertaken?

All this, and more, is not focused on creative writing learning it is focused on control. It is in effect a form of regulation. It comes about because in grounding creative writing understanding in a dichotomy, a separation, we have created contested classrooms not supportive habitats for creative writers and creative writing learning to thrive. Again, think on how many times you've heard someone question the social dynamics of the creative writing workshop. Ask what happens to genres of work that are not easily included in a model of literary fiction or poetry? Certainly some incorporating of popular fiction, screenwriting, and writing for digital media has occurred, to take some examples. But are these genre seen always as equals to the literary staples of the majority of creative writing courses? If not, why not? Are they not produced by the actions and knowledge of creative writing? Are the practices involved in creating excellent examples of completed works in these genre not practices we'd associate with creative writing? Are we not primarily teaching creative writing, rather than primarily literary studies or aesthetics or literacy? Then why would any creative writing practice, and any creative writing result, be less valuable than another if creative writing is our field of learning and teaching?

The monster not the monster movie

Returning to the primal, pre-symbolic condition referenced by Julia Kristeva, the location of the "monstrous," I am reminded of the international star in that influential monster movie franchise, *Godzilla*, the lead monster in such films as *Godzilla vs The Thing* (Honda, 1964), *Godzilla vs Gigan* (Fukuda, 1972), *Godzilla vs Megalon* (Fukuda, 1973). It is not in fact the monsters that are the focus of these films but their battles and what the opponents in them represent. In other words these are adversarial depictions rather than cooperative ones.

Although each monster is presented in these films as abhorrent in some way, the desire to see a victory for one or the other is borne on the question of which is the most acceptable monster. Ultimately that most acceptable monster is shown to be Godzilla. Given we live in a cleaved adult world involving the "self" and the "other," monstrousness is less monstrous if something is upheld that is familiar, symbolically acceptable, and contextualized in terms of our own perceived sense of self. This sense is socially and culturally determined. A clear indication of this is found in representations of Godzilla's gender—which has been defined according to the perceived cultural location of the film audience.

Godzilla, in the Japanese language films in which the monster first appears, is neither female nor male; the creature is gender neutral and is referred to this way. When the films are dubbed or created for an English language audience the monster is depicted as male and referred to as such. It would take more research and more space here to extrapolate this fact into a viable argument concerning women in Japanese films or monsters in Japanese culture or the role of maleness in English language films about aggression. What is immediately and specifically clear, however, is that something is changed for the monster when the cultural context of the viewer is perceived as different.

Fred Botting points out that "monsters appear in literary and political writings to signal both a terrible threat to established orders and a call to arms that demands the unification and protection of *authorized values*."[4] (my italics). Thus via the appearance of a monster a signal is being sent regarding a threat. That notion of a threat is a direct reference to the abject. When a monster is transported across cultures, however, some things change and some things remain the same, in that "authorized values" are not necessarily culturally universal. Godzilla's gender thus changes, according to cultural context, and it could be suggested that this gender change is related to the English language, Western audience the film-makers are imagining.

It is intriguing to wonder what relevance this has to the "monstrous-feminine,"[5] as Barbara Creed describes it in her *The Monstrous-Feminine: Film, Feminism, Psychoanalysis* (1993), and in relation to a further consideration that might be given to the subject of gender and monstrousness in a reading of such works as Jane Caputi's *Goddesses and Monsters: Women, Myth, Power and Popular Culture* (2004).

But to our creative writing matter at hand here, the contested creative writing classroom in our Western educational world, which itself involves a cultural, social, and pedagogic order, regularly reveals evidence of a casting out of the condition of completeness in the declarative name of rejecting the abject, the primal, the monstrous. In such a contested creative writing classroom as we see in our educational institutions (and I refer here primarily to Western, English language classrooms) the equality of creative knowledge and critical knowledge is constantly challenged, quite frequently with work encouraged, responded to, and graded according to a struggle or sense of hostility. For example, where we refer to a "creative dissertation" or to a critical "exegesis" or to submission of "creative work" or to a "critical essay" in a creative writing class we are not talking about the process of creating and thinking about creating, we are talking about the ordering of cultural constructs and of their maintenance, and because of this recognizing artifacts that relate to this dichotomy.

Work is encouraged to be seen as incomplete. We hear reference to adages supporting this, such as in versions of the fiction-writing note "a novel is never complete only abandoned," and a considerable reverence for drafting, where any piece of work is never truly finished but always in motion, always refusing completeness. Completeness in that sense is presented as a kind of exclusion from the writerly self, a subject-object condition, and in that sense it too encapsulates the abject. Indeed, if someone produces a piece of work in a creative writing class in first draft and says it is a completed piece of work the notion of the piece arriving complete is often rejected or viewed with skepticism, despite the recognition that creative practice can involve either Beethovenian method (that is, working and reworking on the page/ screen) or Mozartian method (that is, working and reworking in the mind and then writing done). Here the monstrous, the abject is somehow unfit. With the labor absent, both creative and critical understanding can be questioned.

The contested classroom is a monster movie not the monster. It is a staged embattlement, directed indoctrination, a gladiatorial narrative borne on the back of promoting and maintaining such binaries as *The Self vs Others*; *Physical Actions vs Material Results*; *Editing-In vs Edited-Out*; *Imagination vs Intellect*; *Success vs Failure*. It is a challenge to the truth of creative writing and a subversion of a reality of completeness that runs counter to the stages of creative writing learning development, and in an analogical way counter to our wider inherent learning processes from limited knowledge and simple physical motor activities, onward to the use of language, memory, and the imagination, to discovering the external world and recognizing systems of symbols that represent and define; finally, to a point where we can assess life's variables, formulate hypotheses, and think about abstractions.

The contested classroom, where *Individual v Text*, pits experiential life against paperwork, individual against individual, one truth against another, teacher against student. Is it any wonder we still struggle to resolve questions about how to advance the quality of the creative writing workshop experience? Creative writing lore says this: "embattlement, indoctrination, apprehension, fear, inculcation, consternation, portent, darkness, adversariness, edification, foreboding, combativeness, anxiety, are all located here. Whatever else positive we might in our personal and communal enthusiasm invoke, these things also are what we are telling you about the nature of creative writing and about creative writing learning."

Teaching creative writing with Godzilla

Nature has an order. A power to restore balance.

"DR. ICHIRO SERIZAWA," *GODZILLA* (1954, 1977, 2014)

Creative writing can be defined as "the actions of writing creatively, informed by the human imagination and the intellect, employing both personal and cultural knowledge, and creating a variety of results, some private, some public, some tentative and some in various ways complete."[6] To enable a creative writing learning experience that is true to the nature of creative writing, that gives our students the best sense of and encouragement in creative writing, we need to teach to the monster, and teach with the monster, not teach to the gladiatorial monster movie.

By this I mean we must now acknowledge the completeness that has been previously undermined in the dichotomous linguistic, symbolic world in which we live, and which we have specifically referenced, developed, and maintained through promoting the separation of the creative and the critical, through cleaving creative writing actions and creative writing artifacts, and through endorsing, sometimes with considerable moral zeal, an identity for ourselves and our field borne on such destructive dichotomy. All this has produced spurious creative writing lore. While undoubtedly our classrooms, as social spaces, will remain places of cultural construction and socially structured identities, they can also become places of real equity and real inclusion, where subject and object are one, and communication occurs rather than combat.

To represent what is needed today, I thus invoke Godzilla. Not simply because Godzilla is the monstrous, the abject, but because Godzilla's monstrousness provides a pre-historical grounding, untainted by the baggage of much current and dubious creative writing lore, existing before we imposed symbolic, representational, constructed, and frequently reactionary notions on our creative writing teaching and learning. Godzilla, because neither specifically gendered nor representationally specific (even the original

Japanese for the monster, *Gojira* is a combination of the Japanese word for gorilla and the word for whale), this internationally recognized monster offers us an analogical model for that which openly combines the imagination and the intellect, and does so without binary definition or ideals of separation. Godzilla, because although the monster will defend humankind, where humankind and it have shared allegiances, it will just as quickly find humankind questionable, unclear or unconvincing, and question humankind's motives. Godzilla because the morality it shows is no morality at all, according to established lore; but, rather, it is natural morality born out of empirical evidence, founded on actuality not on imposed constructs, and delivered without subterfuge.

If we can teach with Godzilla, if our classrooms can become habitats of a primal Godzillan monstrousness, informed not by adversarial notions but by a natural process in which the doing of creative writing and an understanding of it are part of the same experience, then we have reached a new and more genuine place in our creative writing teaching. In this space our students (and we) will be more likely to move from moments of limited knowledge to a greater knowledge, onward to the increasingly skilled use of language, memory, and the imagination, to a point of being able to think more expertly both in concrete and abstract terms about what they are doing. Such thinking will not be presented as separations on which their identities and ours as creative writers are said to somehow depend. It will no longer be a case of manipulating the paperwork to cloak the reality of the actions we have undertaken and the understanding we have employed. Rather, we as creative writers and teachers of creative writing will be part of an experience, perhaps even on more occasions responsible for a classroom experience, in which it is not apprehension, not fear of the abject, the reject, or the "other" that is at the core of what we do; but, rather, a celebration of human ingenuity. A Godzillan habitat, favoring neither idealism nor physicalism, supporting both the creative and the intellectual, the mind and the body, the self and those around us, without boundaries, and without the bellicosity of much of the creative writing lore we have now for too long accepted.

Notes

1 Pete Docter, David Silverman and Lee Unkrich. *Monsters Inc*. Pixar, 2001.

2 Julia Kristeva. *Powers of Horror: An Essay on Abjection*, New York: Columbia University Press, 1982, 35.

3 Julia Kristeva. *Powers of Horror: An Essay on Abjection*, New York: Columbia University Press, 1982, 207.

4 Fred Botting. *Making Monstrous: Frankenstein, Criticism, Theory*, Manchester: Manchester University Press, 1991, 51.

5 Barbara Creed. *The Monstrous-Feminine: Film, Feminism, Psychoanalysis*, London: Routledge, 1993, 1.

6 Graeme Harper. "Teaching Creative Writing," in Rodney H. Jones (ed.), *The Routledge Handbook of Language and Creativity*, Abington: Routledge, 2016, 498–9.

References

Botting, Fred. *Making Monstrous: Frankenstein, Criticism, Theory*, Manchester: Manchester University Press, 1991.

Caputi, Jane. *Goddesses and Monsters: Women, Myth, Power and Popular Culture*, Madison: Popular Press, (2004).

Creed, Barbara. *The Monstrous-Feminine: Film, Feminism, Psychoanalysis*, London: Routledge, 1993.

Docter, Pete, David Silverman and Lee Unkrich. *Monsters Inc*. Pixar, 2001.

Fukuda, Jun. *Godzilla v Gigan*. Toho, 1972.

Fukuda, Jun. *Godzilla vs Megalon*. Toho, 1973.

Harper, Graeme. "Teaching Creative Writing," in Rodney H. Jones (ed.), *The Routledge Handbook of Language and Creativity*, Abington: Routledge, 2016.

Honda, Ishirô. *Godzilla v the Thing* (originally entitled *Mothra v Godzilla*). Toho, 1964.

Kristeva, Julia. *Powers of Horror: An Essay on Abjection*, New York: Columbia University Press, 1982.

Piaget, Jean. "Piaget's theory," in P. Mussen (ed.), *Handbook of Child Psychology* (4th edition, Vol. 1). New York: Wiley, 1983.

Tsutsui, William. *Godzilla on My Mind: Fifty Years of the King of Monsters*. New York: Palgrave Macmillan, 2004.

17

Myths, Mirrors, and Metaphors:

The Education of the Creative Writing Teacher

Rebecca Manery

Since the establishment of the first graduate creative writing program at the University of Iowa in 1936, the iconic scene of creative writing education has been the gathering of student writers and an experienced—often eminent—writer around a table to critique student work in progress. The metaphor of the creative writing teacher as a Master Craftsperson who oversees the apprenticeship of student writers in a writer's workshop was reified at Iowa and remains prevalent today.

It has been assumed that, if the creative writing teacher is a writer of sufficient talent, no training is required for such a method of instruction. Thus, while seminars or courses in pedagogy are routinely required for graduate students of composition, most new instructors of creative writing rely on their often unexamined beliefs about teaching and writing, a mirroring of their own creative writing education, and the ubiquitous metaphor of the creative writing classroom as a workshop as the foundation for their teaching practice. The lore that insists that creative writing teachers need only their instincts and experience as students and practitioners of creative writing to be effective teachers of creative writing has resulted in teaching based on myths, mirrors, and a single metaphor.

Recognizing the need for "a deep revision of what it means to teach and learn creative writing," Wendy Bishop was an early advocate of creative writing pedagogy training. In 1994 she envisioned a pedagogy seminar that would cover the basics of course design, assessment, and running a workshop, but would also take new teachers "beyond the boundaries of what they themselves have experienced into investigations of alternatives, into deeper understandings of students, into broader examinations of cultures, politics, and institutional systems" (Bishop, 1994, 291–292). Kelly Ritter's 1999 survey of twenty-five U.S. creative writing doctoral programs revealed that only four offered pedagogical training in creative writing. Ritter concluded that "it seems unlikely that a Ph.D. recipient in this field might be upon graduation a well-trained teacher of creative writing" (Ritter, 2001, 207).

Although they remain a small minority, a growing number of graduate creative writing programs in the United States, Canada, and the United Kingdom now offer creative writing pedagogy courses. As of June 2016 I had identified thirty-eight such programs (Table 17.1). While the expanding

TABLE 17.1 *Creative writing programs that offer a course in creative writing pedagogy*

U.S. Programs (33)	Canadian Programs (1)	United Kingdom Programs (4)
Antioch University	University of Calgary	Keele University
Ball State University		Kingston University
Boise State University		Northumbria University
Bowling Green University		University of Gloucestershire
Chatham University		
Colorado State University		
Florida Atlantic University		
Georgia College and University		
Illinois State University		
Indiana University		
National University		
Oklahoma City University		
Purdue University		
Regis University (Mile High Low-Residency Program)		
Salem State University		
San Francisco State University		
Seton Hill University		
Southern Illinois University		

Spalding University

University of Central Arkansas

University of Central Florida

University of Cincinnati

University of Massachusetts
(Amherst)

University of Massachusetts
(Boston)

University of Nebraska

University of New Mexico

University of North Carolina
(Wilmington)

University of North Dakota

University of Pittsburgh

University of South Florida

University of Southwestern
Louisiana

Western Kentucky University

Western State Colorado University

number of creative writing pedagogy courses is encouraging, little is known about them. Beyond course listings, syllabi shared by the few instructors who teach such a course, and a single journal article, I could find no information about what is taught in creative writing pedagogy courses and why. This information gap gives rise to a number of questions, including: *Who teaches the creative writing pedagogy course, and how? Who takes the course, and to what end? What do reading lists and assignments for the creative writing pedagogy course tell us about the learning outcomes valued in such courses? How do teacher conceptions and communities of practice shape what is taught and learned in the creative writing pedagogy course? And, perhaps most importantly: Do such courses contribute to the "deep revision of what it means to teach and learn creative writing" that Bishop envisioned over twenty years ago?*

In search of answers to these questions, I conducted qualitative interviews with seven teachers of creative writing pedagogy and analysed their course syllabi. Because Pajares has argued powerfully that teachers' beliefs and conceptions strongly influence their behavior in the classroom (Pajares,

1992), I was interested in understanding how creative writing pedagogy teachers' beliefs and conceptions may have influenced how they teach their subject. In an earlier article, I described the variation I discovered in creative writing pedagogy teachers' conceptions of teaching and learning in terms of categories of pedagogic identity (Manery, 2015). In this chapter, I review and extend that discussion by presenting data that fill in some of the gaps in our knowledge of creative writing pedagogy courses, even as they raise other questions. In offering these findings, I hope to encourage reflection on whether creative writing pedagogy courses can promote the deeper understanding of creative writing pedagogy that Wendy Bishop envisioned.

In spite of broad support for such courses by creative writing scholars (Bizzaro, 2004; Vanderslice, 2011; Donnelly, 2012), creative writing pedagogy courses are a relatively recent addition to the 79-year history of graduate creative writing education; 1996 was the earliest year any of the teachers in my study sample had taught a creative writing pedagogy course. None of the creative writing pedagogy teachers who participated in the study had taken such a course themselves. I could discover no authoritative source of information that could answer even basic questions—where and when was the first creative writing pedagogy course offered? How many are currently offered?—with anything like certainty. While a new wave of creative writing scholars has brought fresh ideas and energy to the developing field alternatively known as Creative Writing or Creative Writing Studies, the question of whether—and how—creative writing pedagogy courses can impact teaching within the discipline has remained unanswered even as a growing number of graduate programs have begun to offer such courses. For this reason alone, then, I believe this study contributes to a greater understanding of a relatively unexamined subject.

The creative writing pedagogy course: A review of the literature

As early as 1994, Wendy Bishop called for the establishment of creative writing pedagogy seminars to better prepare teachers of creative writing. Declaring her hope for "nothing less than to change our profession," she affirmed that:

> learning to teach better is tough, exhilarating, and possible. I'm talking here about the need I see for a deep revision of what it means to teach and learn creative writing, a reprioritization of products and processes, a curriculum that investigates itself, that denounces old premises, topples myths, renames, and reaffirms (Bishop, 1994, 291–2).

The seminar Bishop envisioned would:

> address theory, research, and practice; it can and should include writing
> and workshopping; it should address what we know and what we need to
> know—how to design courses, how to grade; it should take a student and
> a teacher beyond the boundaries of what they themselves have experienced
> into investigation of alternatives, into deeper understandings of students,
> into broader examinations of cultures, politics, and institutional systems
> (Bishop, 1994, 292).

Bishop envisioned the creative writing pedagogy seminar or course as a
community of practice where writer-scholar-teachers could investigate not
only what and how we teach creative writing, but why. She blamed "our
failure to invest in creative writing education courses" for "the difficulty of
accumulating and reflecting on knowledge in this field" (Bishop, 2011, 240).
While Bishop shares testimonials from students in her own pedagogy
seminar, (Bishop, 1994, 293–4) she does not provide specifics about what
her own seminar entailed or provide a model for a course in creative writing
pedagogy that would achieve her ambitious aims. This study is, in part, an
attempt to fill that gap.

In 2001, Kelly Ritter became the first scholar to publish a study on creative
writing pedagogy courses. Her 1999 survey of twenty-five U.S. creative
writing PhD programs revealed that only four offered any teacher training
specifically for creative writing, although most required candidates to
complete a course in composition pedagogy. She concluded that "most U.S.
universities have no specific training in place that would prepare candidates
to enter the creative writing classroom even remotely as well prepared as
their rhetoric and composition PhD counterparts" (Ritter, 2001, 213).

Ritter's study has been important in calling attention to the lack of
emphasis on teacher training in even creative writing PhD programs, but as
a map of the current state of creative writing pedagogy communities of
practice, it has significant limitations. First, Ritter looked only at the twenty-
five U.S. creative writing PhD programs then in existence; her survey did not
include MFA programs which, at least today, are as, or more likely to,
include a pedagogy course than PhD programs. Second, Ritter was primarily
interested in pointing out the rarity of creative writing pedagogy courses
rather than describing courses already in existence. While she provides some
specifics about teacher training available to creative writing students in the
University of Georgia's PhD program and for graduate student instructors
at the University of Michigan (which has no PhD program in Creative
Writing and whose pedagogic training is geared toward the teaching of
composition), she does not include detailed descriptions of course objectives,
reading lists, and assignments. Finally, Ritter's study was conducted in 1999;
the information she gathered then is no longer current. For instance, Western
Michigan University, listed as one of the four PhD programs to include a

course in creative writing pedagogy, no longer offers such a course. At the same time, the number of creative writing PhD programs has grown from twenty-five to forty-two, meaning that Ritter's study examined only slightly more than half of the PhD programs now in existence. Ritter's study is one of only a few published sources of information about creative writing pedagogy courses, but that information is eighteen years old.

Another published source is "English 890," Kwame Dawes and Christy Friend's 2003 article describing a course they co-taught at the University of South Carolina. Published as part of *Composition Studies*' Course Designs Series, it includes a wealth of detail: a syllabus complete with a course description, major assignments, reading list, topic listings, and course schedule; a critical statement; and reflective comments by both teachers. Even among creative writing pedagogy courses, Dawes and Friend's course was unusual as a teaching collaboration between a well-known poet and a composition specialist. The course, described as "a broad-ranging introduction to theories, research, and methods of teaching creative writing" was open to MA and PhD English students, creative writing MFA students, and graduate students in English Education. As such, it included consideration of teaching in primary and secondary schools and community settings as well as in undergraduate and graduate creative writing programs. Topics included: creative writing processes; teaching, learning, responding to, and assessing creative writing; creative writing as literary art, therapy, and sociopolitical activity; and professional issues. In addition to its team-taught design, some of the course's most distinguishing features were its incorporation of readings from creative writing, composition, education, and creativity studies; a variety of writing assignments in creative and academic genres; a requirement that all students "develop and actually teach creative writing lessons at sites of their choice", and a "rich mix of theories, research and practice that would help students draw on the resources of both composition and creative writing to approach their writing and their teaching in more thoughtful ways" (Dawes and Friend, 2003, 116). Drawing on scholarship by Wendy Bishop, Tim Mayers, and Harriet Malinowitz, Dawes and Friend "believed that an interdisciplinary seminar on creative writing pedagogy would provide a space to extend the conversations and collaborative projects already underway and to more rigorously explore connections between our two fields" (115). While many scholars have suggested connecting creative writing and composition pedagogies, Dawes and Friend's course actually did so, opening a space for productive conversation with students from composition, creative writing, and English education.

What actually happened in the course was both unexpected and instructive. Friend explains that, in the third week in the course, class opinion divided on the issue of who is qualified to teach creative writing. The MFA students, comfortable with the master/apprentice model most familiar in creative writing programs, insisted that only published creative writers were qualified to teach creative writing to anyone but beginning students and children. Some non-MFA students disagreed, believing there were more similarities than differences in the teaching of creative writing and composition. Students on both sides of the divide took offense, believing their own qualifications for teaching had been questioned. Friend admitted that "the class atmosphere for a significant portion of the semester was quite uncomfortable," although she felt that divisions had largely dissolved by the time students were presenting the results of their teaching experiences to one another.

The unanticipated polarization of students in this otherwise carefully designed course exemplifies the need for—and the difficulty of—changing perceptions about creative writing pedagogy. "Both Kwame and I failed to foresee the degree to which we and our students would be unable to avoid reproducing the conflicting aesthetics, values, and pedagogical perspectives of the traditions in which we'd been trained," Friend acknowledged. "We were both, I think, shocked that the 'genius writer/apprentice' model of teaching—which we were trying to move past—reared its head so often in our class discussions" (120). Dawes concluded, "What should be clear is that the pedagogy of teaching creative writing is in desperate need of critical attention" (123).

Unfortunately, critical attention is precisely what the pedagogy of teaching creative writing has lacked. My interest in addressing this gap was the departure point for this study of creative writing pedagogy teachers' conceptions of writing and teaching and how those conceptions inform their teaching practice. By conducting and analysing semi-structured interviews with these teachers and examining their creative writing pedagogy course syllabi, I sought to understand what is taught in creative writing pedagogy courses, the range of teaching conceptions held by creative writing pedagogy teachers, and how variations in conception may influence variations in teaching practice.

Admittedly, the seven teachers of creative writing pedagogy in my study do not represent all of the thinking about creative writing pedagogy in the field, although my sample represents more than one-fifth of U.S. programs and nearly one-seventh of creative writing programs worldwide that include a course in creative pedagogy (at least, those I have discovered through my own search of the Internet and informal surveys conducted at two AWP Book Fairs). Nevertheless, the interviews and syllabi of these seven teachers represent a wide variety of conceptions of creative writing pedagogy which led, in turn, to a broad range of readings, activities, and intended outcomes as I will discuss later in this chapter. First, however, I will briefly review the variance in teaching conceptions I discovered in the data.

Pedagogic identity in creative writing pedagogy classrooms

In my study, I identified five distinct conceptions of teaching creative writing which I describe as categories of *pedagogic identity*. I borrow the term "pedagogic identity" from the work of Zukas and Malcolm in adult education. In 2002 they surveyed the literature on post-secondary teacher education and identified five common "pedagogic identities." Although they don't explicitly define this term, Zukas and Malcolm define pedagogy as "a critical understanding of the social, policy and institutional context, as well as a critical approach to the content and process of the educational/training transaction" (Malcolm and Zukas, 2001, 40) and "identities" as "'versions' of the educator" (Zukas and Malcolm, 2002, 2). Pedagogic identities thus represent variations in how educators understand and perform teaching within a broader social context. For my purposes, I define pedagogic identity as *"teachers' beliefs and understandings of creative writing pedagogy, including their conceptions of themselves and others as creative writing and creative writing pedagogy teachers."*

I first learned of Zukas and Malcolm's work from Rebecca O'Rourke's article, "Creative Writing as a Site of Pedagogic Identity and Pedagogic Learning." O'Rourke, a teacher of creative writing in Adult and Continuing Education at the UK university where Zukas and Malcolm began their research, asserts that "Pedagogic identity becomes a way of articulating the specific histories, politics, and values embodied by individual teachers: ways of being, as well as doing" (O'Rourke, 2007, 504). Using the concept of pedagogic identity to describe changes in her identity as a teacher at a time of institutional flux, O'Rourke concludes that "pedagogy is not just a question of how; it is also a question of who, of what, and of why" (504). In other words, a study of pedagogy must take into consideration the people involved and the context within which they interact. O'Rourke recommends pedagogic identity as "a potentially useful concept with which to explore the fascinating and prescient questions of what happens, and why, in a creative writing classroom" (511–12). I agree with O'Rourke that Zukas and Malcolm's conception of pedagogic identity is a useful way to think about teachers' conceptions of teaching and themselves and others as teachers.

In my study, I argue that the creative writing pedagogy classroom is *a community of practice where pedagogic identities are formed*. I assert that creative writing pedagogy teachers' conceptions of pedagogic identity can, in part, determine the development of their students' pedagogic identities. Because individuals are shaped by communities of practice and shape them in return, creative writing pedagogy teachers' conceptions have the potential to influence understandings of teaching and learning within Creative Writing as an academic discipline.

Five pedagogic identities

I identified five pedagogic identities from a phenomenographic analysis of my study data. I named these pedagogic identities Expert Practitioner,

Change Agent, Facilitator, Co-Constructor of Knowledge, and Vocational Trainer. I identified three subtypes within the category of Expert Practitioner: Master Craftsperson, Famous Writer, and Teacher/Artist. In Table 17.2 I present each category along with a primary goal of instruction and a primary value as a quick means of defining the categories and understanding how they differ from one another.

It is important to stress that these categories do not represent individual teachers but variations in conception. All of the study participants made statements that represent more than one pedagogic identity; some participants made statements in support of several. This is to be expected, in part because teaching is a complex activity and in part because identities are not static. Many of the study participants acknowledged that their teaching conceptions and practices had changed over time. Some pedagogic identities (such as Famous Author) were not represented by any of the subject participants, but were referred to in the interviews as a type of creative writing teacher often found in creative writing programs or, in the case of Teacher/Artist, as a potential alternative to the Master Craftsperson.

It should also be clear that these pedagogic identities do not represent an exhaustive catalog of teaching conceptions in Creative Writing. Rather, they represent five dominant conceptions found in the data. I fully expect that with additional time and research, these categories will require revision. Tenuous as it may be, the set of categories presented here provides a useful tool for understanding variation in teaching conceptions of creative writing pedagogy teachers and suggests possible guidelines for the creative writing pedagogy course. In the next section I describe each identity and subcategory in more detail.

TABLE 17.2 *Categories of creative writing pedagogic identity*

Pedagogic Identity	Goal of Instruction	Values

Expert Practitioner
  Subtype 1: Master Craftsperson
  Subtype 2: Famous Author
  Subtype 3: Teacher/Artist
	Developing Art/Craft	Talent/Skill

Change Agent	Changing Conceptions	Understanding
Facilitator	Presenting an Array of Options	Choice
Co-Constructor of Knowledge	Expanding the Field of Knowledge	Discovery
Vocational Trainer	Preparing Students for Job Market	Marketability

Pedagogic identity profiles

I. Expert Practitioner

Expert Practitioners draw primarily on their own experiences as writers and students of creative writing to shape their teaching practice and encourage creative writing pedagogy students to do the same. Expert Practitioners believe that students learn by doing and by observing experts at work. Giving students the opportunity to practice and demonstrate their skills as authentically as possible is more important than theories of writing and/or teaching, historical and current developments in the field, keeping up with or contributing to creative writing pedagogy scholarship, or the sociopolitical context in which teaching and writing takes place. Because they give highest priority to the learning of practical skills through observation and practice, Expert Practitioners may focus on the "nuts and bolts" of writing syllabi and developing lesson plans. Expert Practitioners derive their authority from their creative writing, not their scholarship. Therefore, they may feel uncomfortable talking about theories of pedagogy.

I identified three subtypes within the category of Expert Practitioner:

Subtype 1: Master Craftsperson   The Master Craftsperson is a subtype of the Expert Practitioner who views the master/apprentice relationship as an apt metaphor for the relationship between teacher and student. The Master Craftsperson supports the metaphor of the creative writing classroom as a workshop and the practical pedagogical approach that follows from this metaphor.

Subtype 2: Famous Writer   One study participant described the Famous Writer as "somebody who's known or was known at some point"; in other words, a writer who has achieved substantial recognition for his or her literary achievements. Famous Writers may rely on the appeal of their celebrity and "teach by osmosis" rather than invest in their teaching.

Subtype 3: Teacher/Artist   Teacher/Artists make a clear distinction between writing as art and other forms of writing and direct their teaching toward the goal of making art. While they focus on skill development like other subtypes of the Expert Practitioner, Teacher/Artists share the perspective of teachers in other arts disciplines that, through the practice of art and direct instruction by experienced writers, even students who do not seem to possess natural aptitude can learn to become writers.

II. Change Agent

The Change Agent's primary goal is to challenge what they see as myths and misconceptions about writers and writing and to make students aware of the social, political, and economic arenas in which they operate. Change Agents challenge traditional conceptions and practices and direct students toward their own preferred conceptions and teaching practices. Change Agents value knowledge of disciplinary history and scholarship as well as sociopolitical forces that shape teaching and learning in creative writing communities of practice. By helping students develop an awareness of the history and context within which creative writing communities of practice are situated, Change Agents encourage students to critically reflect on their own conceptions and advocate for pedagogic reform.

III. Facilitator

Facilitators maintain a neutral stance toward pedagogic conceptions and practices. They introduce students to an array of options, but do not push students toward any particular conception or practice. As such, the primary focus for Facilitators is to allow students to "try out" alternatives and select teaching approaches that suit their beliefs about teaching or their personalities.

IV. Co-Constructor of Knowledge

Co-Constructors of Knowledge are interested in innovative teaching practices. They themselves may teach and think about teaching "outside the norm." They are not as interested in reforming misconceptions as in promoting an open-ended inquiry in which they are co-participants rather than leaders. Co-Constructors playfully engage their students in imagining as-yet undiscovered teaching conceptions and practices, encouraging conceptual change without the expectation that students will adopt a particular conception. Co-Constructors recognize that they cannot change students' conceptions for them, but they encourage students to reflect on their conceptions and investigate new possibilities for teaching and learning that bring about conceptual change.

V. Vocational Trainer

Vocational Trainers consider one of their primary responsibilities as creative writing pedagogy teachers as providing students with the tools and knowledge they need to get and keep jobs as creative writing teachers. They use their own experience of being on the job market to guide students to create artifacts and practice routines that will demonstrate their fitness for teaching. Vocational Trainers may try to acquaint students with the politics of English Departments in an effort to help them make themselves appealing to search committee members who are not creative writers and who may regard creative writers as uninterested in teaching or the functioning of the department. A secondary goal may be to convince students to seek meaningful employment elsewhere given the paucity of available creative writing teaching positions.

I will once again emphasize that the pedagogic identities described above do not represent individual study participants. All of the creative writing pedagogy teachers in my study held conceptions that correlate with more than one pedagogic identity. Some study participants showed a strong affinity for a particular pedagogic identity while other participants had conceptions that matched several categories of description.

Creative writing teachers may embrace more than one identity at the same time or different identities at different times.

These pedagogic identities were drawn from seven interview transcripts and course syllabi. As such, they do not represent all possible creative writing pedagogic identities. The range of pedagogic identities does, however, challenge the conception of creative writing pedagogy as monolithic. It is clear that the familiar metaphor of the creative writing teacher as Master Craftsperson is not the only possibility available to creative writing teachers.

I now turn to a brief consideration of similarities and differences in creative writing pedagogy courses based on required reading lists and course assignments.

Creative writing pedagogy course comparisons

Required reading

A comparison of the required reading lists for the seven creative writing pedagogy courses represented in my study revealed a surprising variety of assigned texts given the limited body of creative writing pedagogy texts available. While pre-2005 creative writing pedagogy texts, works of craft criticism, and disciplinary histories frequently appear on required reading lists, far less common are texts on theory, cultural studies, education, and current events related to post-secondary teaching. The most surprising finding of this comparison was that not a single reading appeared on every teacher's reading list despite the limited number of creative writing texts available. In fact, only three authors and a pair of co-authors were represented on three or more lists. One author, Wendy Bishop, appeared on six of seven reading lists although she is represented by four different texts. This is not surprising given Bishop's iconic status among scholars of creative writing pedagogy. However, Bishop died in 2003, meaning that all of these texts were published at least thirteen years ago and in some cases far earlier.

With only four of the seven teachers including at least one creative writing pedagogy text published in 2005 or after, this text comparison raises concerns that some creative writing pedagogy teachers may be unaware of current trends in creative writing pedagogy scholarship, a gap that may reflect the distance between many creative writing teachers and creative writing scholars as well as the uncertain status of Creative Writing as an academic discipline.

Course assignments

Comparing course assignments also led to some surprising findings. First, only one assignment—written reflections on readings and class discussions—was required in every course. All but one of the seven teachers asked students to create creative writing exercises or lesson plans, share a book or resource with the class via a report or presentation, and write at least one formal paper. I found it quite surprising that two of the seven teachers did not require pedagogy students to create a syllabus or write a teaching statement. Only three teachers out of seven required students to lead discussions, assemble portfolios, make observations of other teachers, or teach a unit or lesson to undergraduates. The lack of teaching practice in four of the seven pedagogy courses is somewhat offset by the chance some of these students had to teach undergraduate creative writing courses, but teaching assignments were not granted to all students and in some courses no such opportunity was available. Three teachers went to considerable trouble to give their students a chance to teach at least one lesson to undergraduates, while other teachers did not emphasize practical experience in teaching.

Variation in course assignments reflects differences in pedagogic values and goals. In Table 17.3, I suggest how the assignments found in the course syllabi of my study participants align with the values and goals of the five pedagogic identities I identified above.

TABLE 17.3 *Sample assignments and pedagogic identity goal alignment*

Creative Writing Pedagogy Assignments	Pedagogic Identities Whose Pedagogic Goals Align with Assignment
Observe an experienced creative writing teacher and report to the class	Expert Practitioner, Co-Constructor of Knowledge
Observe teacher in another arts discipline and report to the class	Expert Practitioner, Co-Constructor of Knowledge, Change Agent
Develop a lesson plan and teach it	Expert Practitioner, Vocational Coach
Create portfolios and/or artifacts such as syllabi and teaching statements	Vocational Coach, Expert Practitioner

(*continued*)

TABLE 17.3 (*Continued*)

Creative Writing Pedagogy Assignments	Pedagogic Identities Whose Pedagogic Goals Align with Assignment
Read a variety of readings and become acquainted with several classroom resources	Facilitator, Change Agent
Select a reading (and/or resource) to present to the class	Co-Constructor of Knowledge, Facilitator
Construct a "dream" syllabus for an ideal writing course, then create a "real" syllabus that incorporates elements of the "dream" syllabus	Co-Constructor of Knowledge, Change Agent
Read and discuss creative writing pedagogy history and current contexts	Change Agent
Read articles critical of workshop pedagogy and/or the "writer as anointed" mythology	Change Agent

Findings and implications

One of my principal motivations for conducting this study of the conceptions of creative writing pedagogy teachers was to discover whether creative writing pedagogy courses reinforce traditional beliefs and practices of creative writing instruction or whether they critically examine these pedagogic traditions in ways that have the potential to transform the teaching and learning of creative writing.

What I discovered by interviewing seven creative writing pedagogy teachers and examining their course syllabi is that there is significant variation in creative writing pedagogy teachers' conceptions and practices of teaching which I have described in terms of categories of pedagogic identity.

While these findings are necessarily limited by the study sample, the degree of variation found among just seven teachers of creative writing pedagogy recommends further research. From the evidence of the interview transcripts and syllabi of my study participants, I found:

1. There is very little consistency in how creative writing pedagogy courses are integrated into and supported by creative writing programs. Programs varied in how often the creative writing pedagogy course was offered, who was eligible to enroll, whether (and for whom) the course was required, and whether or not the program provided creative writing pedagogy students with opportunities to teach. My data show significant variation across programs in all of these categories as well as puzzling inconsistencies within programs. For instance, at one university creative writing doctoral students are guaranteed an opportunity to teach an introductory course in creative writing but are not required to take the creative writing pedagogy course; at the same time, graduate education majors are required to take the course but are not given the opportunity to teach creative writing. At another university, all MFA students must enroll in an online creative writing pedagogy course, but none are afforded the opportunity to teach. This variation makes cross-program comparisons difficult. It suggests that students who have completed courses in creative writing pedagogy may vary significantly in their preparedness to teach depending, in part, on the course parameters set by their graduate programs as well as the larger social context within which teaching and learning take place.

2. There is significant variation in how the creative writing pedagogy teachers design and teach creative writing pedagogy courses.   I found significant variation in both the required readings and activities assigned by the creative writing pedagogy teachers in my study. There was also very little overlap in the authors represented on the reading lists. The absence of any standard text in creative writing pedagogy may be due to the fact that Creative Writing is still establishing itself as an academic discipline, but it also likely indicates that the division between creative writing pedagogy scholarship and the practice of teaching creative writing has yet to be bridged.

While there was more consistency in assigned activities than assigned readings, there were also surprising gaps. Only one activity—written reflections—was assigned in all seven courses. Six of the seven teachers assigned formal papers; reports or reviews on books or resources; and the creation of a lesson plan, activity, or exercise for a creative writing class. Two teachers did not include the creation of a syllabus or teaching statement in their list of assignments, documents that are essential for job hunters as well as practicing teachers. Four teachers did not include teaching practice, teacher observation, student-led discussions, or the creation of portfolios in their course design. Only one teacher included all ten types of assignments surveyed in her course.

The variety of readings and assignments in creative writing pedagogy courses is not necessarily suggestive of differences in quality, but it does suggest a lack of consistency in the educational aims of such courses. While I am not advocating that creative writing pedagogy courses be standardized, the wide variation in the content of these courses suggests that students of creative writing pedagogy in different programs will experience widely variant preparation for teaching creative writing. A further examination of this variance—and particularly gaps in coverage—would be useful in considering which aspects of creative writing pedagogy have been prioritized and which have received less attention.

3. There is uneven representation of current creative writing pedagogy scholarship in required course readings of the creative writing pedagogy courses. Only four of the seven study participants assigned creative writing pedagogy books published since 2005, while only three assigned articles from peer-reviewed journals. The uneven use of current scholarship suggests that even creative writing faculty members who choose to teach creative writing pedagogy (and thus presumably have an interest in pedagogy) are not always aware of the full range of scholarship available. This is not entirely surprising since many of the books on creative writing pedagogy published in the past fifteen years originated abroad and are difficult to find unless one is already aware that they exist.

The paucity of current creative writing pedagogy scholarship on many reading lists also suggests the limitations of global creative writing communities of practice such as AWP. Creative writing pedagogy scholarship is minimally represented in the AWP Book Fair and seldom reviewed or discussed in the AWP *Writer's Chronicle*, but the newly established Creative Writing Studies Organization, whose *Journal of Creative Writing Studies* became the first U.S. peer-reviewed journal of creative writing scholarship, could potentially play a role in circulating and promoting creative writing pedagogy scholarship within U.S. creative writing programs.

4. Creative writing pedagogy teachers have varied conceptions of teaching that influence their teaching choices and goals. The principal finding of this study is that creative writing pedagogy teachers have different conceptions of teaching creative writing that influence how they teach creative writing pedagogy. I categorize these conceptions as five pedagogic identities. As I discussed earlier, the pedagogic identities I identified from the data are Expert Practitioner, Facilitator, Change Agent, Co-Constructor of Knowledge, and Vocational Trainer. I identified three subtypes within the category of Expert Practitioner: Master Craftsperson, Famous Author, and Teacher/Artist.

What may be most significant about these various pedagogic identities is how differently they represent creative writing teachers from the monolithic Master Craftsperson, by far the most common depiction of the creative writing teacher in the literature. For instance, the pedagogic identities of Facilitator, Change Agent, and Co-Constructor of Knowledge suggest models for teacher-student relationships far different from the master/apprentice model so familiar to the creative writing students in Friend and Dawes' pedagogy class. The Co-Constructor of Knowledge in particular presents an interesting contrast to the Master Craftsperson. Where the Master Craftsperson is the authority who hands down knowledge to apprentices, the Co-Constructor shares both authority and responsibility with students for constructing new knowledge. The Master Craftsperson upholds tradition; the Co-Constructor of Knowledge is poised for discovery.

By becoming aware of the various pedagogic identities discussed, enacted, and developed within creative writing pedagogy courses, future creative writing teachers have the opportunity to challenge the image of the Master Craftsperson and with it, the workshop approach to teaching that the Craftsperson represents. While further research is needed, it is possible that the different pedagogic identities that creative writing pedagogy students are exposed to or see modeled can influence the development of their own pedagogic identities in ways that encourage pedagogical innovation.

5. Creative writing pedagogy courses can challenge or reinforce traditional conceptions and practices of creative writing instruction.   As I mentioned above, one of my principal motivations for this study was to discover whether the creative writing pedagogy course is a site where conceptions and practices of teaching creative writing can change and develop. Do creative writing pedagogy courses encourage the development of new conceptions and practices or reinforce existing pedagogy? Some of the participants in my study described changes in their students' attitudes and approaches to teaching that seemed to indicate that their students had undergone a significant conceptual shift. However, the simple presence of a creative writing pedagogy class on a program's course list is no guarantee that graduates will develop more complex understandings of creative writing pedagogy that could lead to the "deep revision" of creative writing pedagogy that Wendy Bishop envisioned (Bishop, 1994, 291).

Clearly there is a need for continued research into how creative writing pedagogy is taught in graduate creative writing programs. My hope is that this preliminary study can encourage teachers of creative writing pedagogy to critically examine their conceptions of teachers and teaching; engage with other practitioners in imagining alternative possibilities for teaching and research; and encourage their students to do the same.

The Master Craftsperson held up as the epitome of the creative writing teacher is only one of the pedagogic identities being modeled and explored in creative writing pedagogy courses. Within the limitations of the creative writing communities of practice of which they are members, creative writing pedagogy teachers can create spaces in which future teachers of creative writing can develop pedagogic identities and imagine possibilities for creative writing education that extend well beyond the Master Craftsperson and the writer's workshop.

Bibliography

Bishop, Wendy. "Afterword—Colors of a Different Horse: On Learning to Like Teaching Creative Writing." *Colors of a Different Horse: Rethinking Creative Writing Theory and Pedagogy.* Ed. Wendy Bishop and Hans Ostrom. Urbana, IL: NCTE, 1994. 280–95.

Bishop, Wendy. The More Things Change . . . or Shoot Out at the Pedagogy and Theory Corral." *Composing Ourselves as Writer-Teacher-Writers: Starting with Wendy Bishop.* Eds, Patrick Bizzaro, Alys Culhane and Devan Cook. New York: Hampton Press, 2011, 237–48.

Bizzaro, Patrick. "Research and Reflection in English Studies: The Special Case of Creative Writing." *College English* 66.3 (2004): 294–309.

Dawes, Kwame, and Christy Friend. "English 890: Studies in Composition and Rhetoric: 'Teaching Creative Writing: Theories and Practices.'" *Composition Studies* 31.2 (Fall 2003): 107–24.

Donnelly, Dianne. *Establishing Creative Writing Studies as an Academic Discipline.* Bristol: Multilingual Matters, 2012.

Malcolm, Janice, and Miriam Zukas. "Bridging Pedagogic Gaps: Conceptual Discontinuities in Higher Education." *Teaching in Higher Education,* 6.1 (2001): 33–42.

Manery, Rebecca. "Revisiting the Pedagogy and Theory Corral: Creative Writing Pedagogy Teachers' Conceptions of Pedagogic Identity." *New Writing: International Journal for the Practice and Theory of Creative Writing,* 12.2 (2015): 205–15.

O'Rourke, Rebecca. "Creative Writing as a Site of Pedagogic Identity and Pedagogic Learning." *Pedagogy* 7.3 (2007): 501–12.

Pajares, M. Frank. "Teachers' Beliefs and Educational Research: Cleaning Up a Messy Construct." *Review of Educational Research,* 62.1 (1992): 307–32.

Ritter, Kelly. "Professional Writers/Writing Professionals: Revamping Teacher Training in Creative Writing Programs." *College English* 64.2 (Nov. 2001): 205–227.

Vanderslice, Stephanie. *Rethinking Creative Writing in Higher Education: Programs and Practices that Work.* Wicken, Ely, Cambs: The Professional and Higher Partnership Ltd. 2011.

Zukas, Miriam, and Janice Malcolm. "Pedagogies for Lifelong Learning: Building Bridges or Building Walls?" *Supporting Lifelong Learning* Vol. 1, *Perspectives on Learning,* eds, Roger Harrison, Anne Hanson, Fiona Reeve, and Julia Clarke. London: Routledge (2002): 203–18.

INDEX

Page numbers in *italic* refer to tables.